Advance Praise for *From Dynasties to Democracy*

'Rarely in India does one chance upon political chronicles that are as much history from above as they are history from below – offering insights not only into political intrigues at the highest echelons of power but also into the diurnal struggles of ordinary people in a land often caught between the imperatives of electoral democracy and the archaic compulsions of feudalism, casteism and communalism.

In *From Dynasties to Democracy: Politics, Caste and Power Struggles in Rajasthan*, Deep Mukherjee and Tabeenah Anjum weld together a journalistic quest of ten years with five years of painstaking research to pen an enthralling and luminous political and socio-economic history of India's largest state. Scholarly and spellbinding in equal measure, this is a magisterial one-volume account of one of India's most important regions – an infinitely rich repository of culture, literature and history … the authors reveal a Rajasthan that is neither the romanticized desert kingdom of tourist brochures nor merely a region mired in the vestiges of feudalism, but a propulsive political laboratory – where dynastic legacies tussle with grassroots assertion; where caste remains both a burden and a vehicle of mobilization; and where democracy, far from being a settled fact, is a fragile, contested and hard-won achievement. The result is a work at once panoramic in scope and intimate in detail: one that illumines not only Rajasthan but also the enduring dilemmas of Indian democracy itself.'

– **Shashi Tharoor**, Member of Parliament, author of *Our Living Constitution*

'The rich tapestry of Rajasthan's colourful past comes to life in this insightful, nuanced and in-depth book – as do its evolving political aspirations and assertions.'

– **Namita Gokhale**, writer and co-founder, Jaipur Literature Festival

'*From Dynasties to Democracy* is a very fine piece of work combining a deep knowledge of Rajasthan politics with sociological expertise. The authors analyse the state's trajectory in a very sophisticated manner

– the individual case studies they have selected illustrate vividly the points they are making.'

– **Christophe Jaffrelot**, political scientist, author of *Gujarat Under Modi: Laboratory of Today's India*

'Tabeenah Anjum and Deep Mukherjee have filled an important gap in contemporary political writing with this detailed book on Rajasthan's fascinating political history. In-depth research, rare anecdotes and access to primary players make this a riveting account of a complex state that deserves a book of style and substance.'

– **Rajdeep Sardesai**, author and Consulting Editor, *India Today*

'Drawing on decades of reporting from Rajasthan's villages, assembly corridors and political backrooms, Tabeenah Anjum and Deep Mukherjee offer an intimate portrait of one state's political ecosystem in *From Dynasties to Democracy: Politics, Caste and Power Struggles in Rajasthan*. From the enduring feudal networks that shape voter behaviour to the caste arithmetic that determines ministerial berths, this is politics as it actually unfolds on the ground. Their book reveals what we miss when we reduce Indian politics to a national spectacle. Until we understand our states, we cannot truly understand our democracy.'

– **Hartosh Singh Bal**, author and Executive Editor, *The Caravan*

'Keenly researched, deftly presented and boldly argued, *From Dynasties to Democracies* is one of the finest works on contemporary Indian politics. From the vaulted ceilings of palaces to the whispering corridors of Indira Gandhi Bhavan, Tabeenah Anjum and Deep Mukherjee's remarkable deep dive into the contentious political history of Rajasthan offers insights not only into the inner workings of one of the country's most inscrutable states but into the transformation of the Indian political landscape since Independence.'

– **Anish Gawande**, national spokesperson for the Nationalist Congress Party (Sharadchandra Pawar) and co-founder, Pink List India

'This book is a fine example of storytelling being used to explain politics and changing lives in a region known more for its past than its present. It is meticulously researched and vividly written, with journalistic flair and an academic's eye for detail and nuance.'

– **Samar Halarnkar,** Founding Editor, Article 14

'Engaging and essential. This volume by Anjum and Mukherjee speaks not only of their singular project but also of rare insights from a state that has long needed a socio-political narrative such as this one. For those wishing to get a sense of the weave and weft of Rajasthan's politics, this makes for a pathbreaking reference.'

– **Sankarshan Thakur**, author and Editor in Chief, *The Telegraph*

'From feudal echoes to fiery elections, *From Dynasties to Democracy* charts Rajasthan's political evolution with gripping clarity. In this landscape of shifting allegiances and enduring legacies, the desert sands continue to shape India's democratic landscape.'

– **Om Thanvi**, author, former Executive Editor, *Jansatta*, former Vice Chancellor, Haridev Joshi University of Journalism and Mass Communication, Jaipur

'The renowned journalists Tabeenah Anjum and Deep Mukherjee's book, *From Dynasties to Democracy: Politics, Caste and Power Struggles in Rajasthan*, not only imparts knowledge about Rajasthan's past and present together but also acquaints the reader with its entire political landscape – from feudal rule to today's democratic state. This book reveals the intricate relationships between Rajasthan's caste-based and feudal society and its politics, while also foregrounding the role of political parties. By supplementing the account of this significant journey of Rajasthan from monarchy to democracy with deep research and insight, Tabeenah and Deep have accomplished something unique. This is a magnificent and comprehensive tale of the making of Rajasthan. Every person who wishes to learn about the state must read this book.'

– **Bhanwar Meghwanshi**, author and social activist

'Rajasthan has been a neglected state when it comes to journalistic as well as academic writing on Indian politics. The state's politics has several paradoxes. Despite giving pro-Hindu politics one of its first electoral successes in independent India, why did Rajasthan not end up becoming a hegemonic state for BJP the way neighbouring Gujarat and Madhya Pradesh did? Despite a highly caste stratified society, why didn't social justice-based parties take root in Rajasthan the way they did in Uttar Pradesh and Bihar? These are some of the questions that have been answered in Deep Mukherjee and Tabeenah Anjum's excellent book. Perhaps the most remarkable part of the book is how seamlessly the authors navigate between the micro realities and the big picture and from contemporary happenings to the historical backstory. The authors vividly describe political events and personalities while also laying down their underlying structures. This is the most comprehensive book on the politics of Rajasthan and absolutely essential reading for those interested in Indian politics.'

– **Aditya Menon**, senior journalist and Political Editor, *The Quint*

'Rajasthan's complex political journey has long lacked a comprehensive chronicle. *From Dynasties to Democracy* changes that. Mukherjee and Anjum have produced a political history that doesn't sacrifice readability for rigour. Their decade of ground reportage shines through, from Rajput assertion to Jat land struggles, from Congress factionalism to the making of leaders like Gehlot, Raje and Pilot. They write with the authority of reporters who've covered the ground and the clarity [required] to make it accessible. From Maharana Pratap's contested legacy to why Jats have never held the CM's chair, this book reveals how feudal pasts shape democratic presents. Essential reading for understanding Indian politics.'

– **Radhika Bordia**, senior journalist and writer

FROM **DYNASTIES** TO **DEMOCRACY**

Deep Mukherjee is a senior journalist, presently associated with *The Wire* as an assistant editor. He has long served as the Rajasthan correspondent for *The Indian Express* and has also worked with *Hindustan Times* and *DNA*. He covers issues of national importance, pertaining primarily to politics, human rights, gender, atrocities against marginalized communities, impact of government policies and schemes, labour and farmer suicides. A UNICEF Development Journalism Fellowship awardee, Deep has highlighted the plight of child labourers working in the lac bangle industry in Jaipur and stone quarries of Rajasthan through his investigative reportage. He constantly strives to illuminate those perspectives that usually remain confined to the periphery or get lost in the din of the mainstream, especially oppressed voices and the daily struggles of the underprivileged. His work is aimed at mapping the political and administrative history of various communities through the narrativization and contextualization of individual experiences.

Aside from his journalistic endeavours, Deep occasionally writes for literary journals and opinion pieces for news outlets and loves to travel.

Tabeenah Anjum is a journalist with over fifteen years of experience across print and multimedia outfits. She reports on politics, gender, human rights, migrant rights and issues impacting marginalized communities from Rajasthan and neighbouring states. Presently, she writes for *Outlook* magazine and contributes long-form reportage for *The Quint*, *Article 14*, *Times of India Plus*, *The Gaon Connection*, BBC, *Countercurrents*, *Caravan* and *Telegraph*. She was the bureau incharge of *Deccan Herald* in Rajasthan until 2020 and continues to write opinion pieces for the newspaper.

A passionate photographer, she is the recipient of the National Award in Photography (2015) conferred by the Ministry of Information and Broadcasting, Government of India, and the Maharaja Sawai Ram Singh II Award (2017) for excellence in journalism and photography. Her photographs have been exhibited in India, Nepal and South Australia.

She has also published research papers on the media in reputed international journals, including a chapter on 'Journalism of Tolerance:

Reporting About Refugees and Immigrants' in *Xenophobia in the Media* (2024), published by Routledge. She has served as the co-course director of the Basics of Visual Storytelling course at Film and Television Institute of India, Pune, since 2019 and conducts visual storytelling workshops across India and abroad.

She has a master's in journalism from University of Rajasthan and has completed her PhD in 2016. Anjum has been teaching as an adjunct professor at Haridev Joshi University of Journalism and Mass Communication, Jaipur, since 2022. She also taught at the University of South Australia, Adelaide, in 2019 and the University of Sakarya, Turkey, in 2022.

Born and raised in Kashmir, Anjum is currently based in Rajasthan, where her journey in journalism first took root and inspired this book, her non-fiction debut.

FROM **DYNASTIES** TO **DEMOCRACY**

Politics, Caste** and **Power Struggles

in RAJASTHAN

DEEP MUKHERJEE

TABEENAH ANJUM

MACMILLAN

First published in 2025 by Macmillan
an imprint of Pan Macmillan Publishing India Private Limited
707 Kailash Building
26 K. G. Marg, New Delhi 110001
www.panmacmillan.co.in

Pan Macmillan, The Smithson, 6 Briset Street, Farringdon, London EC1M 5NR
Associated companies throughout the world
www.panmacmillan.com

ISBN 978-93-6113-584-2

1 3 5 7 9 8 6 4 2

Typeset in Dante MT Std by R. Ajith Kumar, New Delhi
Printed and bound in India by Thomson Press India Ltd.

FSC www.fsc.org
MIX
Paper | Supporting responsible forestry
FSC® C010615

To my father, Swapan Kumar Mukherjee, and mother, Sangeeta Mukherjee, for their love, support and encouragement. They undertook immense struggles just to see me happy. This book would not have been possible without them.

To my grandmother Kamala Mukherjee, whose love shaped me in my childhood days.

To my doting grandfather Ahmadullah Qureshi, whose clinic in Kashmir and conversations with patients were my first lessons in listening to real stories during my childhood. His old Osmond radio became my first classroom in journalism, where I discovered the meaning of news, truth and empathy.

To my grandmother Begum Atiqa Qureshi, who taught me the value of time, restraint and the power of silence.

To my parents, Fehmida Fazili and Mohd Ishaq Qureshi, for their unwavering faith, patience, prayers and encouragement that sustained me through every draft and doubt. This book exists because you never stopped believing in my dream.

To the people of Rajasthan
whose stories, struggles and unyielding spirit gave this book its soul.

CONTENTS

INTRODUCTION

THE MENTION OF RAJASTHAN, INDIA'S LARGEST STATE BY AREA, spanning across 3,42,239 square kilometres, often evokes images of vast deserts, camels, majestic forts and a vibrant culture. Beyond this colourful façade, however, lies a deeply nuanced and diverse political landscape shaped by centuries of feudal rule, caste dynamics and power struggles. The topography of the state is varied and challenging – the wheat fields of the Shekhawati region give way to the hilly Alwar and Bharatpur regions, nestled amidst the mightyAravallis, before we encounter the cityscape of the capital, Jaipur and, eventually, the endless stretches of sandy desert in the western districts of Barmer and Jaisalmer – an apt reflection of the state's political landscape, which is equally confounding and rife with contradiction.

Having worked as journalists covering the state's affairs for over a decade, we have found its complex history and enduring impact on contemporary Indian politics endlessly fascinating, but sadly, not particularly well-known or understood, especially outside the region. The uniqueness of Rajasthan's politics stems from its long feudal past, which sets it apart from other Hindi heartland states. Rajputana, as the region was popularly known until the state was officially recognized and rechristened as Rajasthan in 1949, persists in memory to this day. Its echoes can be seen in the way Rajasthani society is structured, how its inter-community dynamics have evolved, its distinct challenges while integrating into the democratic republic, individual-driven electoral campaigns and responses to events of national consequence. Through this book, we have attempted to trace the footsteps of the state's political identity on the sands of time, combining the best of our more than a decade of reportage experience with five years of extensive research, as it has transitioned from a state of princely dynasties to one of hard-fought democratic battles.

At the time when India won its independence, Rajasthan was a collection of princely states, known as Rajputana – each with their own kings, *jagirdars* (land owners) and administrative institutions that had faced minimal interference from the British government in their day-to-day functioning – and was substantially different from other areas of the country. While the national freedom movement had been at its peak in the first half of the twentieth century, Rajputana was undergoing a different kind of freedom struggle of its own, led by *kisan sabhas* (farmers' unions) and *praja mandals* (people's organizations) that were challenging the authority of royalty and feudal systems.

The Indian National Congress, the main political party that had garnered massive public support for its part in the freedom movement elsewhere in the country, could not hope to match the influence and power held by Rajputana's royalty. The kings ruled over vast swathes of land and each had their own armies, government officers and jagirdars to boot, to whom they had entrusted the management of large fiefdoms. The region's complex caste system further complicated feudal rule and relegated several communities to the lowest rungs of society, with no way to demand justice for the atrocities committed against them.

It eventually became apparent that freedom from colonial rule was imminent and the rulers of Rajputana realized that their kingdoms would soon be integrated into democratic India. At the same time, the agrarian class, which did not have any rights over the lands they tilled, began to agitate for freedom from the *jagirdari* system and realized that associating with the Congress could aid them in their efforts. The merger of farmers' organizations such as the Marwar Kisan Sabha ultimately led to the Congress emerging as a bankable electoral force in Rajputana. However, the feudal rulers managed to find an ingenious way back into the seats of power. Democracy, the very phenomenon that had ended their unquestioned rule, presented them with an opportunity to utilize their centuries-old influence to become a deciding force in the state's politics. In 1952, several of them contested the first assembly elections and the general elections as independent candidates. They not only emerged victorious but also managed to dent the fortunes of the Congress, which was invincible in other regions of the country at the time.

Rajasthan was among the very few states where the largest party in post-Independence India represented the peasants and the working class in the state and yet did not win a thumping majority in the first assembly elections. The Congress barely managed to scrape through to form a government. The jagirdars and royals permanently cemented their role in the state's politics with this win. They continued to play a crucial role in subsequent elections, leveraging their ideological tilt towards Hindutva to lay and later strengthen the foundations of anti-Congress politics in Rajasthan. This is evidenced in the success of non-Congress political parties, such as the Ram Rajya Parishad, Swatantra Party and Jan Sangh. Several founding members of the Jan Sangh, that later became the Bharatiya Janata Party (BJP), were from Rajasthan.

Since the late 1990s, the state had achieved a peculiar equilibrium – for twenty-seven years, the incumbent party had consistently been voted out every five years. The clear political demarcations between communities, which had sprung up after the abolition of the jagirdari system and initiation of land reforms, had also become much less rigid. The state BJP, previously home to Rajput leaders almost exclusively, now had several leaders from the Jat community, which had traditionally supported the Congress and formed the largest chunk of its cadre. Similarly, the Congress too began to court Rajput leaders to join its ranks.

And yet, the ground reality showed traces of the state's feudal past – the business of heritage hotels gaining widespread popularity, incidents of Dalit wedding processions being attacked for violating caste norms by having the groom ride a horse, and the erstwhile royals dragging old feuds from pre-Independence times into electoral politics.

Despite caste being the primary driving factor in the political arena, a magician's son from a minority caste became a three-time chief minister, while the most numerically dominant community nurses the grudge of never getting to occupy the CM's chair even once. A woman hailing from the erstwhile royal family in the neighbouring state of Madhya Pradesh became the chief minister twice and continues to be among the most powerful leaders Rajasthan has seen, despite belonging to a male-dominated party.

Another significant feature of the state's political landscape is the public's preference for larger-than-life personalities. Be it former chief ministers Bhairon Singh Shekhawat, Ashok Gehlot, Vasundhara Raje, or younger leaders such as Sachin Pilot and Diya Kumari – the charisma of individual politicians has always captured the imagination of the public. At times, this strong fan following has even compelled their respective political parties to surrender to their will. This resulted in the achievement of formidable feats, such as Shekhawat overcoming the demands of the RSS, Raje quelling dissent against her leadership and Gehlot outfoxing the Congress high command to prevent a change of guard.

A stroll along the streets of Jaipur's Civil Lines lined with the bungalows of current and former chief ministers and other politically connected families is akin to tracing the path of the state's politics. Old, well-known names from the BJP give way to relatively new ones, reflecting the generational transition the party is undergoing in the state, with the elevation of Bhajan Lal Sharma, a first-time MLA, to the chief minister's post in 2023. The Congress's decade-long tussle between the old guard and younger leaders continues and the peaceful locality betrays nothing of the inner conflict, generations of its members residing beside one another in apparent harmony.

This book charts the course of the political events from 1947 to the present day, when Rajasthan is at yet another crucial turning point in its history. It is based on five years of extensive interviews with both former and present politicians from the state and individuals who witnessed major historical events on the ground, and information gleaned from rummaging through mountains of old news reports and dusty old records of state assembly proceedings. The book recounts the details of this long and eventful history while also contextualizing it for the reader by providing the background to important issues such as caste and religious fault lines, the condition of marginalized communities and factionalism and rivalries within political parties – all significant factors affecting the politics in the state. The facts herein are further supplemented with stories of real happenings on-ground, which we have been documenting for years as reporters, and with anecdotes from our experience of covering six assembly and Lok Sabha elections, incidents of caste atrocities, Adivasi assertion, fight for gender rights, refugee rights, curfews, riots, lynchings, and stories of hope and resilience – all of which barely feature in the media outside this region.

This book is the first single, in-depth account (written in English) of the political journey of Rajasthan that not only embeds the state within the larger framework of Indian politics, but also critically examines the role played by regional factors in its specific context from the very first elections in 1952 to the present times and thus reveals the grand tapestry of the state as never seen before.

1

RAJPUT PRIDE AND ELECTORAL MIGHT

Old Rulers, New Turf

'*PATTHAR KO JO KAR DE PAANI, JAI* BHAWANI, *JAI* BHAWANI! (THE ONE who can transform stone into water, Jai Bhawani!)' echoed through the streets as a large group marched briskly past St Xavier's School, Jaipur, their hands gesticulating violently as they sloganeered on their way to the Rajput Sabha Bhawan.

It was 17 November 2017 and the Shree Rajput Karni Sena was having a field day protesting against the Bollywood movie *Padmaavat*. Angry young men, many of whom were barely in their late teens, clad in ripped jeans with coaching centre bags slung over their shoulders, were seen flinging shoes and chanting slogans at a photo of the director, Sanjay Leela Bhansali. On the previous day, Mahipal Singh Makrana, the then state president of the Karni Sena – he later became the national president of the outfit – had threatened to chop off the lead actress Deepika Padukone's nose[1] for her 'incendiary remarks'– she played the role of the thirteenth-century Rajput queen, Padmini, in the movie.[2]

Makrana, who claims to be a gold medallist from the University of Rajasthan,[3] had been generous with the theatrics, alternating between threats and sermons, pumping his fists, daring other actors who had come out in support of Bhansali, to confront him. '*Tu idhar aa ja, tera gussa shant kar denge* (You come here, we will calm your rage),' he said, in his signature beret at a press conference inside the Rajput Sabha Bhawan, targeting actor Hrithik Roshan.[4] He accused Bhansali of distorting history and showing Rani Padmini in a bad light. In the street outside, the police were silent spectators as the tall, bearded figure of Narayan Singh Divrala – the Divrala (also Deorala) suffix an allusion to the village where he was born – the then Jaipur district president of the Karni Sena, walked towards an effigy of Bhansali made by young members of the outfit using his photos and a wooden pole. It had been mangled from the constant kicks and punches it had received from the mobs. Standing beside it, Singh took in the television cameras before flashing a grin and shouting 'Jai Bhawani' at the top of his voice. He lit the fire.[5] 'It was me who had slapped Bhansali when he came to Jaipur,' Singh was heard bragging on the occasion.[6]

Thirty years before this incident, another fire had been lit in Divrala, which had sent shockwaves across the country and brought Rajput might onto the streets. 16 September 1987 saw lakhs from the ruling community of the erstwhile Rajputana gather to celebrate Chunari Mahotsav,* defying prohibitory orders by the high court. It had been thirteen days since eighteen-year-old Roop Kanwar's tragic death by *sati* on her husband Maal Singh's funeral pyre in front of hundreds of villagers and thousands following in procession towards the pyre, including some Rajasthan politicians.[7]

Following Kanwar's death, a Jaipur women's collective comprising academics and activists organized a massive demonstration against the practice of sati and filed a petition

---

* Now an annual ritual in Divrala that attracts lakhs of pilgrims, the Chunari Mahotsav began with Roop Kanwar's relatives – including her father, Bal Singh Rathore, who was informed of his daughter's death only after the fact – consecrating the couple's pyre on 16 September by pouring *Gangajal* and milk and wrapping a chunari over a *trishul* planted at the spot. The *sati sthal* (site) saw nearly 2 lakh visitors that day.

against the Chunari Mahotsav at the Rajasthan High Court that led to the ban. Lad Kumari Jain, former chairperson of the Rajasthan State Women's Commission and the woman behind the petition, recalled in an interview how her husband picked up a call on their landline phone and was met with a threat: 'If your wife goes to the court, *khoon kharaba ho jayega* (there will be bloodshed)'.[8] She also said that government officials had told Rajput outfits to expedite the celebrations, leading to the gathering at the sati sthal on the morning of 16 September. In addition, the women's protest march was met with a counter march by Rajput organizations, including youths carrying unsheathed swords, protesting for their right to worship Goddess Sati.[9]

Three decades later, Roop Kanwar was still revered as a goddess among the Rajputs, despite civil society maintaining that she had been forcibly placed on the funeral pyre by relatives, who, to this day, command respect from their community for being related to '*sati mata*'.[10] Roop Kanwar's death is the last documented case of sati in India. A fact-finding team sent to Divrala by the Bombay Union of Journalists (BUJ)[11] days after the event noted in its report that the sati sthal comprised a raised brick platform with a saffron canopy over it. In the centre was a *trishul* with a red-and-gold chunari draped over it, resembling the figure of a woman. Seven Rajput youth carrying rusty swords circled the site day and night in two-hour shifts for the next few days.

The fire of Roop Kanwar and Maal Singh's funeral pyre forged the political careers of leaders from both the Congress and BJP stables, with some of them going on to become multiple-term MLAs and cabinet ministers. To the late Lokendra Singh Kalvi, the founder of the Karni Sena, Roop Kanwar was a '*devi*', but Deepika Padukone was a '*naachnewali* (dancing girl)'.[12] Kalvi – once a national-level basketball player who often mentioned his six feet five inches height during conversations – was the son of former MP Kalyan Singh Kalvi, who was at the forefront of the pro-sati protests in the late 1980s.[13] Till the time of his death in 2023, Kalvi maintained that Rajputs are the 'actual victims'. He said that it is a misconception that all Rajputs were kings or jagirdars. A major grouse of his was that in movies the Thakur is often portrayed as a despicable villain.[14]

The emergence of pressure groups such as the Kalvi-led Karni Sena – named after Karni Mata, a deity worshipped by the Rajputs – in recent years are a reflection of the consistent anger felt by Rajput youngsters at the mismatch between their fabled past glory and current commoner status. Accounting for more than 8 per cent of the population, Rajputs have high representation in government services, judiciary and governance. In sharp contradiction, according to Satish Kumar, the director of the Centre for Dalit Rights in Jaipur, it took more than fifty years after Independence for the Rajasthan High Court to get a judge from a Scheduled Caste (SC), despite the fact that Dalits comprise 17.8 per cent of the state's population.[15] The state has consistently remained among the top three in the country – along with Uttar Pradesh and Bihar – for atrocities committed against Dalits.

So why does the Rajput community, which has ruled over the region for a thousand years, feel victimized? The answer to this question lies in the 1947 accession of princely states to the newly created Indian nation, when the royal families of Rajasthan negotiated with the Indian government over the terms and conditions of their merger into the state. They had to surrender their titles, lands and a large part of their assets to the Indian government so the land could be redistributed equitably among farmers, who, in pre-independent India, had served Rajput royalty without any ownership rights over the farmlands.

However, come Independence, Rajput royalty found a different avenue to continue their rule despite a legal end being put to their kingship – democracy.

Feudalocracy

A six-seater Beechcraft Bonanza plane flew low over the arid landscape of Jodhpur on 26 January 1952, dangerously close to the ground. Nearly five years had passed since India's Independence, but the passengers of this aircraft had managed to retain their royal stature. The pilot of the aircraft, Maharaja Hanwant Singh of Jodhpur, was a self-assured man. In line with his father Maharaja Umaid Singh's ways – who was accompanied by hundreds of servants and more than fifty ponies when he travelled abroad – he put his personal fleet of aircrafts on flamboyant display during his independent election campaign in the run up to the 1952 general elections.[16] Running on very little sleep, he was confident of a landslide victory over his rival, Rajasthan's best-known freedom fighter and the incumbent chief minister, Jai Narain Vyas. He had been met with immense love and reverence by the people while on his campaign trail[17] and was basking in the afterglow as he flew with his second wife, Zubeida, an actress he had met in Bombay. Since she was a Muslim, his clan had not been happy with her inclusion in the family, but the maharaja had paid no heed to their disapproval and managed to have their marriage solemnized despite these hurdles. Zubeida was renamed Vidya Rani and the couple lived at the historic Mehrangarh Fort, overlooking Jodhpur's Brahmapuri, home to the ancient houses painted blue that gave the city its moniker of 'Blue City'.

The transition from royalty to democracy was painful for the ruler, who fought tooth and nail to retain his royal status, even meeting with Muhammad Ali Jinnah during Partition discussions to explore the option of joining Pakistan if that would aid him in his mission. Jinnah assured him he was eager to make Jodhpur a part of Pakistan, but the maharaja had ultimately changed his mind and decided to sign the treaty of accession with India. His anger at the prospect of acceding to India has been well-documented by V. P. Menon, who was the Secretary, Ministry of States, under Saradar Vallabhbai Patel and his man Friday during the integration of princely states. Hanwant Singh initially refused to accept the terms in the Instrument of Accession, even threatening Menon with a revolver. He was admonished for his recklessness, after which he reluctantly signed the document agreeing to integrate Jodhpur into Rajasthan.[18]

When the date for the elections finally drew near, the *janata* (subjects) of Jodhpur never once considered refusing their Thakur sahab what he had come to their doorstep soliciting, according to Congress leader and former cabinet minister Pratap Singh Khachariyawas, a vocal Rajput politician whose political career was also propelled by the pro-sati protests.[19] Turbaned men abandoned their hookahs at the sight of the royal, lunging to touch his feet. Veiled women clutched the ends of their long *ghoonghats* while chanting *mantras* and showering him with vermillion. The maharaja ridiculed the Congress in his speeches, cautioning his subjects against voting for the party by invoking the sacred cow. He told the electorate:

> Congress is permitting the erection of a factory where hundreds of cows will be killed … to solve the food problem. The cow is like our mother. Perhaps Congress will next suggest that we should kill our mothers and eat them. … The slavery of the British was a thousand times better than the Freedom of today … I swear by the Goddess Chamunda that if elected I will continue to serve the people as my ancestors have done for seven hundred years.[20]

The young royal of Jodhpur inspired other royal families and jagirdars to consider the merit in using electoral politics as a means to retain their influence despite losing their power to the Indian constitution. A party founded by a godman from Uttar Pradesh would soon give them the banner to take on the Congress.

For Rajputs, the very thought of people with non-royal lineage and bureaucrats deciding their fate was revolting. Even the smallest of jagirdars had absolute power over the villages they governed. A report compiled on the abolition of jagirdari in Rajasthan by former Uttar Pradesh chief minister G. B. Pant in 1953 puts the total number of *jagirs* (land holdings) in the state at 16,780.[21] Land reform acts now threatened to disenfranchise the Rajputs and transfer the vast swathes of lands under their governance to the authority of the Indian government. Along with this, freedom fighters and future chief ministers, including Jai Narain Vyas, aggressively resisted the jagirdari system as well, leading to further alienation of the Rajputs from the new Indian state. Vyas led the Marwar Hitkarini Sabha, which demanded accountability from the ruler of Jodhpur. He was subsequently arrested and exiled from the princely state in the 1930s, but by the time of Independence had become the face of Congress in Rajasthan. Elsewhere, praja mandals formed by farmers mounted further pressure on the jagirdars, particularly in Shekhawati Rajasthan comprising Sikar, Jhunjhunu and Churu districts. Activist Kailash Mina, whose hometown Neem Ka Thana in Sikar district was ruled by the erstwhile Patan *thikana* (jagir), highlights the Dalits' discontentment with jagirdari, mentioning how the erstwhile jagirdars and their administrations perpetrated horrifying atrocities against marginalized SC and ST communities. His community, Meena, had even been classified as a criminal tribe by the British, which further made it vulnerable to arbitrary arrests and punishments during the rule of the jagirdars.

The Marwar Hitkarini Sabha demanded in 1929 that a legislative assembly overseen by the maharaja be created and elections to the municipal boards be held, all the while allowing freedom of speech to flourish. The Jodhpur royal family was compelled to bury the hatchet with Vyas, since his stature had risen considerably during his exile. In 1948, Vyas was made the prime minister of Jodhpur state, reflecting the growing pro-democratic sentiments in Rajasthan. In March 1951, Vyas, being a close friend of Nehru's, was made the chief minister of the state, and retained his position at the helm till the first general and state assembly elections in 1952. He had closely observed the clout of the Maharaja, and despite his consistently firm anti-feudalistic stance, as CM, he thought it necessary to find a middle ground with the royalty to ensure peaceful governance.

He entered negotiations with Hanwant Singh about allowing jagirdars to contest elections on 10 per cent of Congress's tickets, inviting fierce opposition from stalwart Congress leader Manikya Lal Verma. Later, he even let the Rajasthan Kshatriya Mahasabha nominate a member to his ministry during his first term as CM. However, any hope of the Rajput jagirdars joining the Congress was dashed on the eve of the first general elections, when the Jat-dominated Marwar Kisan Sabha merged with the Congress, giving the party a much-needed base in western Rajasthan. The Rajput jagirdars had been embroiled in numerous confrontations with Jat farmers who were tenants but didn't have any right over the land they tilled – there was no chance the two communities would be on the same side.

With an alliance with Congress no longer possible, the Rajputs rallied behind the Akhil Bharatiya Ram Rajya Parishad (RRP) founded in 1947 by Swami Karpatri, a monk who was a fierce critic of secularism and aspired to restore Ram *rajya* (a utopian idea of good governance as purportedly under the rule of Lord Ram). RRP's Ram Rajya imagined a state governed along Hindu religious lines, which put the party naturally at odds with the Congress under Jawaharlal Nehru, who was advocating for a modern, democratic republic system. With Hanwant Singh contesting as an independent candidate for the Lok Sabha and assembly elections, other royals and jagirdars followed suit, either standing as independents or under the banner of the RRP, leading to Rajasthan giving the fledgling party its biggest tally of seats in India. The Rajasthan Kshatriya Mahasabha also pledged its support to the RRP, helping it emerge as an unlikely challenger to the Congress, which enjoyed widespread, undisputed public support. Meanwhile, Hanwant Singh picked a group of Rajput men to contest as independent candidates in the areas comprising the present-day districts of Jodhpur, Pali, Jalore, Jaisalmer and Barmer.

The banner of the 500-year-old rule of the clan of Rao Jodha, the founder of Jodhpur, flew high once again when the twenty-seventh maharaja of Jodhpur defeated the incumbent chief minister of Rajasthan Jai Narain Vyas from the Jodhpur City B assembly constituency. Hanwant Singh received 11,786 votes in the elections, while Vyas lost his deposit after polling a mere 3,159 votes. He had contested from two constituencies and had lost from both – the Jalore A seat being won by a Rajput candidate fielded by the RRP.

The Congress, which won 364 seats in the first Indian general elections and comfortably formed the government in most states, was shocked by the outcome in Rajasthan. In the 160-member state assembly, the Congress bagged eighty-two seats, a majority by just two MLAs. In the Lok Sabha elections, it could win only eleven seats – half of the total constituencies. Powered by Rajput jagirdars, the RRP had won twenty-four seats, making the little-known party the principal opposition in the Rajasthan assembly. There were also thirty-five independents – enough to form their own party – and, interestingly, more than twenty of them were Rajputs from Jodhpur and other districts of Western Rajasthan, handpicked and supported by the maharaja himself. With fifty-four MLAs, the Rajputs comprised one-third of the Rajasthan assembly.

The maharaja of Jodhpur had been successful in his mission to establish a feudalocracy in Rajasthan – the throne had remained uncontested and the doors of democracy had been flung open for the former feudal lords. But as fate would have it, the architect of the victory was never able to enjoy its glory.

Hanwant Singh and Zubeida's Beechcraft Bonanza airplane crashed over Sumerpur, in Pali district, on 26 January 1952, killing both passengers before the election results were declared.*

A Rajput Political Renaissance

One can see the cogs of the state machinery churning day in and day out in Civil Lines, Jaipur – a devoted party *karyakarta* (worker) putting up hoardings; senior ministers in their sixth or seventh terms in the assembly finishing their breakfast on their sprawling manicured lawns; people from faraway districts, clad in dhotis and their off-colour sturdy *juttis*, queuing up to air their grievances before their elected leaders. They await an audience with the important occupants of these heavily guarded stately mansions, relying on the strength of caste ties or being native to the leaders' constituencies. They carry photocopies of legal documents, FIRs, case records in plastic bags, seeking respite from long-drawn court battles or speedier investigation from the police into pending cases their lives may depend on.

The jovial, bespectacled Abhimanyu Singh Rajvi is presently in his early thirties and a third-generation Rajput politician.† He flashes a smile as he walks past an elderly visitor on the lawns of

* Fifty years later, the memory of this tragedy would come alive in the Shyam Benegal-directed *Zubeidaa* (2001).

† Abhimanyu has followed in Shekhawat and his father's footsteps. He was formerly the vice president of the Bharatiya Janata Yuva Morcha (BJYM), the youth wing of the BJP, and his English fluency and popularity among Delhi's elite circles makes him the rightful, charismatic heir to the family's political legacy.

his maternal grandfather and three-time Rajasthan chief minister Bhairon Singh Shekhawat's bungalow. He makes a joke in chaste Rajasthani and the elder showers his blessings on him in reply. Abhimanyu's father and Shekhawat's son-in-law, Narpat Singh Rajvi, was formerly an MLA and cabinet minister.

Abhimanyu recalls with some fondness how his grandfather would deal with the huge crowds of people gathering at their gates every day to meet him, interacting with them individually, addressing them by their names – all while performing his usual functions of clearing files brought in by officials and bureaucrats. Shekhawat was a founding member of the BJP, former Rajasthan CM and Vice President of India, and his grandson proudly proclaims that the Rajput community has not seen a leader like him.

It is hard to dispute his grand claim. The veteran leader passed away in 2010 and we are yet to see a contemporary parallel who has influenced Rajasthan's political landscape in a comparable way. If Hanwant Singh paved the way for the Rajputs' grand entry into democratic politics, Shekhawat – fondly addressed as 'Babosa' by his partymen and the public owing to his stature as a father figure in the state's politics – was the able navigator who guided the community across the rocky terrains of electoral and coalition politics through the following decades and cemented their position. Shekhawat was a sub-inspector in the then State Police of Sikar and a distant relative of the jagirdar of Khachariyawas, a village in Sikar district. He successfully contested the 1952 elections from Danta Ramgarh on the ticket of the Bharatiya Jan Sangh (BJS) – the BJP's predecessor – selling his motorcycle to raise money for his election campaign.[22]

As an MLA, and later as the leader of opposition, Shekhawat vociferously took on the Congress and cornered subsequent state governments in the 1950s and '60s over issues such as corruption and law and order in the state. Emerging as a moderate yet unapologetic voice for the Rajput community in the wake of the abolition of the jagirdari system, Shekhawat highlighted the hatred being spread against the jagirdars, even though he supported the move to redistribute their jagirs among tenant farmers. With his exceptional oratorial skills, he alerted the Rajasthan assembly in December 1956 to the 'discrimination' faced by the jagirdars after they had been robbed of their power and income. 'I can surely say that at this point of time, what is an issue of class divide will take the form of a struggle in the future,' he said.[23] This was the first instance of a public representative giving political legitimacy to the narrative of Rajput victimhood, a thought that continues to fuel the ideology of outfits such as Karni Sena in present day.

Throughout the 1960s, members of Rajasthan's royal families continued to venture into electoral politics, becoming multiple-time MPs and MLAs. In 1962, Gayatri Devi, the Maharani consort of Jaipur through her marriage to the erstwhile Maharaja Sawai Man Singh II, bagged a thumping victory from the Jaipur Lok Sabha seat. She contested on a Swatantra Party ticket and went on to comfortably win two more terms from the constituency. Her long-time associate Dharmendra Kanwar recalls that the Rajmata was disappointed to bear witness to the prohibition of privy purses for former kings by the Congress and supported the need for political opposition.[24] The highest point for the Rajputs came in 1977, when Shekhawat was first elected chief minister of the state, riding the wave in favour of the Janata Party after Emergency was declared.

The fact that from the very first elections, when the first non-Congress government was formed, all opposition leaders were Rajputs is evidence of the community's shared anger towards the grand old party. In the later years of the twentieth century, more and more Rajput jagirdar families chose to join politics to protect their business interests and influence. While it is not up for debate that the Rajput elite struggled after the abolition of privy purses by Indira Gandhi, by the 1990s they had found other avenues to bolster their financial situation. In post-liberalization India, the hospitality industry boomed and many ancient havelis belonging to jagirdars and royalty were converted to heritage hotels. These were lucrative holiday destinations for foreign tourists, who had no qualms about splurging to get a taste of the royal life in erstwhile Rajputana.

Just a few hundred metres from the present-day residence of Shekhawat's family is the official bungalow of Diya Kumari, the BJP's rising star and, more recently, the deputy CM of Rajasthan in the wake of the 2023 assembly elections. She is Sawai Man Singh II's granddaughter from his eldest son, following in her step-grandmother Gayatri Devi's footsteps. She was brought into politics by former CM Vasundhara Raje in 2013, when she contested and won on a BJP ticket from Sawai Madhopur and became an MLA. Incidentally, Raje herself belongs to the Scindia royal family, former rulers of Gwalior, Madhya Pradesh, and was the first royal to become the Rajasthan CM.

However, Diya Kumari fell out with Raje after the Jaipur Development Authority (JDA) sealed the Rajmahal Palace hotel – her family's property – in 2016, when Raje was the chief minister. As the impasse continued, the erstwhile royal family roped in the Karni Sena, which organized a huge rally in Jaipur, reminding the state government of Rajput muscle. In response, her mother, Padmini Devi, the former Queen consort through her marriage to the Maharaja Sawai Bhawani Singh, expressed her gratitude for the people's support: 'I am overwhelmed by the support from all over Rajasthan. My family is hurt by the high-handed action of JDA at the Rajmahal Palace.' Diya Kumari's son Padmanabh Singh, who was made the titular King of Jaipur after Bhawani Singh's death, was also at the forefront of the rally. Diya Kumari distanced herself from the rally since she was a member of the ruling BJP government, but her community's displeasure at the Raje administration was clear.[25]

In 2019, Kumari became the BJP MP from Rajsamand. She claimed that her family were the direct descendants of Lord Ram, through his son Kush, and were hence named Kushwahas and Kachwahas. She claimed that the relevant documentary proof about their lineage was kept in the City Palace Museum.[26]

The tradition of former royals joining politics has continued till date – Jaipur, Jodhpur, Udaipur, Kota, Alwar and the Jat-ruled Bharatpur and Dholpur have all at some point in the state's history been elected to power as allies of either the BJP or Congress. What started in 1952 with a group of forward-looking jagirdars, rulers and the RRP has now become a permanent key feature of the state's political milieu.

'Kamal ka phool, hamaari bhool'

The monsoon had draped the hilly terrain leading to Udaipur with a thick coat of greenery. Shrubs and creepers covered this historic battlefield which had once witnessed the legendary battle between two kings that inspired a plethora of literature, poetry and political rhetoric. The narrow mountainous pass of Haldighati is flanked by rocks the colour of turmeric, giving it the name that has now become synonymous with the clash of Maharana Pratap and Akbar's forces in June 1576. This event is a watershed moment for the Rajput community and even today, swells the community's youth with pride – the Maharana's bravery against the huge forces of the Mughal Emperor Akbar makes for an impressive example of the Rajputs' glorious legacy. It is no wonder then that the community mobilizes readily to defend this narrative of their history, and any missteps come at a high cost to Rajasthan's leaders, as was demonstrated in 2018.

Four months prior to the assembly elections that year, Raje announced the Rajasthan Gaurav Yatra to help her fight widespread anti-incumbency sentiments and defeat a resurgent Congress under Sachin Pilot. In June 2016, CM Raje and then union defence minister Rajnath Singh unveiled a statue of Maharana Pratap in Gogunda, once the capital of Pratap's kingdom, 30 kilometres from Haldighati.[27] The statue showed the Maharana atop his loyal horse, Chetak, with hands raised and spear pointed upwards. It was a token of gratitude to the Rajput community for steadfastly supporting the BJP, and before that, its predecessor Bharatiya Jan Sangh. Raje herself hailed from a *kshatriya* family and often described herself as a 'Rajput *ki beti*' (daughter of Rajputs) to woo the community, which comprised the biggest chunk of anti-Congress voters in the state amongst all caste groups.

Despite the Congress fielding Rajputs in every election since 1952 and also awarding them important ministerial berths, the community's first choice has always been the BJP. Once settled into power after winning a thumping majority of 163 seats in the 2013 assembly elections, the Raje government continued with its overtures towards the influential community. Vasudev Devnani, a former college professor, was the Minister of State for Education in the Raje government with a knack for rewriting history. While launching a special issue of *Pathey Kan*, an RSS-affiliated magazine, in 2017, Devnani said that there was no doubt that Maharana Pratap had won the battle of Haldighati.[28] Leaders such as Devnani, who had a strong RSS background, wanted their tenure to be productive in terms of furthering the Sangh's ideology, and knew that by invoking Maharana Pratap, the BJP would only strengthen its relationship with the Rajputs. Almost all his public speeches included diatribes against 'invader Mughals' and scorn for 'anti-nationals'. He was unapologetic about making changes in school textbooks, removing Nehru from the syllabus of one class, declaring his intent to introduce a chapter on the 2016 demonetization and to ensure that school students are taught about the unmistakable victory of the Maharana over Akbar.[29]

The Rajput community was pleased by the glorification of Maharana Pratap in political discourse and continued to lend its wholehearted support to the government in all its endeavours. In 2017, Rajasthan textbooks were altered to change the outcome of the battle of Haldighati, with the revised textbook not mentioning Pratap's retreat from the battlefield – a fact that is generally accepted by most historians.[30] It appeared that nothing could dull the spark between the Rajputs and BJP – until the unthinkable happened. As Raje's Gaurav Yatra reached Haldighati in August 2018, it was greeted by the unexpected sight of sloganeering Rajputs.[31] '*Kamal ka phool, hamaari bhool* (The lotus is our mistake)', they chanted.

But what had caused this sudden change of heart?

The man who drove a wedge between the BJP and Rajputs was Anandpal Singh. A gangster whose extortion and bootlegging operations had frequently incited gang wars in the the Shekhawati region in the mid-2000s, Singh was an unlikely spoilsport in the decades-long alliance between the party and the community. He was widely viewed as a larger-than-life Robin Hood-like character owing to the immensely popular stories of his exploits peddled by the media. This led to young Rajput men idolizing him.[32]

In September 2015, Singh made a daring escape from police custody as he was being conveyed to a high-security prison facility after a court hearing. The escape – along with his penchant for posing for photos with weapons and appearing for interviews with reporters, speaking in broken English – made him an icon among Rajput youth, who hailed him for his bravery and claimed he was a victim of the system. The BJP government, which came under severe fire after Singh's mockery of the law, was forced to act fast. A flashpoint came in June 2017, when the Rajasthan Police killed him in an encounter in Churu district. Armed with an AK-47, Singh had fired at the police till his last breath, even critically injuring a commando from the Rajasthan Armed Constabulary. Singh's death led to massive protests by Rajput outfits, including a rally at his village Sanvrad, Nagaur district, where things quickly got out of control and violence ensued. The angry mob attacked the then Nagaur SP IPS Paris Deshmukh, who was narrowly saved by his gunman, but sustained injuries. One person died in the violence. The Rajputs spilled out onto the streets, vowing to teach the BJP a lesson.

Ironically, Anandpal Singh was a Ravana, a Rajput sub-caste that is not considered at par with the upper echelons of the caste, yet he had oddly managed to unite the community in his death. 'I would like to thank bhai Anandpal Singh, whose martyrdom demolished the barriers between the Ravana Rajput and Rajput communities and made us united,' Ravana Rajput leader Gajendra Singh Sankhla thundered in a community meet after Singh's death.[33]

August 2018, when Raje's Rajasthan Gaurav Yatra entered the hamlets of Mewar to ask the people to vote for the BJP, seemed the opportune time to remind the party of the extent of the displeasure felt by the party's oldest allies at Singh's 'fake' encounter. Simultaneously, in Jaipur, the Shree Rajput Sabha – the highest decision-making Rajput body – was flashing a poster of an inverted lotus with a red line struck through it. The Rajputs had vowed to correct their past mistake of helping the lotus flourish. The late Giriraj Singh Lotwara, the president of the Rajput Sabha till his passing in 2021, had echoed the community's sentiment that the BJP took them for granted. Over the next few months, Rajput leaders reached out to villages, blocks and tehsils to tell their brethren it was time to break ranks with the BJP and demonstrate the community's might. In the 2018 elections, the BJP fielded twenty-six Rajput candidates, but only ten of them could make it to the assembly.

In a spectacular display of unity, the community had demonstrated that there could be no ruling government in Rajasthan without the Rajputs.

Seventy years after the first elections in Rajasthan, the Kshatriya Yuvak Sangh gathered at a ground in Jaipur in December 2021 to mark their diamond jubilee celebration; the sea of saffron turbans surrounding the stage presented a formidable picture of the Rajput community's strength. Founded in 1944 by Tan Singh of Barmer, who later went on to become an MLA and MP, the Sangh describes itself as a non-political organization. However, everything about this gathering was political – Rajput leaders from both the Congress and the BJP were in attendance. A minister in the then Ashok Gehlot government, Pratap Singh Khachariyawas, sat beside BJP MP and union minister Gajendra Singh Shekhawat, who had defeated Gehlot's son Vaibhav in the 2019 Lok Sabha elections from his home turf, Jodhpur.*

Young men in sunglasses could be seen clicking selfies as the politicians addressed the massive crowds one by one, confining their speeches to the time slots assigned to them by the organization's leaders. The elders appealed to the politicians from the opposing parties to prioritize the community over political divides.

The thousands of people in attendance were not just celebrating the host organization, but the might of their community, which had survived the abolition of jagirs, the nation's independence and the institution of statehood and successfully merged their feudal past with the contemporary reality of electoral politics.

* Back in 2018, when Shekhawat's appointment as the state BJP president was stalled by Raje, Bhagwan Singh Rolsabsar, the patron of the Kshatriya Yuvak Sangh, had said that whoever had opposed his announcement will be opposed by the (Rajput) samaj. His words rang true as Raje was ousted months after the statement of the veteran community leader.

2

TILLERS AND KINGMAKERS

The Jat Vote

JUST A KILOMETRE AWAY FROM THE CHIEF MINISTER'S RESIDENCE IN Jaipur's Civil Lines, a steady trail of cars and two-wheelers moves sluggishly underneath the elevated Metro track that divides the road into two. The cluttered road often causes traffic jams outside Baldev Plaza, popularly known as Orbit Mall – a large, yellow structure with two triangles protruding from its roof. One of the earliest malls built in Jaipur, the building houses a plethora of shops, along with a passport seva kendra.

On this foggy January afternoon, Raghuvendra Mirdha sits at his desk in his office in the mall's basement, dressed impeccably in formal attire. He is in his early fifties and, gazing upon a timeworn bust of a turbaned man with a sharp moustache, he says with pride, 'It all started with him, my great grandfather'. The man he speaks of, immortalized in bronze, is Baldev Ram Mirdha, founder of the Marwar Kisan Sabha and an architect of the movement that led to the political empowerment of the Jat community in Rajasthan. He is also known to have popularized the Mirdha name in the state's political history, with various MPs, MLAs and ministers bearing the family surname over the last sixty years. Now here he is, resting in the basement of the mall that derived its name from him, watching over his grandson as he manages it. Their family owns all the office spaces in the building and has rented them out to various vendors.

Raghuvendra is a businessman and the youngest scion of a political family whose clout once transcended the state's boundaries to reach all the way to the Parliament in Delhi. This was during the era in which several larger-than-life Jat leaders from Rajasthan were members of the Congress party. His father Harendra Mirdha is a former minister and the incumbent MLA from Nagaur,[1] while his grandfather Ram Niwas Mirdha – Baldev Ram's son – was a multiple-time union minister and former speaker of the Rajasthan Legislative assembly.

But by now, the title Mirdha has lost much of its sheen, becoming largely restricted to historical electoral data and academic institutions named after the political stalwarts. Even so, any account of the many dimensions of Jat politics in Rajasthan will be incomplete without the story of the Mirdha clan.

Comprising more than 10 per cent of the state's population and holding the largest share of seats for any single caste within its 200-member assembly, the Jats are one of the most formidable forces in Rajasthan politics. The foundation for Jat assertion and dominance was laid by Baldev Ram Mirdha with the founding of the Marwar Kisan Sabha, which served as a body of primarily Jat farmers in the Marwar region of western Rajasthan. Owing to the fact that Baldev Ram Mirdha had a high-ranking job in the Jodhpur princely state as a deputy inspector general, he had considerable repute and influence in his community. Over the years, the Marwar Kisan Sabha became the biggest farmers' organization in western Rajasthan to vocalize the struggles and defend the rights of the peasants tilling the lands of Rajput jagirdars. The organization was eventually taken into the Congress's fold in 1951.

In the early twentieth century, however, the Jats of western Rajasthan could typically be seen labouring on farmlands they did not own and were not known to obtain formal education. Baldev Ram was, in fact, one of the first Jats to break with this tradition by passing matriculation in the English medium and emphasizing the significance of education to the community. He leveraged his close relationship with the royal family of Jodhpur to arrange for grants and facilitate the authorization of secondary schools for the children of farmers, predominantly Jats. This led to the establishment of Jat schools and boarding houses in areas such as Merta, Nagaur, Parbatsar and Barmer in the western region of the state.[2]

Before Independence, Rajputana – as the region comprising modern-day Rajasthan was called then – was a collection of princely states. Vast swathes of land entrusted to jagirdars by the king were called jagirs, and at times, even comprised several villages. The feudal lords, primarily belonging to the Rajput community, owed their allegiance to the king of the princely state and enjoyed unbridled power over their jagirs. The remaining land was ruled by the king himself and was known as Khalsa land.

Barring eastern Rajasthan's twin princely states of Bharatpur and Dholpur, which were under Jat rulers, Rajputs have always constituted the region's royalty. Even as late as 1950, 72.5 per cent land and 76.7 per cent of villages in Baldev Ram Mirdha's Jodhpur division were under the jagirdari system, and therefore under Rajput rule. In the Shekhawati region, which was a part of the princely state of Jaipur at the time, 50.4 per cent of the land was under the hold of jagirdars, with the rest being in the king's direct control.

The first signs of change and Jat empowerment were brought in by praja mandals in eastern Rajasthan and kisan sabhas in the west. Towards the end of the 1920s, awareness among the public, especially the more affluent section of the urban populations, started to increase due to the spread of English education and social reform movements unfolding across the country. Airing public grievances related to welfare policies of the princely states became more widespread and demands for greater say in the policy decisions grew. Despite the fact that this movement didn't have any one figurehead, but was led by multiple prominent citizens, caste panchayats and freedom fighters, it drove the establishment of local administrative bodies known as praja mandals in the urban areas of Rajputana. In addition to the well-represented upper castes, such as Brahmins and Vaishyas, these bodies also comprised Jat leaders such as former MLA Ranmal Singh from Sikar, one of the last surviving members of the Jaipur division Praja Mandal until his death in 2024 at the age of 101.

Two years before his demise, Singh recalled how, as members of the Praja Mandal, they spoke fearlessly against the excesses committed by the jagirdars and braved constant threat to fight for the rights of farmers.

> I joined the Praja Mandal because I could no longer watch the jagirdars treat farmers as if they were their subjects, not human beings. We wanted dignity, not charity. At Molyasi, when their men came with lathis and rifles to stop our meeting, I kept speaking. They hit me, and blood ran down my face, but I shouted, 'Mahatma Gandhi Zindabad'. They could break my bones, [but] not my resolve. That day I understood that freedom is not given – it is taken by those who refuse to bow.[3]

In Molyasi village in Sikar, a Praja Mandal-organized farmers' meeting in 1945 was brutally attacked by jagirdars armed with lathis and rifles in an episode that came to be remembered as the Molyasi Kand. The incident, which was brought to light by *Lokvani*, a newspaper published from Jaipur by Devi Shankar Tiwari,* the

* Devi Shankar Tiwari was a freedom fighter from Jaipur, Rajasthan. Throughout his life, he remained independently associated with newspapers. He served as the education, health and finance minister from 1946–49. Source: Devi Shankar Tiwari, Indian Culture, Government of India. Available at: https://indianculture.gov.in/node/2820547.

chairperson of the praja mandal, symbolized the growing defiance of Shekhawati's peasants against feudal oppression.

There were also the more rural-centric kisan sabhas, which were established specifically to advocate for farmers' rights. By the early 1930s, Jats comprised not only the backbone of the kisan sabhas in the Jodhpur division, but also played a significant role within the praja mandals, thereby elevating their political importance in the region.

Since Baldev Ram Mirdha had leveraged his status and connections to build more facilities for the predominantly rural Jat population, such as hostels and secondary schools, he had earned the unwavering loyalty of his community. As defiance against feudalism strengthened, the winds of change swept through the Shekhawati region as well, 300 kilometres away from Jodhpur. Here, awareness about land and civil rights was instilled in the Jat farmers by organizations such as the Arya Samaj and the All India Jat Mahasabha in the 1920s and '30s. Some of these organizations have considerable influence in the region to this day, as demonstrated by the two-time victory in Lok Sabha polls bagged by Sumedhanand Saraswati – former BJP MP from Sikar and an Arya Samaj monk – in 2014 and 2019.

The historic city of Sikar is considered to be the heart of the Shekhawati region for many reasons. In 1934, an unthinkable sight awaited its jagirdars – Jat farmers defied the law of the thikana by riding elephants during a massive religious ceremony, the Jat Prajapati Maha Yagna, organized for publicly pledging their resolve to attain land rights, literacy and political representation.[4] Men, women and children from every corner of Rajputana participated in the mega event – a display not only of the growing unity and mobilization among the Jat community, but also of an emphatic break with caste norms which dictated that only Brahmins could preside over religious ceremonies.

This invited the ire of the Rajput jagirdars, who had ordered the thikana police to crack down on the increasingly defiant Jat farmer population. In 1935, Jats from Khudan village attacked a contingent of revenue officials out to collect tax and more than 100 of them were arrested, and several died during the police crackdown. The same year, in Khudi village, the thikana police attacked villagers after a Jat groom defied custom and rode a mare on his wedding, further angering the already unsettled Rajputs.

It was leaders such as Sardar Harlal Singh – among the first Jat leaders to join the upper caste-dominated praja mandal – who realized that the community's struggle for freedom from the jagirdari system aligned with the objectives of the larger freedom struggle against the British that was raging in the country in the first four decades of the twentieth century. The desire for change in the status quo led to their increased participation in the praja mandals and eventually in the Congress, which had been trying hard to broaden its influence in the feudal politics of Rajputana since the late 1920s.

Baldev Ram Mirdha resigned from the Jodhpur princely state's police service in 1947. By then, his rank as a highly decorated government servant had given him unrivalled clout within the Jat community of this region. The Second World War had just ended and a large number of Jat soldiers had returned to their villages after serving abroad and begun to participate in increasingly intense debates about ideas of democracy and freedom from the oppressive feudal system. The Marwar Kisan Sabha under Baldev Ram Mirdha's leadership expanded to include other peasant castes, such as the Bishnois and Malis. These developments also coincided with citizen-driven movements in Jodhpur, with the public vying for more autonomy and participation in the princely state's civic and political decisions.

The Marwar Hitkarini Sabha, led by Jai Narain Vyas – the most powerful Congress leader in the region between 1938–42 – had established the Marwar Lok Parishad in 1938, which was to work in coordination with the king of Jodhpur as his official advisors on public issues.[5] Nathu Ram Mirdha, a relative of Baldev Ram Mirdha's, was appointed the minister of the agriculture sector. However, the Lok Parishad's activities were brought to an abrupt end in 1942 after the arrest of its most prominent leaders, including Vyas himself, due to its anti-jagirdar campaign.

In subsequent decades, Nathu Ram Mirdha emerged as one of the tallest and most well-known Jat politicians from Rajasthan. Shortly after, the Marwar Kisan Sabha was founded in 1946, and many more kisan sabhas sprouted across Rajasthan over a decade, serving as unifying platforms for the large farming community. This enabled the Jats to combine their numerical strength and their desire to break free from the shackles of the jagirdari system to create a unique coalition with Congress leaders such as Vyas and Manikya Lal Verma, who steadfastly opposed both British rule and Rajputana's feudal system and even braved imprisonment and exile to persevere in their demand for increased citizen participation in governance. With other farming communities and a national party on their side, they forever altered the political landscape of Rajasthan.

Finally, just before India's first general elections in 1951–52, the Congress got its biggest boost to date in Rajasthan. The Marwar Kisan Sabha merged with the party, making it the first choice of Jat voters for many years to come and firmly establishing the Jat community as a major political power. One of the conditions of this merger was the right to nominate 50 per cent of the candidates from constituencies in the Jodhpur division, thereby rendering the support of Jats indispensable to the Congress in Rajasthan.

Jats Versus Rajputs: The Origins of a Historic Rivalry

In reply to a question in the state assembly in October 1952, then chief minister of Rajasthan Tika Ram Paliwal informed the House that thirty-one instances of violence between jagirdars and farmers had been recorded in the past three months. 'The reasons behind the attacks are both financial and political. One reason is that section which was powerful, they are trying to grab land by force at a time when the era has changed. The second reason is that due to voting rights, even that section which earlier didn't know much is fighting for their rights over the fact that farmers have the right over land,' said Paliwal.[6]

The jagirdar MLAs launched a scathing attack against Chief Minister Paliwal for his statement, alleging that Congress workers were involved in these skirmishes. The CM termed these allegations as 'imaginary'.[7] This was among the first signs of the Jat–Rajput rivalry firmly taking root in Rajasthan's political system and manifesting in violent ways. The former feudal ruling class and their erstwhile serfs were now on equal footing and at loggerheads under the democratic system.

After the country became independent and the Congress came to power, propelled by the support of farming communities, the jagirdari system met its inevitable end. The Congress passed the Rajasthan Land Reforms and Resumption of Jagirs Act in 1952, leading to the abolition of jagirs and redistribution of lands among those who farmed them. As a direct result of this, the Jats became immensely powerful as new owners of the vast lands they laboured on in both eastern and western Rajasthan.

The next two decades saw the Jats emerging as a potent political force as well. After Baldev Ram Mirdha's passing in 1953, his legacy was carried forward by his son, Ram Niwas Mirdha, and nephew Nathu Ram Mirdha. Ram Niwas served as the speaker of the

Rajasthan assembly for two consecutive terms, while Nathu Ram became a legislator and minister multiple times, even heading the state Congress at one time. Other Jat leaders, including Kumbha Ram Arya and Parasram Maderna, ensured that the community's ascent remained unabated in the state's politics. While former Rajput jagirdars who joined electoral politics remained a powerful lobby, the Jats were part of the ruling party and held important portfolios in the government, thus emerging as a force to reckon with in the state's political milieu.

'The movement against feudalism had resulted in the spread of education and a sense of serving the community. When I first got elected to the assembly in the 1950s, I would go to my constituency driving a jeep, trying to resolve the grievances of people. Village elders would tell others to give their vote to the *chhori* (girl). I loved horse riding, believed in principle-based politics and always kept raising issues impacting farmers,' recalls one of the earliest women Jat leaders in the state, nine-time MLA and former speaker of the Rajasthan assembly Sumitra Singh.[8]

In February 1970, the murder of a Rajput student, Dilip Singh, on the Rajasthan University campus resulted in the sharp polarization of student politics along Rajput–Jat caste lines for several years. Singh died at a hospital a fortnight after being allegedly assaulted by a group of Jat students at the Vivekanand hostel, University of Rajasthan. Later, the trial court noted that long-standing farmer agitation in northern Rajasthan's Sri Ganganagar district had been the cause for discord between Singh and the accused. This rivalry between the two groups of students was a reflection of the larger conflict unfolding in the state as a result of shifting power structures. Rajput students such as Singh came from long lineages of erstwhile jagirdars. The Jat assertion and eventual abolition of the jagirdari system flung open the doors of colleges and universities to young Jat students from different regions of the state, establishing these spaces as new arenas for state politics to play out. Among those accused of assaulting and killing Singh were future Jat politicians Mahipal Maderna and Vijay Poonia. During the trial, the prosecution alleged that Maderna had transported the weapons used to kill Singh in a car owned by his father Parasram Maderna, a sitting cabinet minister in the Congress government.[9] Poonia's mother was a veteran MLA. Both the accused were subsequently acquitted.

The Rajput–Jat rivalry within the ranks of the Congress party led to senior Jat leaders, such as Kumbharam Arya, who had helped the party grow after the Marwar Kisan Sabha was merged into it, leaving after the Congress inducted former jagirdars to enhance its popularity in the region. The true barometer of this age-old feud between the two dominant castes, however, sits on the western edge of the state – the Barmer–Jaisalmer Lok Sabha seat. The home turf of former foreign minister and founding member of the BJP Jaswant Singh, the two districts of Barmer and Jaisalmer have been home to large populations of both Jat and Rajput communities. The region has had the distinction of electing stalwart Jat leaders, such as Ram Niwas Mirdha, and Rajput strongmen, like Kalyan Singh Kalvi, to the Lok Sabha.

Over the past twenty years, the battle for Barmer has become synonymous with the caste contest. Kalyan Singh Kalvi's son Lokendra Singh Kalvi – the founder of the Karni Sena, a Rajput pressure group – chose Barmer for his foray into parliamentary politics, but lost to Jat leader Colonel Sonaram Choudhary in 1998. In 2004, Jaswant Singh's son Manvendra defeated Choudhary, even though the firebrand leader had gone on to win the Barmer seat four times since his first victory. In the 2019 elections, Manvendra, who switched to the Congress after the BJP sidelined his father, lost the elections from Barmer to Jat leader Kailash Choudhary, who subsequently became a union minister. In 2024, the seat was won by Congress's Ummeda Ram Beniwal, a Jat leader. However, the Rajput vote was also consolidated and went to Ravindra Singh Bhati, a young Rajput leader, who decided to contest the Lok Sabha polls as an independent from a constituency in Barmer and stood second in the overall electoral contest – ahead of the BJP. This was despite the fact that the BJP had fielded sitting union minister Kailash Choudhary, also a Jat.[10] The Rajput voters had chosen to vote for the young independent candidate from their own community over more experienced Jat leaders.

In the caste-driven political landscape of Rajasthan, when a big leader from a particular community contests the election from a small constituency, the effects can be felt across the surrounding region, sometimes proving beneficial for their party at a state level. For instance, when Ram Niwas Mirdha contested the 1991 Lok Sabha elections from Barmer, the Congress also won other districts in western Rajasthan, including Jodhpur and Jalore. Such is the influence of this much-coveted seat.

The Chief Minister's Chair and a Jat Grudge

In early 2012, men were seen scouring the cement bed of a canal for days, wading into the water in their vests, while government officials scanned the scene using metal detectors. After three days, the Central Bureau of Investigation (CBI) found what it was looking for – evidence. Pieces of bones, jewellery, a watch and a human tooth were triumphantly displayed to the media. These items that were fished out of the Rajiv Gandhi Lift Canal in Jodhpur were the last remaining traces of Bhanwari Devi, a thirty-seven-year-old government nurse.[11] The discovery of her belongings sounded the death knell for the career of the powerful politician from one of the most influential political families of Rajasthan.

Parasram Maderna, eighty-five years old at the time, had

enjoyed a whopping nine terms in the state assembly until his son, Mahipal Maderna, the water resources minister of Rajasthan, was arrested in connection with Bhanwari's murder in 2011. Once numbered among the most powerful Jat politicians in Rajasthan, Parasram could only watch as his protégé Chief Minister Ashok Gehlot handed the Bhanwari Devi murder case over to the CBI, which eventually led to his son's arrest and the definite end of his own political career.

Mahipal Maderna had allegedly been in an illicit relationship with Bhanwari, who worked as an auxiliary nurse and midwife at a government hospital. Their affair was outed by a leaked sleaze tape filmed with help from a political rival. Bhanwari attempted to blackmail Mahipal for political gain but disappeared soon after, in September 2011. She had been missing for nearly four months when the CBI discovered her remains.[12] Due to the political clout of the accused – Mahipal Maderna was a sitting minister at the time – an FIR could not be lodged immediately and was only registered after a court order.[13] Mahipal spent a decade in prison while the case was under trial and died of cancer in 2021 as an accused and was never convicted, seven years after his father Parasram's death.[14]*

The Madernas had once charted the course of Jat politics in Rajasthan alongside the Mirdhas. Ram Niwas Mirdha, Baldev Ram Mirdha's son, died four years before Parasram, in 2010. Between the two leaders, there was shared experience of about sixty years of public life, serving as MLA, MP, assembly speaker, cabinet minister and union minister. The two men also shared another common factor – despite being among the strongest contenders to lead the state, neither of them could ever become the chief minister. Their stories reflect the biggest irony of Jat politics in Rajasthan – one of the most dominant communities in politics that helped the Congress firm its foothold in the state was never elected to the

* The case is still under trial at the time of writing.

top post. Brahmins, Rajputs, Kayasths, Dalits and Muslims have all taken turns leading the state. But the Jats, who at the time of Independence had led the fight against jagirdars and weakened feudalism with each of their electoral success stories, were never afforded the opportunity to lead from the helm.

Once the Bhanwari Devi murder case had dealt a deadly blow to the Maderna family's political career, Rajasthan was left with no Jat contender for the chief minister's chair. Parasram Maderna was in the fray to be the chief minister in 1998 as the leader of opposition in the state assembly, but his hopes were dashed, ironically by Ashok Gehlot, who owed much in his career to him. Ever since, the Jat community in the state has been relegated to faceless political influence. While the community continues to have the maximum number of MLAs for any single caste group, it has no contenders for the chief minister's chair.[15]

The 1998 assembly elections in Rajasthan were a defining moment in the state's political history – for the first time since the state had been formed, the Congress had spent eight years out of power. Stalwart Rajput leader and three-time chief minister Bhairon Singh Shekhawat had been at the helm for two consecutive terms, starting from 1990. First, he had formed an alliance with the Janata Dal and then engineered a split in the party, securing the support of the twenty-five MLAs of the Janata Dal (Digvijay) the second time around. Congress had struggled in the opposition, dwarfed by the country-wide Ram Temple movement and the decline in the popularity of the party after the Bofors scandal hit the Rajiv Gandhi government. Both these controversies bolstered support for the BJP in the Hindi heartland and the anti-Congress politics of the Janata Dal.

After two continuous stints as the assembly speaker, from 1973, Ram Niwas Mirdha missed the chance to be the first Jat chief minister of Rajasthan when Haridev Joshi was elected leader of the Congress Legislature Party (CLP). Joshi, a Brahmin, went on to become a three-time chief minister while Ram Niwas had to remain content with ministerial berths in both the state and union governments. Disillusionment with the Congress was on the rise among the Jats. Some of the stalwart leaders of the party, such as Nathu Ram Mirdha, had left over differences with the leadership and joined other outfits such as Lok Dal and Janata Dal, taking large chunks of the Jat support base with them. By the mid-1990s, Parasram Maderna was the only Jat Congress leader of the same stature as the Mirdhas in the state who had a shot at bagging the chief ministerial post. After serving as the Pradesh Congress Committee (PCC) president in the initial years of Shekhawat's tenure, Maderna became the leader of the opposition in the state assembly – pitted directly against the Rajput CM. At the same time, the young Ashok Gehlot was appointed the state Congress president.

So what role did Parasram Maderna play in the making of Ashok Gehlot? In a 1998 interview, he recalled how he had supported Gehlot's candidature for the 1980 Lok Sabha elections from the Jodhpur parliamentary constituency. When it came to matters of the Congress in the Jodhpur division, the Maderna family always had the last word. Neither Gehlot's OBC status nor his Mali caste held as much political muscle as a consolidated Jat vote bank, so Maderna went from village to village introducing Gehlot to the electorate and beseeching the public to vote the young leader into office.

As anti-incumbency in the wake of the eight-year-long rule of the Shekhawat regime thinned its chances of retaining power for a third term in 1998, the Jat electorate started looking to Maderna to become the first chief minister from the community in Rajasthan. 'I have not looked towards Delhi. [The real] India and Rajasthan are found in villages, I look towards these villages,' the leader had said before the state assembly in December 1993, on becoming the leader of the opposition.[16] During his tenure as the opposition leader, Maderna attacked the BJP on its communalism and other issues and accused Chief Minister Bhairon Singh Shekhawat of running a government supported on the crutches of independent candidates.[17]

As the 1998 elections approached, the Jats, who in recent years had begun veering towards the BJP, returned to the Congress fold to bolster Maderna's claim to the chief minister's chair. When the results were declared, it became evident that the Maderna factor had worked – the Jats voted overwhelmingly in favour of the Congress with him as its face. Never in the history of Rajasthan had the Congress got a mandate akin to 1998, when it won 153 seats; more than three-fourths of the assembly. Shekhawat's BJP was decimated with thirty-three seats, ending the three-time chief minister's reign in the desert state.

What followed thereafter, however, did not further endear the Congress to the Jats. The party high command under its newly appointed president Sonia Gandhi chose Ashok Gehlot –the state Congress president at the time – to be the chief minister over Maderna. As a consolation prize, the senior leader was later made the assembly speaker. In the later 2000s, former MP and union minister Sis Ram Ola was seen by some sections of the Shekhawati Jat community to be the rightful claimant for the top post, but due to his advanced age and Gehlot's firm hold over the state Congress, the possibility was soon abandoned.

The anger at Parasram Maderna being denied the chief ministership definitively diverted Jat loyalty away from the Congress. In 1999, when former prime minister Atal Bihari Vajpayee announced at a massive rally in Sikar district that his government would provide reservation for the Jats of Rajasthan, the community warmed up to the BJP. Four years later, when BJP's chief ministerial candidate Vasundhara Raje reached out to the Jats during her election campaign and described herself as a '*Jaton ki bahu*' (daughter-in-law of Jats), the community rushed to support her. The 2003 election results came as a resounding reinforcement of the Jat community's new allegiances – the BJP won 120 seats. A section of Jats continued to share a turbulent relationship with Gehlot after Mahipal Maderna was ousted from office in 2011 following murder allegations. Several gathered in Jodhpur to demand Gehlot's resignation as chief minister, accusing him of targeting the community, in a show of solidarity that transcended party lines, with Congress leaders such as Sonaram Choudhary standing tall against the CM.[18]

To date, the community continues to hope that one of their own will occupy bungalow number 8, Civil Lines, the chief minister's residence.

Jat Politics 2.0: From Kisan Sabhas to Farmer Movements

'Vasundhara and Gehlot have been in an alliance for 22 years. Both of them have protected each other over the years ...'[19] The above allegation may come as a surprise to most people. It is hard to fathom how two chief ministers from rival parties could ever be in league with each other. However, this is what Hanuman Beniwal has built his brand of politics on – not mincing his words and not shying away from punching above his weight.

Unlike other stalwart Jat leaders in the state from the Mirdha, Maderna and Ola families, Beniwal has never held a ministerial post in his three-decade-long political career. And yet, at present, he is the only Jat leader in the state whose aura somewhat resembles that of these erstwhile politicians from the Jat community – powerhouses in New Delhi whose influence stretched all the way from Marwar, Shekhawati, to neighbouring states, such as Haryana.

The tall, bearded Beniwal has a knack for switching from '*tum*' to '*tu*' during his interactions with the public and is quick to dismiss both the Congress and BJP, batting for a third force in the state. It takes a certain amount of audacity to try to be a third option in a bipolar state like Rajasthan, where no other political party apart from the Congress and BJP has ever managed to make significant inroads, let alone think of forming the government. Therefore, it was no insignificant feat when two months after he formed the Rashtriya Loktantrik Party (RLP) in October 2018, Beniwal's new outfit won three seats in the state assembly. In 2022, Beniwal was confident that '80–90 per cent of the votes from the Jat community will be for the RLP', referring to the assembly elections due the next year.[20]

The Nagaur district is nestled in western Rajasthan and has remained the epicentre of Jat politics in the state for more than half a century. Once a stronghold of the direct and distant relatives of Marwar Kisan Sabha founder Baldev Ram Mirdha, the outcome of the electoral battle in Nagaur decides the course of Jat politics in Rajasthan. Between 1971 and 1996, Nathu Ram Mirdha won six Lok Sabha elections, contesting on both Congress and Janata Dal tickets. In the 1977 Lok Sabha elections held after the Emergency, Nagaur was the only seat where the Congress wasn't defeated despite a massive countrywide wave against the party and Nathu Ram Mirdha emerged victorious. The other members of the Mirdha family who won the seat include Ram Niwas Mirdha, Baldev Ram Mirdha's son who defeated Nathu Ram in the 1984 Lok Sabha elections. Five years later, Nathu Ram won the seat back.

Beniwal's influence can be gauged from the fact that even the Narendra Modi-led BJP, which got a record 303 seats in the 2019 Lok Sabha elections, chose not to field a candidate against Beniwal from Nagaur, and instead entered into an alliance with him. 'The BJP received 30 lakh votes in different constituencies across Rajasthan because of my name. Jat voters have a significant influence in 20 to 21 Lok Sabha seats. When I went to campaign for BJP candidates, all the party's top leaders used to stand at the helipad to receive me … BJP leaders have asked me to merge the RLP with them, but I refused straightaway. When the BJP requires support, it comes to my door,' Beniwal says in his trademark manner, not willing to take the BJP seriously.[21]

But why did the BJP drop its sitting MP from Nagaur in the 2019 election and enter into an alliance with Beniwal's RLP, which had only three seats in the assembly? The answer lies in the image that Beniwal has managed to successfully cultivate for himself, which has won him immense popularity among Jat youth. He is the son of Ram Dev Choudhary, who was a close associate and mentee of Nathu Ram Mirdha's and later became a two-term MLA from the Congress and the Lok Dal after switching parties along with his mentor. Beniwal became an MP in 2019 after defeating Jyoti Mirdha, Nathu Ram's granddaughter.

Starting from the 1970s, the University of Rajasthan has been a hotbed of student politics and a gateway for young aspiring politicians to be initiated into mainstream electoral politics. With most caste groups having their own hostels in the state capital of Jaipur, the university elections inevitably reflected the larger caste-driven political scenario of the state. In 1997, Beniwal became the president of Rajasthan University, making clear his intentions of following in his father's footsteps. The 1990s were entirely forgettable for the Mirdha clan, which was experiencing a lull in its political journey with Ram Niwas Mirdha and Nathu Ram Mirdha – its two patriarchs – ageing, and the Congress also seeing an ebb in its fortunes after being kept out of power in Rajasthan for eight years until 1998. The lowest point for the family came in 1995, when Ram Niwas Mirdha's son Rajendra Mirdha was kidnapped by proponents of Khalistan.

While the Mirdha family was on a decline, Beniwal's stars were ascending. In the aftermath of an alleged gangrape inside the J. C. Bose hostel, University of Rajasthan, student leader Beniwal hit the streets, albeit not to side with the victim. Most of the accused in the case belonged to the Jat community, prompting Beniwal to claim that the community was being targeted and 'innocents' were being harassed by the police.

Some Jat legislators too were quick to pitch in. Condemning the gangrape, then Congress MLA from Kishangarh Jagdeep Dhankhar – who would later become the Governor of West Bengal and subsequently the Vice President of India during the Narendra Modi-led BJP regime, before abruptly resigning in 2025 – said on 9 September 1997 that the twenty-six-year-old victim had arrived at the hostel on a motorcycle and in response to the warden's enquiries, had boldly stated that she had come to meet her boyfriend. Spelling out the implications of his statement, he went on: 'What happened is wrong. Nobody can approve of it. But to call this rape, tomorrow if some death happens by accident during driving a car on the road should it be called murder?' Dhankhar's remarks caused a furore in the assembly. Senior legislator Kamla Beniwal – also a Jat, who went on to become the Governor of Gujarat – criticized the MLA, reminding him of his responsibility as a political leader in the situation: 'The subject of the discussion is to condemn such a serious incident and to tell the government the kind of action that should be taken. What kind of a perspective are you presenting?'[22]

Finally, in 2012, a court convicted several people in the infamous case and sentenced them to ten years' imprisonment.[23]

After his stint with student politics, Beniwal started his mainstream electoral career with the Haryana-based Indian National Lok Dal (INLD), formed by former deputy prime minister of India, Choudhary Devi Lal. Contesting from his father's former constituency Mundwa in Nagaur, Beniwal lost the 2003 assembly elections. Five years later, when the Mundwa seat was discontinued after delimitation, Beniwal won the 2008 assembly elections on a BJP ticket, but later fell out with former Rajasthan CM Vasundhara Raje.

Predictably, if there is one subject on which Beniwal can speak for hours, it's Vasundhara Raje. In Raje's five-decade-long political career in Rajasthan, first as an MP and then as chief minister, no other leader has targeted her in as scathing and personal a manner as Beniwal has in the past decade. 'I was with Raje (in the BJP) when she became the CM for the first time in 2003. At first, she called for the end of corruption in the Gehlot government but indulged in corruption herself. Gehlot set up a commission to probe graft allegations against Raje but nothing came out of it (the commission was dismissed after court orders),' Beniwal said,[24] repeating his allegation that Gehlot and Raje are from rival political parties in name, but go soft when it comes to each other.

The high points of Beniwal's four-year-old party are winning three seats in the 2018 assembly elections, bagging the Nagaur Lok Sabha constituency in the 2019 parliamentary elections in alliance with the BJP and thereafter breaking away from the NDA in December 2020 to support the farmer protests.

So what fuelled Beniwal's rise as a Jat leader and his popularity among the youth?

As explained previously, Rajasthan politics is driven strongly by the public perception of a leader. At a time when no true heir to the politics of Jat stalwarts such as Mirdha and Maderna is in sight, despite the large number of MLAs in the assembly, the community is resentful of the two national parties. Beniwal is well aware of how power works in Jatland. The best example of his political acumen are the circumstances under which he allied with the BJP in 2019 and then left the NDA – acknowledging later that it was an alliance of convenience.[25] Five years later, he allied with the Congress and INDIA bloc to win the Nagaur parliamentary seat, demonstrating that he was a slippery ally who will choose the path that best suits his immediate political interests.

Beniwal's consistency in raising the core issues that are affecting Jats, such as farm laws or the centre's Agniveer scheme – which allows the recruitment of young individuals to work as soldiers in the army on short-term contractual basis – in addition to his constant deriding of the Congress and BJP have earned him the respect of many community members who refused to take him seriously until a few years ago. In the absence of any other prominent leaders, Beniwal has emerged as the dark horse in the battle to uphold the Jatland legacy. But despite managing to carve out a support base for himself within his community, the fate of Beniwal's party echoed the largely bipolar nature of Rajasthan's politics dominated by the Congress and BJP. While the RLP did manage to win three seats in the 2018 assembly elections, it could only win one in the 2023 assembly elections – the candidate being Beniwal himself. After Beniwal allied with the INDIA bloc and went on to win the Nagaur parliamentary constituency for a second time in the 2024 Lok Sabha elections, his party's strength in the assembly was reduced to zero following the defeat of Kanika Beniwal, his spouse, in the by-elections.

Irrespective of Beniwal's changing fortunes, the Jat community today remains a deciding factor in the Shekhawati region and western Rajasthan, where the first farmers' movements started. The political strength of the community was demonstrated in both the 2023 assembly elections and the 2024 Lok Sabha elections. While the Congress lost the 2023 assembly elections, it still won the Shekhawati belt, capturing the majority of seats in districts such as Sikar, Jhunjhunu and Churu owing to the Jat anger against the BJP on issues such as the farmers' protest and Agniveer scheme.

Advocate Akhil Chaudhary, human rights lawyer and grandson of Jat leader Ranmal Singh, who was formerly an MLA from Sikar, a member of the erstwhile praja mandal and a lifelong crusader for farmers' rights, says that the Shekhawati region has been the crucible of farmers' movements in Rajasthan. Based on his experience of being involved in the 2020 farmers' agitation, Chaudhary notes that issues such as minimum support price (MSP) and government procurement continue to shape the political and economic landscape of rural Rajasthan. He argues that the Agniveer scheme, which curtailed long-term opportunities in the armed forces, has deeply alienated thousands of Jat youths who once saw military service as a path of dignity and security. Farmers in Rajasthan, particularly in the Shekhawati region, now face a convergence of crises that extend far beyond policy debates. Alongside MSP and procurement, rising input costs, depleting groundwater, erratic monsoons and mounting debt have also contributed to making agriculture increasingly precarious. Rural youth, caught between a stagnant farming economy and shrinking avenues of alternative employment, find themselves trapped in uncertainty, where both the plough and the uniform appear to be out of their reach. These intertwined economic and social pressures are not just indicators of hardship, but rather are reshaping political choices, migration trends and sustenance in rural areas itself.[26]

The discontent arising from these conditions was visible in the 2023 assembly and 2024 Lok Sabha elections. Such was the Jat anger against the BJP in 2024 that the saffron party lost Sikar, Churu, Jhunjhunu and Barmer – Jat-dominated constituencies that it had won comfortably in 2014 and 2019. Even the CPI (M), a non-entity in the state's politics, managed to win against the party in Sikar as a Congress ally.[27]

Over time, other Jat leaders have emerged as well, such as Govind Singh Dotasra – who has established Laxmangarh as his bastion and risen to the rank of the PCC president in 2020 – and Harish Chaudhary, a Jat politician from western Rajasthan who is a vocal advocate for the rights of OBC communities.

While the community's dream of a Jat chief minister of Rajasthan remains unfulfilled, it has demonstrated that no political party that wants to stay in power can ignore it.

3

A HOUSE DIVIDED

The Congress Conundrum

AT FIRST GLANCE, THE NONDESCRIPT TWO-STOREY BUILDING BLENDS perfectly with the ever-busy Sansar Chandra Road. Autorickshaws honk as they make their way out of the Walled City of Jaipur, and bus drivers compete to get to the next stop first so they can get more passengers. It is only after seeing the Congress party symbol atop hoardings and police barricades placed near the gate that the significance of Indira Gandhi Bhawan begins to dawn.

For more than five decades now, this ancient structure has served as the headquarters of the Congress in Rajasthan, seeing as many as nine chief ministers from the party pass through its doors. Occasionally, Congress Sewa Dal members can be seen sitting at the nearby roadside tea stalls, wiping the sweat off their foreheads with their trademark Gandhi caps. Meanwhile, within the damp, dark interiors of the Congress office, a group of party staff members are typing away on desktop computers drafting press releases for the media and official orders on behalf of the president of the Rajasthan Pradesh Congress Committee (RPCC). The Congress has ruled over Rajasthan for fifty years – two decades more than its present arch-rival, the BJP – and the building at the Sansar Chandra Road has steadfastly remained its main office for the entire duration.

The history of the Congress party in Rajasthan is significantly different from how the party set down roots in other states. From the early twentieth century to Independence, at a time when a nationwide movement was raging against the British, freedom fighters in Rajasthan, including influential leaders such as Jai Narain Vyas, Manikya Lal Verma and Gokulbhai Bhatt, were fighting a two-pronged battle. One was against British supremacy and the second was against the feudal kings of the Rajputana. As detailed in Chapter 1, the feudal system had been in place for centuries before the arrival of the British, but was bolstered further after the kings pledged their allegiances to the colonial government. Political agents were appointed to these states, who, apart from being the eyes and ears of the British government, also kept a close watch on the administration of the princely states. As a result of this unbridled power, the Rajput royalty and jagirdars had the last word in the everyday matters of their respective territories.

A people's movement that could challenge this well-established feudal regime needed large-scale public participation and a strong organization with deep roots in rural India and the capability to lead a charge of such magnitude. It was here that caste played the most crucial unifying factor – the Jats were the primary farming community in the region and hence the best-placed to spearhead this proletarian revolution. The native tongues of the various princely states in the region were different, although they were all dialects of Rajasthani – including Dhundhari, Shekhawati and Marwari. While the Rajput identity was common to all princely states, some areas of modern-day Rajasthan were under the rule of different caste and religious groups. For example, the royal families of Bharatpur and Dholpur were Jats and the Nawab of Tonk ruled over the only Muslim state in the Rajputana. Each state fiercely maintained its distinctness and individuality, even under British Raj, and often clashed with their fellow Rajputs. The jagirdars, who paid taxes to the central court of the king of the princely state, were royalty in their own areas, but were also divided along caste lines, wherein various gotras and sub-gotras were arranged in a hierarchy.

The longing for political consciousness and autonomy started growing among the urban populace of the Rajputana, coinciding with the return of a large number of soldiers of the British Indian Army deployed in the First and Second World Wars and uniting them with the rural populations in a collective desire to move away from the feudal system. This led to the birth of the praja mandals – the earliest forms of the Congress in this region.

Praja Mandals and Kisan Sabhas

Freedom fighters such as Jai Narayan Vyas, along with educated, well-read youth who wanted reforms in the feudal system, founded the Marwar Hitkarini Sabha in 1923 with the hope of effecting change. The Marwar Lok Parishad or the Popular Government of Jodhpur is one such example, which saw Vyas, a fierce critic of the king's rule and the feudal system, becoming the prime minister of the Jodhpur state in 1948 and ensuring the representation of other reformists in the government. While Vyas was leading the push against feudal rule in Marwar, his contemporary and friend Manikya Lal Verma was organizing the Bijolia movement against excessive taxation by the state in Mewar, comprising the modern-day areas of the Udaipur division. Both Vyas and Verma went on to become stalwart leaders of the Congress, with the former serving as the chief minister of Rajasthan twice, from 1951–52 and 1952–54.

By the 1940s, the various movements organized by the praja mandals had created a clamour for change. With the independence of India imminent as well as the eventual accession of the erstwhile states of Rajputana, it became apparent that the age-old jagirdari system would soon become a thing of the past. There was now a need for an organization which was formidable enough to take on the collective might of the Rajput royalty. At this time, the praja mandal's activities had also combined with the freedom movement of the Congress party at the national level. Evidence of this was seen in 1938, when the Jaipur princely state administration didn't allow freedom fighter and Mahatma Gandhi's associate Jamnalal Bajaj into the state. Bajaj disregarded the ban and tried to enter Jaipur, leading to his arrest and detention, which prompted the launch of a satyagraha in the state and created a new base of supporters who had not been part of the other protests in the region.[1]

The praja mandals, several of which later merged into the Rajputana Prantiya Sabha, played a crucial role in spreading awareness about civil liberties and introducing a tradition of dissent among the urban populations of the princely states. But the movement was largely dominated by upper caste elites and, apart from some representation of Jat leaders such as Sardar Harlal Singh, there was negligible representation of scheduled castes and other marginalized communities.

The praja mandals finally became a part of the Congress in April 1948, at the Bombay session of the All India Congress Committee (AICC).[2] Around the same time as the praja mandals activities, the farmers' agitation for land rights was being spearheaded by predominantly Jat organizations, such as the Marwar Kisan Sabha and All India Jat Mahasabha, in western and eastern Rajasthan.

After Independence, as the first general elections approached and the erstwhile Rajput royalty decided to step into the electoral arena, their formidable clout over the electorate became a cause for worry for the praja mandal elites, whose influence had not yet permeated into the rural areas. It was at this moment that the Congress and Jat farmers' outfits joined hands to form an alliance which transformed the Congress into a powerful political force overnight. The party now had the support of the huge rural farming class.

Jai Narayan Vyas and Post-Independence Political Climes

On the morning of 6 November 1954, a group of Congress MLAs committed an unprecedented act – they ousted Jai Narain Vyas, then chief minister and the party's best-known face in Rajasthan from the party's fold.

A freedom fighter, crusader against feudal rule and friend to India's first prime minister, Jawaharlal Nehru, Vyas went from being a journalist, poet and writer to chief minister of Rajasthan at the time of its first assembly elections in 1952. In his first term as CM, Vyas announced that the jagirdari system would be abolished, inviting sharp opposition from the Rajput groups. But the Congress held its ground and stood by Vyas's ideological stance against feudal rule. This stance also earned him the grudging respect of the state's royalty. His popularity was such that even some of the princely state rulers, who were sworn enemies of the Congress, had acknowledged that leaders like Vyas were the future.

In 1937, Maharaja Ganga Singh, the erstwhile king of Bikaner, wrote to Sir Donald M. Field, the then chief minister of Jodhpur – the letter reflects the grudging respect that the royals had for Vyas's commitment to fighting against feudalism. He described Vyas, with whom he himself had many grudges, as a 'self-made man, honest and true to his conscience' and urged Field to adopt a more lenient stance towards Vyas's rebellious activities in his hometown that had led to his exile, ordered by the king of Jodhpur. He called to end Vyas's exile, stating:

> Let me tell you, Sir Donald, that neither the glorified pillars of the Princely order nor the loftiest pillars among the Regency Bucks are going to survive these proletarian firebrands. Yet the mantle of centuries-old sovereignty in India is going to fall upon them and

> some of us will, in all probability, look towards them for justice and fair play.[3]

Vyas lost the elections from two constituencies to Rajput royalty and, in his stead, Congress leader Tika Ram Paliwal was made CM in November 1952. However, his stature enabled him to contest and win a by-poll from Kishangarh in the same year and take back the reins of chief ministership.

Ironically, despite fighting his entire life against Rajput jagirdars and even being exiled from his hometown by the king of Jodhpur, it was softening his stand on feudalism in later years that cost Vyas his party's favour. In what was one of the earliest instances of rising factionalism within the Congress, Jat leader Kumbha Ram Arya, along with Manikya Lal Verma, freedom fighter and once a close friend of Vyas, and Mohan Lal Sukhadia of Udaipur, around whom other party leaders rallied, closed ranks and ended Vyas's tenure as chief minister. In the election for the CLP leader, Vyas received fifty-one votes, while Sukhadia got fifty-nine votes, making him the new face of the state.

Months before Vyas was forced to relinquish the top post, he had become the object of Jat anger after negotiating the entry of former jagirdars into Congress, which he had felt was necessary for the expansion of the party in Rajasthan. To remedy the party's weak majority in the Rajasthan assembly, Vyas ensured the absorption of twenty-two jagirdar MLAs into the Congress in 1954. Jat leaders were furious over this move and felt betrayed by the Congress, which had been able to make inroads into this region solely due to its vocal allyship with the anti-feudal movement spearheaded by the Jat community.

Congress spokesperson Swarnim Chaturvedi, an advocate by profession, is a regular at the Sansar Chand Road office of the PCC. His family has been associated with the Congress for three generations. Six decades ago, his grandfather Narayan Chaturvedi had been an MLA from Chaksu in Jaipur and one of former CM Tika Ram Paliwal's loyalists who had voted against Vyas in the CLP elections. Relentless power struggles and change in leadership have characterized Rajasthan Congress ever since the party gained a foothold in the state. Now in his seventies, Swarnim's father, Ashok Chaturvedi, still remembers the time he met CM Tika Ram Paliwal as a child. He also recounts a later encounter, when the leader – now no longer the CM – had visited their home, sometime in 1954. When Paliwal got ready to leave, Narayan Chaturvedi asked his son to drop the leader to the bus stand. Paliwal rode pillion on Ashok's scooter until they caught up with a bus. Paliwal thanked Ashok for the lift, gestured to the bus to stop and boarded it. Today, it is unimaginable that a former chief minister would ride pillion on a scooter or board a public bus.

Chaturvedi's memory sheds a unique light on the political climate around 1954. Despite the fact that a well-respected leader such as Vyas was forced to step down from his position by his own party, the people who had planned his ouster had nevertheless touched his feet as they bade him farewell. 'We touched the feet of Vyas ji and asked for forgiveness. We told him that your stature is much higher than the leader of the Congress legislature party. We should forget whatever happened,' Mathura Das Mathur, one of the main architects of the ouster of Vyas had said, as documented by journalist Vijay Bhandari.[4]

Bhandari also details how a day after his resignation, Vyas left his official accommodation with just one briefcase and later returned to Jodhpur by train. He was made the PCC president in 1956 in a bid to restore some semblance of his former glory, but Vyas could never become chief minister again. Bhanu Kapil, an associate professor and head of the department of history at B. N. University, Udaipur, describes Vyas as 'a great freedom fighter who, through his newspapers and writings, had taken on the mighty feudal kings of Rajputana. But he was not a shrewd politician.'[5] Despite being the leader who made the Congress a formidable political force in the princely states, Vyas fell prey to factionalism within the party.

Once the seed of infighting had been sowed in the Congress, it was not deterred by actions such as a show of respect by leaders who opposed Vyas. The Jats had been instrumental in forging an alliance with Sukhadia to facilitate Vyas's removal from office and were naturally miffed with Sukhadia for adopting the same course as the former CM – bringing more Rajput jagirdars into Congress. Stalwart Jat leader Kumbha Ram Arya's daughter-in-law, former Congress MLA Suchitra Arya, details her father-in-law's role in merging the praja mandals into the Congress, which transformed the party into a political force to reckon with. In his capacity as the state revenue minister, Arya had overseen the abolition of the jagirdari system, and noticing CM Sukhadia invite those very jagirdars and feudal lords into the Congress prompted him to diverge from the party leader.[6]

Over the next decade, the power struggle between Sukhadia and Arya remained constant, reaching a flashpoint in 1966. Arya left the Congress and formed the Janta Party (not to be confused with the Janata Party that defeated the Congress in 1977) with other leaders such as Ram Karan Joshi, Daulat Ram Saran and, most interestingly, the erstwhile maharaja of Jhalawar Harish Chandra Singh, whose presence in the Congress had once been unacceptable to Arya. The CM also fell out with his mentor Manikya Lal Verma, a contemporary of Vyas's who had been instrumental in bringing him to power. Verma eventually became a member of the Rajya Sabha and distanced himself from the state's politics. With the exit of its founding leaders, Sukhadia became the tallest politician in the party. Settling comfortably in his chair, he went on to become the longest-serving CM of Rajasthan.

The Sukhadia Era

An unlikely name in a party of larger-than-life leaders, thirty-eight-year-old Mohan Lal Sukhadia was an 'accidental chief minister', first rising to occupy office in 1954. When he finally relinquished the post after seventeen years, Sukhadia had set the record for the longest-serving chief minister of Rajasthan, a feat that is yet to be surpassed by the next generation of leaders. After the first four chief ministers of Rajasthan – Heera Lal Shastri, bureaucrat C. S. Venkatachar, Tika Ram Paliwal and Jai Narain Vyas – in the seven years following Independence, it was his political ingenuity that enabled Sukhadia to maintain his power during his nearly two-decade-long tenure. Despite being surrounded by party members who were ready to go for his jugular at the slightest opportunity, Sukhadia, a protégé of Manikya Lal Verma, would always manage to pull a new trick out of his hat and keep his rivals on their toes.

'Sukhadia is central to the study of Rajasthan politics,' according to Kamakhya Lal Kamal, who gives him credit for stabilizing and strengthening Congress rule over the state from the time he assumed chief ministership in November 1954.[7] Contrary to popular belief, soon after occupying office, Sukhadia showed the first indication that he was not the kind of chief minister who would allow himself to be steered by Jat leaders like Arya. After assuming charge as CM, he included Ram Niwas Mirdha in his cabinet. Since Mirdha had been introduced into politics by Nathu Ram Mirdha, his fresh face helped Sukhadia create a separate power centre within the Jat lobby, which had thus far been overwhelmingly dominated by Arya, who acted as their spokesman. A few years later, when Jai Narain Vyas was made the president of the PCC,

Sukhadia also made placatory gestures by including some of Vyas's loyalists in his cabinet.

In the 1957 assembly elections, Sukhadia's chief ministership got the approval of the public as the Congress won 119 seats out of the 176 seats in the assembly, a clear gain from its tally of eighty-two seats in 1952. A year after this win, Sukhadia faced yet another challenge – this time from the praja mandal generation of leaders who had founded and facilitated the growth of the Congress in Rajasthan. Jai Narain Vyas, Manikya Lal Verma and former chief ministers Tika Ram Paliwal and Heeralal Shastri, among others, prepared a chargesheet against the Sukhadia government, accusing it of corruption and nepotism. This was the first step in a larger campaign to remove Sukhadia from office, although the move did little to deter the CM. Fresh into his second term with a comfortable majority, Sukhadia happily put his chief ministership to a vote at a CLP meeting and secured the favour of the majority yet again.[8]

In the 1962 elections, however, the Congress suffered a major setback when its tally dropped from 119 seats to just eighty-eight. An analysis of the results of the 1962 and 1967 elections shows a declining trend in the party's popularity, primarily due to a resurgent opposition. The Swatantra Party, led by the erstwhile queen of Jaipur, Gayatri Devi, performed exceedingly well at the polls. Its thirty-six seats in the 1962 election had reached forty-eight by the 1967 polls.

Corruption allegations levelled against Sukhadia, in particular, related to misappropriation of gold at the famous Shrinath Ji temple in Nathdwara, tarnished the chief minister's image.[9] Although the accusations were never proven, in the 1967 elections, the combined strength of the opposition proved to be more than the Congress could overcome. With a total strength of ninety-five MLAs, the opposition staked the claim to form the government. The Congress, despite winning eighty-nine seats, was left with only eighty-eight MLAs after one legislator, who had won from two constituencies, resigned. The governor, however, did not pay heed to the opposition and invited Sukhadia to form the government instead, leading to large-scale protests erupting across Jaipur. In an unprecedented event, police firing in Jaipur's Johari Bazaar resulted in nine casualties in March 1967, after which President's Rule was imposed in the state.

When Sukhadia finally managed to break legislators away from the opposition and into the Congress's fold, the party formed a government in the state for the fourth time.

While he may have served as CM for seventeen years, rising above the affairs of the otherwise infighting-ridden Rajasthan Congress, Sukhadia's downfall arrived with the 1969 presidential elections. The elections had become a proxy battleground with Prime Minister Indira Gandhi and the old-timers in the Congress fighting for control of the party. The Congress's presidential candidate, Neelam Sanjiva Reddy, had the support of then party president S. Nijalingappa and other leaders such as K. Kamaraj, who were part of the anti-Indira group commonly known as 'the Syndicate'. The incumbent vice president V. V. Giri decided to throw his hat into the ring for the presidential elections as well, backed by the tacit support of Indira Gandhi, who asked her fellow Congressmen to vote as per their conscience. V. V. Giri was elected president after defeating Congress's official candidate. Indira Gandhi's message to her party echoed loud and clear: she was the boss. Sukhadia had made the wrong move by supporting Reddy in the presidential elections, which was the last nail in the coffin for his chief ministerial tenure. In July 1971, he was made to resign from his post.[10]

A New CM Every Few Years

Mohan Lal Sukhadia was succeeded by Barkatullah Khan, who was one among a handful of Rajasthan Congress members who voted for V. V. Giri in the presidential elections. The state chief ministership was bestowed upon him as a reward for his loyalty. To date, Khan remains the only Muslim chief minister of Rajasthan. His untimely death at the age of fifty-three in 1973 prematurely ended his tenure and paved the way for senior Congress leader Hari Dev Joshi to become CM. Joshi, a Brahmin, was challenged by Ram Niwas Mirdha during a CLP meeting and thereafter won the internal election, dashing the chances of Rajasthan getting its first Jat chief minister.

In the early 1980s, Jagannath Pahadia, then Rajasthan CM, was invited to attend a literary function at Jaipur's Ravindra Manch auditorium. Among those present and honoured at the function was the legendary Hindi poetess Mahadevi Verma. Senior journalist and editor Om Thanvi, who was with *Rajasthan Patrika* at the time, recalls that Verma had not minced her words while criticizing the deteriorating standards in politics. She urged the public to awaken their political consciousness, urging them with '*Jaago fir ek baar* (Rise once again)'. The CM had felt targeted by her comments as the first – and till date the only – Dalit holder of the top office in the state. When he proceeded to take the dais to deliver his own speech, the audience was surprised at his remarks: he said he found it 'difficult' to understand Verma's poems and was even considering announcing a grant or two for the literary community, until her scathing comments had made him change his mind.

Thanvi had tape-recorded the entire programme. A few days after the event, his editor at the paper asked for the tapes, and he later found out that Sheila Kaul, a relative of Jawaharlal Nehru's and a senior Congress leader, was in Jaipur and had asked for them. Mahadevi Verma regarded Nehru as her elder brother and was hugely revered by PM Indira Gandhi. The fact that Pahadia's comments against her had reached the Congress top brass meant that his days in office were numbered.[11] Sure enough, a few months later, Pahadia was asked to clear out his desk and vacate the chief minister's residence by the PM, who cut his term short after just one year – from June 1980 to July 1981.

Even before this, the CM had faced stiff opposition from his cabinet colleagues, as they refused to adjust to his style of functioning. They resented him for his lack of punctuality and the fact that despite not having been actively involved in the state's politics as an MP, he had been appointed as CM by the Congress high command on Sanjay Gandhi's recommendation. It did not help Pahadia's case that he was not the first chief minister to be parachuted into office by the party leadership. This was a key feature of the story of the Congress in Rajasthan in the 1970s and '80s – the party high command anointed and fired chief ministers at will and no CM ever managed to serve a full term in office, especially in the '80s.

At all points of time in the party's history in Rajasthan, rivalries between state Congress leaders were constantly escalated to the high command. Throughout the 1970s and '80s, leaders would lobby hard to get an appointment with Indira and Sanjay Gandhi, and later with Rajiv, to apprise them of the 'misgovernance' by their rivals. This was one of the primary factors in Pahadia's exit from office as well. Mohan Lal Sukhadia was a powerful influence even after he had stepped away from electoral politics a decade earlier. After seventeen years in office, Sukhadia had an army of trusted lieutenants, such as Heeralal Devpura, who helped him stay abreast of even the smallest happenings in the state. After a few stints as governor of various states, Sukhadia forayed into electoral politics once again, winning the 1980 Lok Sabha elections from Udaipur. Around this time, state Congress leaders approached him with complaints against CM Pahadia, which he dutifully relayed to the party high command and the Congress parliamentary board, of which he was a part. Subsequently Pahadia was removed from office. Thereafter, Shiv Charan Mathur was made CM in 1981 in yet another instance where his loyalty to the party was rewarded with the charge of the state.

It was an unprecedented occurrence: the helicopter of a sitting CM lay mangled on the ground in Bharatpur – once the kingdom of Jat ruler, Maharaja Suraj Mal, a name that invokes pride and respect in the community to this day. The helicopter had fallen prey to the wrath of Raja Man Singh, Suraj Mal's descendant and a seven-time MLA. He was feared by his rivals but loved by the people of his constituency, Deeg.

On the eve of the 1985 assembly elections, Man Singh was fuming because Congress workers had torn his posters and flag to shreds right before CM Shiv Charan Mathur's visit. He felt that he needed to send the party a message. What he did next has since become the stuff of folklore. Man Singh allegedly repeatedly rammed his one-tonne World War II-era weapons carrier jeep into the chief minister's parked helicopter. Thankfully, the pilot managed to escape and there were no casualties.[12]

Undefeated since the first assembly elections in 1952, Man Singh held unbridled power over Bharatpur and was one of the state assembly's most vocal members. His blatant disregard for the government, evident in this act of impunity, angered and stunned Shiv Charan Mathur in equal measure. He had been leading the state comfortably since Pahadia's ouster four years ago. His clamp-down in response went down in history as the infamous 'Bharatpur encounter case'.

A day after destroying the helicopter, Man Singh was driving through a busy market area with his son-in-law and associates, when a flurry of bullets stopped their jeep in its tracks. Over the next few minutes, the Rajasthan police fired several more rounds at the group, killing three people, including the former royal. The fact that the firing was ordered by the Deputy Superintendent of Police,[13] a Rajput, inevitably attached it to the legacy of rivalry between the Jats and Rajputs in the state and incensed the people of Bharatpur. Violence broke out and several police vehicles were torched. Shiv Charan Mathur was left to bear the biggest brunt of all – he was ordered to resign from his post by PM Rajiv Gandhi.

For the next fifteen days after Mathur's resignation, Heeralal Devpura, once a staunch supporter of ex-CM Sukhadia, held fort as CM until the next round of elections were conducted. The public of Deeg, the assembly constituency of the slain Raja Man Singh, voted overwhelmingly in favour of his daughter Krishnendra Kaur, furious at the killing of their beloved Raja sahab. Kaur received more than 44,000 votes, while her closest rival was an independent candidate who got just 687.

By this point in time, it had become tradition in Rajasthan for chief ministers to change every few years. Every time a CM faltered or made a mistake that left the party embarrassed, his many detractors in the Congress would ensure that the high command relieved him of his duties, so someone else could have a shot at the top post. In his five years as Prime Minister of India between 1984–89, Rajiv Gandhi changed the CM of Rajasthan five times, resulting in a game of musical chairs. Despite Man Singh's death in February 1985, however, the Congress managed to win majority with 113 seats in the state assembly in the following elections, primarily owing to the general sense of sympathy towards the party at a national level after Indira Gandhi's assassination in 1984. Once they formed the government in 1985, Heeralal Devpura, who had been the CM in the interim before the elections, was not considered for the post. Instead, former CM Hari Dev Joshi made a comeback, whose government had been dismissed by the Janata Party administration in 1977.

In his second stint as CM, two incidents spelt doom for Joshi. The first was the sati of Roop Kanwar, a Rajput woman in Sikar district's Divrala village, who was burned on her husband's funeral pyre. Her death made international headlines, with activists and women's rights groups slamming the Rajasthan government. Thirteen days after the death of Kanwar, when the government couldn't stop lakhs of Rajputs from organizing a ceremony where the incident took place, Joshi's image was damaged further.

The final push leading to Joshi's ouster came in December 1988, when Prime Minister Rajiv Gandhi held a meeting with his council of ministers in Sariska. Bogged down by the Bofors scandal allegations and from fighting a resurgent opposition, Gandhi gave strict instructions to Joshi that the meeting was to remain an austere affair and he was not to create fanfare or put on an ostentatious display of any sort.

Gandhi drove himself to Sariska from Delhi in an SUV. Making a wrong turn, he arrived at a spot where hundreds of government vehicles were parked in waiting for the reception of Joshi and other dignitaries arriving in Sariska. The PM was furious and publicly rebuked Joshi for defying his orders. A month later, Joshi resigned and Shiv Charan Mathur was reinstated as the chief minister after a cooling-off period of three years since the Bharatpur encounter.

In the following year, Rajasthan saw two more chief ministers' resignations. Mathur resigned after Congress's dismal performance at the 1989 Lok Sabha elections, when the Rajiv Gandhi government was voted out. In Rajasthan, the party had failed to win a single Lok Sabha seat against the Janata Dal and the BJP. In the remaining three months of its tenure as state government, Hari Dev Joshi resigned from his post as the Governor of Assam and rushed to Rajasthan to assume the chief minister's office for a third time.

Ninety days later, the BJP–Janata Dal coalition, led by Bhairon Singh Shekhawat, wrenched power from the hands of the Congress government after a resounding victory in the 1990 assembly elections.

It is clear from these examples that factional feuds and a battle for supremacy among leaders across eras have been constants in the Rajasthan Congress's journey. However, despite its internal divisions, the party has managed to consistently form the government in the state, even when its stature was diminished at the national level. The caste alliances which it helped stitch after Independence too have largely remained intact, ensuring that unlike in states such as Uttar Pradesh or Bihar, no regional party could wrest power from the grand old party in the state.

4

THE SAFFRON SURGE

The Roots of Anti-Congress Sentiments

The Shekhawat Legacy

IN THE FINAL YEARS OF HIS LIFE, JAI BAHADUR SINGH SHEKHAWAT would venture onto the lawns of his residence on Jaipur's Sardar Patel Marg using a walker to support himself. He lived just a few hundred metres away from the Rajasthan BJP headquarters and sat for hours receiving visitors – workers from the Vishwa Hindu Parishad (VHP) and the Sangh Parivar flocking to seek his blessings.

His nephew Pratap Singh, the *prant adhyaksh* of the Hindu Jagran Manch* recalls how his uncle used to devote most of his time to the Sangh. Each morning, he would reach the RSS office by 6 a.m. and cycle down to his own office at the state insurance department thereafter. One of the most important contributions of Jai Bahadur Singh Shekhawat has been the furthering of saffron ideology in Rajasthan and the building of Bharat Mata Mandir, where the VHP office is presently situated, just a few lanes behind his residence. Shekhawat went to jail during Emergency with

* The Hindu Jagran Manch was founded by BJP leader Vinay Katiyar in 1982 and is affiliated with the RSS. They often run campaigns against what they term as 'illegal conversions of Hindus' and organize 'ghar wapsi' events, where people of other religions are converted to Hinduism.

other opposition leaders and dissenters under the Maintenance of Internal Security Act (MISA) and also led a long campaign against cow slaughter, going on to become a well-known RSS leader. Although he distanced himself from mainstream electoral politics, his main priority remained spreading the values of the Sangh.

When his cousin, the stalwart leader Bhairon Singh Shekhawat offered him a ticket to contest elections from Danta Ramgarh in Sikar, he refused. He passed away in August 2020 at the age of ninety-three, after seeing his dream of a Ram temple being built in Ayodhya fulfilled; the Supreme Court had ruled in its favour the previous year. This was a true triumph of his life's efforts and marked the culmination of a long journey beginning with the very first state assembly elections in 1952, in which the BJS could win only eight seats. Sixty-one years later, in 2013, its successor, the BJP, won 163 seats in the 200-member assembly in the state elections. Just a few months after that, the BJP won all twenty-five Lok Sabha seats in Rajasthan in the 2014 general elections – an extraordinary success it repeated in the 2019 elections to ensure a second term for PM Narendra Modi. Overcoming the vast gap between eight and 163 seats over seven decades was not an easy task for the saffron party – a multi-pronged effort was required.

Over many decades, Bharti Bhawan – the Jaipur RSS headquarters – and the state BJP office on Sardar Patel Marg have nurtured and launched many leaders from all castes to challenge the Congress. The Sangh's dedicated cadre on the ground has played a significant part in the electoral victory of Hindutva proponents.

The Sway of the Sangh

The small room above the office of *Pathey Kan*, a popular fortnightly magazine affiliated with the RSS, housed its patron Manak Chand for many years before the octogenarian passed away in July 2025 the year the RSS turned 100. To describe this room as 'austere' would be an understatement. During his lifetime, apart from few sets of dhoti kurta, there were only photographs adorning its walls – those of RSS founder K. B. Hedgewar, Jan Sangh founder Syama Prasad Mookerjee, M. S. Golwalkar and Bharat Mata – and not much else. Chand was one of the oldest surviving RSS *pracharaks* in Rajasthan. Born in 1942 in a village in Nawan tehsil, Nagaur district, his life story mirrors the rise of the Sangh from the underdogs in the political arena to kingmakers. He was popularly known as Manak ji Bhaisahab in Sangh circles and was a bachelor like all RSS pracharaks, overseeing the publication of *Pathey Kan* for many years.

Chand belonged to the mercantile Maheshwari community and his father was a businessman in Shillong. As a child in 1954 – right after the first elections in 1952 and during Congress's heyday – he went to Kuchaman, Nagaur district, for his studies, where a big *shakha* of the Sangh operated with the support of many big businessmen and government officials. Like most other children, Chand played kabaddi and took part in the daily drills. He recalled that his father had always been a staunch believer of Hindutva ideology and would drive away any Congress party member who came seeking votes. Contrary to other districts, such as Sikar and Jhunjhunu, where many big industrialists – such as Jamnalal Bajaj – were strong supporters of the Congress, Chand said that in the Marwar region, where his home district was located, most of the big industrialists were Hindutva supporters. One of Chand's biggest influences was Hanuman Prasad Poddar – founding editor of *Kalyan*, a monthly Hindi magazine published by the Gorakhpur-based Gita Press – and Golwalkar, whom he first met during one of his visits to Deedwana.

Chand spent nearly sixty years in service of the Sangh as an integral cog in its massive machinery, whose branches twisted and intertwined across all sections of society. With his behind-the-scenes work for the Sangh, Chand contributed to the slow but steady expansion of the influence of the RSS and Jan Sangh – its political wing and the BJP's predecessor – during 1960–70, when these saffron outfits were the proverbial Davids against the Goliath that was the mighty Congress party in power at both the state and at the centre. Chand completed the Tritiya Varsh Sangh Shiksha Varg training at the RSS headquarters in Nagpur, which is mandatory for all aspiring pracharaks. Thereafter, he was appointed the Tonk district pracharak for eleven years between 1966–77.

Chand was among the many Sangh leaders who were arrested during the Emergency under MISA. After he was released from jail, he became the district pracharak in Churu, and witnessed firsthand how the RSS capitalized on anti-Congress sentiments after the Emergency, the formation of the BJP in the 1980s and the party's eventual rise to power in Rajasthan.

Manak Chand's eyes would light up every time he spoke about his early days in the RSS, when the organization did not have much of a foothold in newly independent India. A slight man with a friendly smile, Chand was always dressed in white.

> Before I became a pracharak, I was the *mukhya shikshak* at the shakha at Jaipur's Gangori Bazaar. I would oversee the training in the shakhas and my work also included regularly interacting with the residents in the area, visiting their homes and talking about the Sangh's ideology. Back in those days, our aim was to bring maximum people into the Sangh fold. We would say *har ek Hindu swayamsevak hai* (every Hindu is a swayamsevak).[1]

In those early days, the Congress had immense political capital owing to its role in spearheading the freedom movement. Senior RSS leaders like M. S. Golwalkar, who was the *sarsanghchalak* (chief) at the time when Chand first became involved with the organization, would regularly visit different areas of Rajasthan to oversee and inspect the work of the swayamsevaks.

The task of inducting new members into the RSS was not always easy. The outfit was banned after Mahatma Gandhi's assassination by Nathuram Godse in 1948. Even though the RSS had distanced itself from Godse and has always maintained that he had left the outfit long before the assassination, Chand recalled how even in the 1950s and '60s, the general perception of the Sangh was largely unfavourable. As per his own account of an incident from Pilani in Jhunjhunu district, a group of university students belonging to the Jat community labelled RSS supporters or sympathizers among students as '*Gandhi ke hatyaare* (killers of Gandhi)'.

In fact, Jats, the numerically largest community in the state, have posed the biggest challenge to the RSS's ambitions since the mid-twentieth century, especially in rural areas. While the mid-2000s saw the RSS steadily gain popularity among Rajasthan's OBC communities, the organization is yet to be headed by a sarsanghchalak belonging to this category, even as late as 2025. Thus far, of its six sarsanghchalaks, five have been Brahmins, while one has been a Kshatriya – a serious disadvantage for the outfit since this has hindered its efforts to woo the Jats, who have also been categorized under OBC since 1999. Stalwart Congress leaders from the Jat community, such as Nathu Ram Mirdha and Daulat Ram Saran, took special care to ensure that the Sangh did not find a foothold in their respective regions, according to Chand. Despite this, the RSS endured undeterred, dispatching its army of volunteers – such as Chand – to spread its ideology across villages. These efforts did yield fruit as even Congress supporters in some areas joined forces with the RSS.

For example, in Tonk, Ramkumar Tikkiwal, the younger brother of former Congress MLA Ram Ratan Tikkiwal, was the district *sanghchalak* of the RSS. This was a silent testament to the groundwork laid by the RSS, which enabled it to venture into the electoral arena with its political wing, the Jan Sangh. When Manak Chand was first deputed to the district as its pracharak in 1966, the Jan Sangh was yet to register a victory from this assembly constituency. Tonk has a sizeable Muslim population and was once a princely state ruled by a Muslim nawab. The Sangh would staunchly side with Hindus in case of any confrontations with Muslims, recalled Chand, which would lead to polarization of the electorate along religious lines and help consolidate Hindu votes. Hardworking swayamsevaks like Chand travelled to every village, spreading the ideology of Hindutva at the grassroots. His frequent visits to villages around Tonk earned him the moniker of 'Sangh *waale* Manak ji (Mr Manak from the Sangh)'.

As the 1972 assembly elections rolled around, the religious fault lines started deepening. Chand recalled,

> Swayamsevaks would go to every village before the elections to mobilize people. Balraj Madhok – the former Jan Sangh president – came to Tonk and declared, '*Musalmano, yadi Hinduon ne tai kar liya ki hum sabhi vote Jan Sangh ko denge, toh tum kuch nahi kar sakte* (Muslims, if the Hindus decide that all of us will vote for Jan Sangh, then you will have no power to do anything)' ... *aur wahi hua* (and that is exactly what happened).[2]

The Jan Sangh emerged victorious for the first time from the Tonk constituency in the 1972 assembly elections, with its candidate Ajit Singh winning the seat.

Three years later, after widespread arrests of Sangh functionaries including Chand, who were held in Tonk and Jaipur jails during the Emergency, anti-Congress sentiments were on the rise. Congress was drubbed in both the 1977 Lok Sabha and assembly elections, with the Janata Party – a coalition of Jan Sangh, socialist and communist parties – forming governments across the country. There was no looking back.

By the time he passed away in July 2025, Chand had witnessed the state turn saffron; the mission he had dedicated his entire life to had succeeded. From RSS's austere beginnings as a humble grassroots organization – especially in comparison to the giant that had been the Congress – to a total role reversal wherein a former RSS pracharak was elected as the country's prime minister, Chand had truly seen the world change. He had met Narendra Modi in the late 1980s, when the latter was a young pracharak. Figures like Manak Chand have been instrumental in transforming the Hindutva ideology of the Sangh from a fringe movement into a mainstream force. They were its driving forces through challenging times and it is to their loyalty that the RSS owes its success in Rajasthan. They enabled opportunities for unlikely alliances to surface and joined forces with every anti-Congress movement on the ground, while making overtures to caste groups which constituted the majority of Congress's support base, steadily converting their loyalties to create a mass support base for Hindutva.

Swatantra Party

One day in mid-1956, Gayatri Devi found her husband in a pensive mood. He had just received communication from PM Jawaharlal Nehru and President Rajendra Prasad that the office of the *rajpramukh* – equivalent to the post of governor today – was going to be abolished. The announcement had surprised Man Singh II, who, according to his wife, had been assured that he would be able to retain the office of the rajpramukh for the entirety of his lifetime, since it had been formalized in the Constitution of India.

The post had been created to give the former ruler – in return for having agreed to accede his princely state of Jaipur to India – a sense of stake holding in the government. As the Rajpramukh of Rajasthan, Man Singh II had addressed the very first assembly on

31 March 1952. The humiliation of being stripped of his post and reduced to a commoner in his own kingdom was unbearable for the king, as he expressed in a letter to the PM: 'I find it most distressing that in spite of sincere cooperation and unflinching loyalty on my part throughout the seven years, my official connections with the administration of the state should cease so abruptly.'[3] But the times had changed and Nehru wrote back stating emphatically, 'the Constitution cannot be petrified'.[4] Until then, however, the Congress had been making overtures to the Jaipur royal family. CM Mohan Lal Sukhadia had paid Gayatri Devi a visit in an attempt to convince her to join the Congress and contest elections on the party's ticket from the Jaipur Lok Sabha seat. The erstwhile queen consort was far from convinced – she felt that in many parts of the country, the Congress was beginning to acquire a poor reputation for corruption and nepotism.

> In Rajasthan, as in other places, the ministers put their protégés or people who had helped them in the elections in responsible government jobs which they had neither the education nor the experience to fill capably. It was rumoured that when government contracts were assigned to private companies, they were apt to go to whoever gave the minister concerned the most money under the table. [...] Congress Party, with the achievement of power, had become the Establishment and, as far as I could see, was attracting people who were more concerned with a lucrative career than with achieving good for India.[5]

Gayatri Devi subsequently rejected the chief minister's offer.

Independence movement activist and the last Governor General of India C. Rajagopalachari, popularly known as Rajaji among his followers, founded the Swatantra Party in 1959 with several former Congress members who disagreed with Prime Minister

Nehru's policies. Impressed by Rajagopalachari's unconventional ideas, Gayatri Devi joined the Swatantra Party in early 1961. At the time of her joining, the party was a relatively unknown entity in Rajasthan where anti-Congress politics were steered primarily by the Jan Sangh and the RRP, which had the support of the erstwhile feudal jagirdars. Sudhir Kasliwal, a friend of Gayatri Devi's, revealed that the Maharani kept a photograph of Rajagopalachari in her office at all times. She felt that the Swatantra Party was needed to serve as a platform for anti-Congress political forces in Rajasthan to converge around.[6] Her hunch was correct – within a year of her joining Swatantra Party, the ruling Congress was unsettled at its gathering influence in the state.

The sheer magnitude of the win of the debut force in the 1962 Lok Sabha polls sent shockwaves through the state Congress led by CM Sukhadia. Gayatri Devi, contesting from the Jaipur parliamentary seat, had received more than 1.9 lakh votes, while her opponent from the Congress got only a little more than 35,000 votes. Later, in the assembly elections held in the same year, the Swatantra Party won thirty-six assembly seats – more than double the tally of Jan Sangh, at fifteen seats, which had led the anti-Congress mantle in the state until then. Within a year of becoming active in politics, Gayatri Devi found herself leading the pushback against the Congress.

The appeal of the Ram Rajya Parishad – the first choice for former royals and jagirdars wishing to enter electoral politics, as we saw in Chapter 1 – eventually fizzled out and the elite shifted loyalties to the Swatantra Party. While the Congress was comfortably able to form the government as the single largest party with eighty-eight seats, the Swatantra Party, with the second highest number of seats, was poised to give the Congress its toughest challenge since the creation of Rajasthan. This was a tremendous feat.

Defection and President's Rule

The year 1967 was the first instance in Rajasthan when conscious efforts were made to form a non-Congress government since Independence. It was a significant year for other reasons too – President's Rule was imposed, elected MLAs switched sides and public unrest resulted in the loss of lives. For Gayatri Devi and the Swatantra Party, this could have been their moment of glory if not for the political shrewdness of CM Sukhadia and the might of the Congress government at the centre.

In her memoirs, Devi made her apprehensions about joining forces with the Jan Sangh clear, terming the party 'the extreme rightists', but conceded to understanding the need for it before the 1967 assembly elections. It was, after all, crucial to prevent the anti-Congress vote from being split between two parties in the triangular contest between the Congress, Swatantra Party and Jan Sangh. 'I was particularly worried that an alliance with an avowedly Hindu party like the Jana Sangh would lose us our crucial Muslim vote,' she writes,[7] and also felt at the time that the Jan Sangh resented the fact that the Swatantra Party – whose members were secular-minded – had managed to capture the largest chunk of opposition votes in the state. She felt that allying with the Jan Sangh would be akin to 'political suicide'. Yet, as the 1967 assembly elections approached, the Swatantra Party entered into an alliance for some seats with the Jan Sangh.

The results were bad news for the Congress, which won just eighty-nine of the 184 seats in the assembly. The Swatantra Party won forty-eight seats, and together with other parties such as Jan Sangh, the Samyukta Socialist Party (SSP), independents and the Communist Party of India (CPI), the opposition MLAs outnumbered the Congress – the Congress had won eighty-nine seats in total, while the opposition parties and independents had collectively bagged ninety-five.

Gayatri Devi herself, however, was defeated by Congress leader Damodar Lal Vyas from Malpura, although she retained the Jaipur Lok Sabha seat by a comfortable margin. As opposition parties staked their claim for government formation, then Governor Sampurnanand – a former Congress politician and ex-CM of Uttar Pradesh – invited Sukhadia to form the government instead, citing the reason that the Congress was the single largest party. Massive protests erupted across Jaipur against the Congress, even leading to police firing and the loss of nine lives and the imposition of President's Rule in the state for the first time since Independence.

President's Rule was removed only when some of the opposition MLAs defected to Congress and enabled Sukhadia to form the government with the required numbers. Sudhir Kasliwal, a lifelong photography enthusiast, remembers how a young Ramdas Agarwal – a future stalwart BJP leader of the state – had asked him to bring his camera and positioned him opposite a house in Jaipur's Gandhi Nagar to click photos of the MLAs who were herded at the house.[8] This episode was the first instance of MLAs defecting to another party in Rajasthan, and also the last time the Swatantra Party was a formidable force in the state's politics.

In the following years, Indira Gandhi rose as the sole force to be reckoned with in national politics, thriving despite internal opposition from the Congress's old guard (the Syndicate) and earning public support after the 1971 Indo-Pak war that led to the creation of Bangladesh. It was she who ensured that Sukhadia – who had ruled over Rajasthan for seventeen years by then and was close to the Syndicate – was ousted from power in July 1971.

When the 1972 elections arrived, the Rajasthan Congress was led by Barkatullah Khan, the man handpicked by Indira Gandhi to replace Sukhadia as CM. Buoyed by the public support for Gandhi after the 1971 war, Congress won 145 seats in the assembly, setting a new state record. Swatantra Party could win only eleven seats in the 1972 elections and was never again active in the state. As

Gayatri Devi took a backseat from politics and the Janata Party became the collective voice of the opposition after the Emergency, the Swatantra Party faded into oblivion, but left an undeniable trail of anti-Congress politics in its wake.

The Jan Sangh and BJP's Rise to Power

The Rajasthan chapter of the Bharatiya Jan Sangh was created in September 1951 and within a year, it had garnered enough public support to bag eight seats in the first assembly elections. The legislators contesting on Jan Sangh tickets in the 1952 elections were all Rajputs, which was evidence of the fact that the newly formed party had the trust of the powerful former ruling class, including erstwhile jagirdars, who favoured its ideology. The Jan Sangh also idolized Rajput icons such as Maharana Pratap and extolled the virtues of Hindu rulers of the past, which contributed to its appeal as a platform to take on Jawaharlal Nehru's socialist, anti-feudal, pro-democracy Congress of the 1950s.

The mercantile classes too were traditional supporters of the Jan Sangh, owing to their long association with and patronage of organizations such as the Gita Press, which played a crucial role in propagating Hindutva ideology among the public. Sundar Singh Bhandari was the first convener of the Rajasthan chapter of the Jan Sangh. As elaborated in the preceding sections, the trajectory of the Jan Sangh and its successor BJP in Rajasthan reveals that while the goal of the saffron party has always been to form a government on its own, it has had no qualms in allying with other parties against the Congress, even if their ideologies did not align. An example of this is from the tenure of the very first assembly in Rajasthan after the 1952 elections, when the Jan Sangh, with its eight legislators, became a part of the Samyukta Dal – an opposition party collective. This was despite the fact that the bulk of the Dal was constituted by jagirdars, who wanted to maintain the status quo, while the RSS-backed Jan Sangh was in favour of abolition and a rehabilitation grant for jagirdars to support themselves. The leaders of the Jan Sangh understood the importance of maintaining a united front against the mighty Congress and that every individual win was ultimately a win for their larger Hindutva mission.

Some of the varied issues raised by Jan Sangh legislators during the 1950s and '60s included protests against the shifting of the Rajasthan High Court from Jaipur to Jodhpur, and inflation. It kept expanding its influence in the state, going from eight seats in 1952 to twenty-two seats by 1967. However, in those initial years, the Jan Sangh remained a largely urban phenomenon and failed to give the marginalized adequate representation in its leadership.* Although Dalits and tribals remained out of the Jan Sangh fold for a long time, it was the RSS which steadily brought people from different walks of society into its ideological ambit, creating Jan Sangh voters where none had existed.

The political trajectory of Satish Poonia, the former state president of the BJP in Rajasthan, coincided with the inclusion of the farming communities into the saffron fold and is an effective illustration of how similar shifts were orchestrated over the years. When a young Poonia arrived in Jaipur to study at the Maharaja College in the 1980s, he was in search of a hostel in the capital city that was to be his home until graduation. Hailing from Churu district, Poonia was dazzled by the sheer size of Jaipur and welcomed his first friendships with members of the Akhil Bharatiya Vidyarthi Parishad (ABVP), the student wing of the RSS, with open arms. He fondly remembers how they introduced themselves to him and helped him find a room to stay in, thereby laying the

* As per Professor K. L. Kamal, former vice-chancellor of University of Rajasthan, an analysis of the Jan Sangh's state working committee members for the years 1953–54, 1958–59 and 1965–66 shows that the caste distribution was as follows: thirty-five Brahmins, fifteen Rajputs, twenty-eight Hindus from other castes, four from the peasantry and eight from Scheduled Castes, Scheduled Tribes and Backward Classes.

foundations of his lifelong loyalty to the Sangh and its ideology.[9] Poonia went on to become the state president of the BJP from 2019–23.

In addition to the Emergency and the alliances formed during the Janata Party regime, there was another factor that played a role in turning Rajasthan's farmer communities against the Congress, according to Poonia. In 1999, then PM Atal Bihari Vajpayee announced the inclusion of Jats in the OBC category and thereby granted them the benefits of reservation. This endeared the BJP to the community and enabled the successful induction of youngsters from farming communities into the RSS – a massive feat for the organization. The sudden shift of Jat loyalties and the sight of Jat youngsters aligning with the Hindutva cause surprised many. The late RSS pracharak Manak Chand recalled that people like Poonia, who joined the organization, were called 'filtered Jats' by other members of the community who were still opposed to the Sangh.

As the BJP's fortunes swelled in the 1990s with electoral successes and the Ram Janmabhoomi movement, culminating in the demolition of the Babri mosque, the communities that traditionally supported the Congress saw their fellow members emerge as leaders of the party. From young Jats like Poonia, to the firebrand Dalit Hindutva supporter Madan Dilawar and tribal leaders like Kirodi Lal Meena, the BJP had acquired the favour of communities that had once been staunchly opposed to the RSS. This was made possible by the two-fold approach of Hindutva forces on the ground and in the electoral arena. While a dedicated cadre was busy propagating the ideology on the ground, on the political and governance front, Bhairon Singh Shekhawat was the face of this opposition.

Shekhawat was among the eight MLAs who won on a Jan Sangh ticket in the first assembly elections. He had been in his late twenties at the time and had left his job as a police officer to contest the elections, going on to become the party's greatest asset in the state.

While Shekhawat was not a jagirdar and had even supported the abolition of jagirdari, he was loyal to his community, cautioning the government against letting anti-jagirdar sentiments run rampant in the wake of mass protests. He was also an immensely popular leader, which allowed him the freedom to contest from any assembly constituency and, barring 1972, Shekhawat never lost an assembly election. One year, he would contest from his home district of Sikar, the next from Bali, western Rajasthan, or Dholpur on the easternmost edge of the state. Shekhawat's pan-Rajasthan appeal also greatly helped the Jan Sangh establish itself as the main opposition party in the state.

In 1977, Shekhawat became the CM for the first time in the Janata Party government comprising all opposition forces including the Jan Sangh, the Swatantra Party and breakaway factions of the Congress. Even though his government was dismissed after three years, when Indira Gandhi returned to power, Shekhawat continued to lead anti-Congress politics in the state. His knowledge and experience in governance, paired with his political genius, earned him respect from across party lines. B. D. Kalla* recalls how Shekhawat, as the leader of opposition, would often leave sitting ministers embarrassed after they failed to answer technical questions on laws and policy decisions. He would suddenly ask the minister to define a term in a bill to test their understanding and if the individual had not come prepared, they would fumble and give the opposition the upper hand. Shekhawat himself would always come meticulously prepared. He was also widely admired for his administrative acumen; his poverty alleviation scheme, Antyodai Yojana, won him accolades and cemented his mass appeal, reassuring the public of the ability of the party which had thus far only graced the assembly benches, to produce able leaders who were good administrators.

---

* Senior Congress leader and former Rajasthan minister who served in CM Shiv Charan Mathur's government.

After the formation of the BJP in 1980, Shekhawat continued to be the best bet for the RSS to win the state elections in Rajasthan. In 1990, the Janata Dal MLAs supporting the BJP-led Rajasthan government withdrew their support after the BJP pulled out of the V. P. Singh-led Janata Dal government at the centre.* The Congress viewed this as an opportunity to broach the subject of forming an alliance with the Janata Dal in the state. CM Shekhawat, as his son-in-law and former BJP MLA Narpat Singh Rajvi recalls, acted instantly to engineer a split in the party, forming the splinter Janata Dal (Digvijay) party with twenty-six party MLAs. Overnight, they had the MLAs needed to win the trust vote, effectively dashing any hopes of an alliance with the grand old party. This expert manoeuvre was but another evidence of the saffron front's consistency in grabbing every opportunity to oust the Congress from power. Eventually, their singular focus on the prize was amply rewarded.[10]

And the Tides Turn: BJP CMs and the Rise of the Sangh

Bhairon Singh Shekhawat and Vasundhara Raje, two chief ministers from the saffron fold who ruled Rajasthan for a collective period of more than twenty years, had one factor in common. Both were strong personalities and liked to function independently of the RSS on occasion – this at times resulted in some political decisions being contradictory to the policies of the BJP's ideological parent. This is not to assert that the propagation of RSS's ideology was hindered

* After CM Lalu Yadav ordered the arrest of Advani in Bihar during his *rath yatra* demanding the construction of a Ram Temple in place of the Babri mosque, the relationship between the Janata Dal and the BJP soured. This prompted the BJP to withdraw its support for the Janata Dal at the centre and V. P. Singh to resign from the post of prime minister. In reaction to this, the Janata Dal pulled out of the BJP-led government in Rajasthan.

in any way during their rule, but rather that their personalities were the main driving forces and the Sangh simply did not have as much free rein as it would have liked. This was the primary reason why many BJP leaders with a strong RSS background often did not see eye to eye with the two CMs.

In 1987, in the wake of the Roop Kanwar sati case, Shekhawat openly condemned the practice of sati after some Rajput groups defied the Rajasthan High Court order to organize the Chunri Mahotsav to glorify the horrifying incident. Despite the fact that many right-wing and Hindu outfits had supported the Chunri Mahotsav, Shekhawat took a contrarian stance. However, to ensure he did not lose favour with his Rajput community, he later criticized an ordinance by the state government against the glorification of sati, accusing them of 'singling out Rajputs', thus successfully playing both sides. He kept himself at a distance from protests by right-wing groups in support of the practice of sati throughout, which consolidated his image as a progressive politician.

Similarly, Shekhawat inducted several Muslim leaders into the BJP during the late 1980s and '90s. Despite the RSS's tradition of prevailing over the BJP in most matters, Shekhawat held his ground and encouraged leaders such as Yunus Khan to join the BJP, promoting his image as a relatively secular politician despite being part of the Hindutva fold. Khan had had no plans to join politics and was content working at the Life Insurance Corporation (LIC). However, Shekhwat had been so persuasive that Khan went on to become a two-time minister and a three-time legislator. When the Shekhawat government came to power for a second time in 1990, his council of ministers included Ramzan Khan, who had won the assembly elections on a BJP ticket from the Pushkar constituency. Later in the same year, when Shekhawat saved his government with the help of the Janata Dal (Digvijay) MLAs, by his side stood several Muslim MLAs, including Abdul Hadi, Gulam Mustafa Khan and Nafis Ahmad Khan, who were formerly supporters of the BJP, with Nafis Ahmad Khan even being a minister of state (MoS) in the council of ministers consisting Janata Dal and BJP MLAs in 1990.

At the time, despite the existence of an anti-Shekhawat lobby comprising hardliners such as Ramdas Agarwal and Lalit Kishore Chaturvedi often disagreeing with his policies, the RSS would remain beholden to Shekhawat, whose stature within the party and popularity among the public could not be matched by his colleagues. In several instances, those close to Shekhawat too went against the RSS's decisions, while the veteran leader would choose to look the other way. He adopted the same stance in the case of the Rajasthan University Students' Union presidential election in 1992, when his nephew Pratap Singh Khachariyawas contested as an independent against Satish Poonia, the official candidate of the RSS's student wing, ABVP. CM Shekhawat posed no objections whatsoever to his nephew contesting – and defeating – Poonia.

Shekhawat differed from the hardline BJP leaders in one other aspect – he was willing to induct non-RSS members into the party fold, some of whom even went on to become cabinet ministers. Some such protégés of the leader include Rajendra Rathore, who began his career outside of student politics in the Janata Dal and later became an important ally for anti-Congress forces.

Vasundhara Raje, whom he mentored, was no different in this aspect. In early 2004, in an interview with journalist and news presenter Karan Thapar, Raje was asked for her reaction to VHP leader Praveen Togadia's assertion from 2002 that 'Rajasthan has already become the laboratory of Hindutva' and was slated to follow in the footsteps of Gujarat in the wake of the Godhra riots.[11] Raje dismissed the threat perception, countering it with 'Rajasthan is very clear, it's always been very secular'.[12] The fact that so early on in her term, Raje had no qualms about saying that her government had no Hindutva agenda – a claim that was bound to invite the ire of RSS leaders – showed that the new chief minister liked to do things on her own terms.

During her second term as CM, one of the major issues on which Raje and the RSS disagreed was regarding the removal of ancient temples from the Walled City of Jaipur to pave way for the construction of the Jaipur Metro. RSS leader Vivek Gupta criticized the government's decision, saying that there was anger among the public at the demolition of temples.[13] The RSS summoned nine BJP legislators from Jaipur to its headquarters in Bharati Bhawan, and demanded that they explain their 'inaction' in this regard. It also slammed the government for overlooking 'societal concerns', calling its attitude 'worse than that of Mughal ruler Aurangzeb'.[14]

Cabinet minister Yunus Khan continued to be a point of contention between Raje and RSS-backed BJP leaders as well. In June 2017, Ghanshyam Tiwari, a long-time favourite of the RSS who had been sidelined by Raje, demanded Khan's resignation, accusing him of harbouring associations with the people who had chanted 'anti-national slogan' in Deedwana, Nagaur district – Khan's assembly constituency. While Khan denied the allegations and affirmed his belief that the police would conduct a fair investigation into the incident, the animosity between him and BJP leaders from the RSS cabal continued to increase throughout Raje's tenure.

However, the party's stance shifted as the 2018 state assembly elections approached. For days, there was uncertainty over whether Yunus Khan would get a ticket, despite him being considered the number two in the government after Raje. After much delay Raje only got her way partially. Khan's name was among the last ones to be announced by the party, but the BJP set up his election bid for failure by fielding him from Tonk, which was more than 250 kilometres away from Deedwana, citing a greater need for a suitable candidate to woo the large number of Muslim voters in Tonk. To make the contest even more unfair for Khan, the BJP pitted him against state Congress president Sachin Pilot, who was being touted as the future CM at the time. Predictably, Khan lost the elections by a margin of more than 54,000 votes. In the

2023 assembly elections, he was compelled to resign from the BJP and contest as an independent from the Deedwana assembly constituency, where he won. To this day, when asked to describe Raje in one word, the former BJP leader does not hesitate to say she is 'staunchly secular'.[15]

Until 2018, the RSS remained dwarfed by the strong personalities and independent working styles of leaders such as Shekhawat and Raje. But after Raje's defeat in the 2018 electoral contest, the environment became more conducive for the RSS to move away from chief ministers who belonged to the saffron fold but did not feel obligated to follow the Sangh's mandate. This also coincided with the ascent of Narendra Modi and Amit Shah at the centre and within the BJP. Under their watch, the influence of powerful regional leaders and former chief ministers who had enjoyed long tenures – such as B. S. Yediyurappa, Raman Singh and Shivraj Singh Chouhan – was majorly curbed. As soon became evident from the results of the 2023 assembly elections, the RSS was finally set to establish complete and total control over governance and administration, having eliminated all strong personalities that had the potential to pose a hindrance to its Hindutva agenda.

5

BOVINES AND BLOODSHED

Mob Lynchings and the Communal Cauldron

FOR SOMEONE WHO HAS BEEN ELECTED TO THE ASSEMBLY ONLY ONCE, Gopi Chand Gurjar has left a disproportionately powerful mark on the political landscape of Rajasthan. Now in his early sixties, he has not held public office for more than twenty years, and his only term as an MLA in the Rajasthan assembly was from 1993–98.

A large photo of the godman Jai Gurudev hangs in his office, which is filled with literature and teachings by the controversial guru who was routinely seen with powerful people, including former prime ministers.[1] When Jai Gurudev passed away in 2012, he left behind a ₹4,000-crore empire[2] and thousands of devotees, mostly from the Hindi heartland, especially Uttar Pradesh and Rajasthan. In Rajasthan, Jai Gurudev's slogans 'stop cow slaughter' and 'become a vegetarian' are often found graffitied in public spaces.

Gurjar believes he was sent to the assembly by his guru for a purpose that he has fulfilled, so he spends his days spreading the message of Jai Gurudev, handing out pamphlets to anyone who steps into his office. The 'purpose' he refers to is the enactment of The Rajasthan Bovine Animal (Prohibition of Slaughter and Regulation of Temporary Migration or Export) Act (RB Act) 1995 that prohibits the transportation of cows or bulls outside

Rajasthan.* Elected as a BJP MLA from Nagar constituency in Bharatpur in 1993, Gurjar claims his political career was cut short because then CM Bhairon Singh Shekhawat did not appreciate him arm-twisting the party into passing the RB Act.

Gurjar had managed to convince other BJP MLAs not to budge till the bill against cow smuggling was passed, asserting that the cow was a sentimental subject.[3] The issue escalated to such a degree that the MLAs were willing to resign if their demand was not met. CM Shekhawat had no choice but to pass the law, although he ensured that Gurjar did not get a BJP ticket in the next elections. Content that he had fulfilled his purpose, Gurjar was unperturbed.

Many years before Rajasthan became notorious for cow vigilantism and lynchings of people transporting bovines, Gurjar claims to have formed 'cow protection squads' in Alwar[4] and Bharatpur districts, way back in the 1970s. Every time a suspected case of cow slaughter was brought to his notice, Gurjar would rush to the spot with his squad. He claims that his very name would strike terror into the Meos, who would tell each other, '*Bhaago*, Gopi Gurjar *aa jayega*! (Run or else Gopi Gurjar will come and get you!)'. Mewat, the region comprising parts of Alwar, Bharatpur and bordering regions of Haryana, is home to a large population of Muslims, colloquially called Meos. The region has a history of communal flare-ups, with the Meos often being targeted by Hindutva groups. In the wake of Partition, the Meo community was victim to one of the nation's worst ethnic cleansings. Thousands of Meo Muslims were either killed or forcibly converted during bouts of communal hatred. N. B. Khare, a future head of the Hindu Mahasabha, who was the prime minister of the Alwar estate at

* For more on the Act, see Rajasthan Legislative assembly, 'The Rajasthan Bovine Animal (Prohibition Of Slaughter And Regulation Of Temporary Migration Or Export) (Amendment) Bill, 2018', Bill no. 8 of 2018. Available at: https://prsindia.org/files/bills_acts/bills_states/rajasthan/2018/Bill%208%20of%202018%20Rajasthan.pdf.

the time of the mass violence against the Meos, is believed to have played a part in the gruesome event.

> The Meos who did not run away became Hindus. They were made to recite the Gayatri *mantra* [a Rigvedic chant], swear on the Ganga and drink a mixture called *pañch gab* that included *gaū mūtra, gaū gobar, gaū dūdh*, gaū ghī, and gaū dahī [the five cow products, comprising cow urine, cowdung, milk, clarified butter, and curd]. The Qu'ran had to be put into the flames.[5]

In response to a question raised in the state assembly on 3 November 1952, the then rehabilitation minister of Rajasthan, Amritlal Yadav, informed the House that a total of 2.41 lakh Meo Muslims had been evacuated from Alwar and Bharatpur during the Partition violence. The official records of the Rajasthan assembly mention that at the time of these discussions, several members had also brought to the attention of the House that there were many empty houses in these areas which had been abandoned during the violence, indicating the sheer intensity of the atrocities committed against the community.

In the present times, cow vigilantism is a real threat to the lives of Meo Muslims. Pehlu Khan, Umar Mohammed, Rakbar Khan, Nasir and Junaid are just some of the Meo Muslims who have lost their lives in the last few years as a direct result of cow vigilantism. 'After this bill is passed, our government will be known as "*gaurakshak*". This day will be written in golden letters in the history of Rajasthan's democracy,' Gurjar had claimed in the assembly back in 1995 after the safe passage of the bill.[6]

Not all legislators had shared the enthusiasm of the strongman from Nagar. Then CPI (M) MLA Amra Ram,* also a leader of the All India Kisan Sabha (AIKS), had warned the House that in villages,

* Ram went on to become the MP from Sikar in 2024.

it was common for people to abandon cattle after they stopped producing milk. Cattle-rearers in the state used to sell large number of calves, bulls to other states. 'You will find thousands of stray cattle in Rajasthan's villages which were abandoned by farmers. This bill will also affect buyers from other states who would earlier come to Rajasthan [to buy milch cows but will no longer be able to do so] and farmers would be forced to sell their animals at a lower price,' Ram had predicted.[7] He even offered to adopt the hundreds of stray cattle that were roaming in his home district of Sikar. Two decades later, his prophecy came true when data from Rajasthan's Animal Husbandry Department revealed that at the world-famous Pushkar cattle fair – once a thriving marketplace for cattle traders to sell bovines to dairy farmers – fewer than ten animals were being sold per year.[8]

The appearance of the cow in the desert state's politics has caused political rhetoric to often veer toward supporting vigilantism in recent years. '*Maine khullam khulla chhoot de rakhi hai karyakartaon ko, maaron sa**** ko jo gokashi … Bari bhi karwayenge, zamaanat bhi karwa denge* (I have given a free hand to the workers, kill those [expletive] behind cow slaughter … We will get you acquitted, get you out on bail, too),' former BJP MLA Gyan Dev Ahuja from Ramgarh can be heard saying in a video in 2022.[9] Known for his frequent anti-Meo Muslim statements, Ahuja routinely catches the attention of the media. His promise of 'getting cow vigilantes acquitted' rang with an ominous self-assuredness.

On 14 August 2019, a day before India was going to celebrate its seventy-second Independence Day, a large group of people gathered outside a court in Alwar district. The mood was celebratory. Men exiting the court premises emerged chanting 'Bharat Mata ki Jai' – they had just been acquitted of all charges pertaining to the murder of Pehlu Khan. Local lawyers, dressed in their trademark black coats, soon joined the chorus as TV channel crews zoomed in to focus their cameras on the group. A few kilometres away, Khan's twenty-seven-year-old son, Irshad, broke down while talking about the verdict. When he had left his village Jaisinghpur in Haryana's Nuh district for the court hearing, he had been hopeful that his father would get justice. He was in disbelief at the turn of events, wondering what more evidence was needed – there was a video of his father being subjected to violent assault by the newly acquitted. Situated less than a hundred kilometres from New Delhi, Jaisinghpur was covered in darkness after a power cut, but Khan's house was easy to locate – all one had to do was follow the long wails of the mourning family.

The grainy video of Khan, fifty-five, a Meo Muslim dairy farmer from Haryana, being assaulted near Behror on the Jaipur–Delhi highway had gone viral in April 2017, leaving the country stunned. Khan and his two sons were waylaid by a mob while they were returning to Haryana after purchasing cows from a government-managed cattle market in Jaipur. Two days after being attacked, Khan succumbed to his wounds at a local hospital. Even as the attack on Khan resulted in massive outrage across the country and the then BJP government under Vasundhara Raje was slammed by activists, the political rhetoric emboldened the attackers. It is for this reason that the Pehlu Khan case is crucial to understanding the close relation between cow vigilantes and Rajasthan politics.

Shortly after Khan's lynching, future Punjab governor Gulab Chand Kataria, who was the home minister in Raje's government and an old RSS loyalist, reiterated the claim made by Hindutva groups that Pehlu Khan was a cattle smuggler. Five months later, the Alwar police gave a clean chit to all the six people whom Khan had named as his assailants in his statement to the police before his death.[10]

A day after news broke that the CID-CB of the Rajasthan police had let the six men named by Khan go scot-free, Karwan-e-Mohabbat, a campaign against hate crimes, arrived in Behror – the town where Khan had been attacked. Om Yadav, one of the six alleged assailants, who had been 'absconding' until just a day ago, accompanied by members of local Hindu outfits, began furiously sloganeering against Karwan-e-Mohabbat.

Local police blocked the passage of the campaign, preventing them from reaching the spot where Khan had been attacked. Activist Harsh Mander, who was leading Karwan-e-Mohabbat, staged a dharna beside the busy highway, refusing to budge despite being heckled by the local protesters. 'We won't let you pay tribute to Pehlu Khan. Is he Netaji Subhash Chandra Bose or the men fighting at the borders that people would pay tribute to him?' said one of the protesters as tensions ran high.[11] The police finally took only Mander to the spot near the highway where Khan had been assaulted, and he sat there with folded hands, paying his respects to Khan.

In a town where the majority of the population is from the Yadav community, Khan or the Karwan-e-Mohabbat garnered little sympathy from the public, an overwhelming number of whom regarded Khan as a 'cow smuggler'. Many local media outlets were firmly against Khan as well – days after his death, they described him as a cattle smuggler. 'An apt headline would be: *mohabbat nahin, nafrat ka hai ye karwan* (this is not a campaign of love, but of hatred),' remarked a local reporter in Behror, who worked at a leading vernacular daily.[12] In fact, after Khan died, he and his sons were booked under the RB Act – the same law that Gopi Chand Gurjar had helped pass in the assembly in 1995 – for cattle smuggling and his sons were chargesheeted.

In August 2019, all the men chargesheeted by the police for the murder of Khan had walked free, acquitted by the district court on the basis of benefit of doubt. But the court slammed the police for not taking the video evidence of the attack into account.[13] The botched investigation process is further evident from the difference between the judgments delivered by the district court that tried the six accused and acquitted them, and the verdict of the Juvenile Justice Board (JJB) that convicted two teenagers, who were minors at the time of the killing – the only guilty verdict handed out to anyone involved in the attack on Khan.[14] The two teenagers convicted in the Pehlu Khan lynching case were sent to a special home for three years – the maximum punishment that the board could pronounce in such cases. The FIRs and chargesheets against Khan's sons were subsequently quashed by the Rajasthan High Court in October 2019, which noted that continuation of proceedings would be tantamount to 'abuse of process of law and would result in grave injustice' to Irshad and Aarif.[15]

The JJB in Alwar was scathing in its criticism of some doctors of the private hospital in Behror where Khan was first admitted. Notably, the hospital is owned by Mahesh Sharma, a BJP MP from Gautam Buddh Nagar in Uttar Pradesh. 'Because every doctor has given different statements, it appears that the doctors of Kailash Hospital treated the body of deceased Pehlu Khan as a dummy, wherein injuries were arbitrarily decided and inflicted injuries were arbitrarily treated as minimal. Such statements by the aforementioned doctors also cast suspicion on their medical conduct,' Principal Magistrate Sarita Dhakad said in her verdict. Subsequently, it also issued notices to four doctors of the hospital who had treated Khan. The judgement reads: 'Therefore, doctors of Kailash Hospital Dr Akhil Saxena, Dr B. D. Sharma, Dr R. C. Yadav and Dr Jitendra Butolia should be issued a notice and their answers be sought that for the fulfilment of what objective they changed the reason for death from serious hurt to heart attack.'[16]

Incidentally, in the Alwar court, the statements of these very doctors had a part to play in the acquittal of the six accused. Senior advocate Nasir Ali Naqvi, the counsel for Khan's family in the Rajasthan High Court after the family petitioned for the withdrawal of the cow smuggling accusation against the Khan brothers, remarked on how the conflicting conclusions of the Kailash Hospital doctors and the postmortem report posed a significant challenge for them as prosecutors. The private hospital doctors were presented as their witnesses, but it was the defence that ended up benefitting from their testimonies.[17]

Days after the lynching of Khan, Congress leader Sachin Pilot, who was the president of the RPCC at the time, met with the Governor along with other leaders of his party to demand a CBI probe into Khan's murder. Yet, it was the Congress that gave a party ticket for the 2018 assembly elections from Behror to Dr R. C. Yadav – one of the doctors who would later be issued a notice by the JJB in the Pehlu Khan case. Om Yadav, among the six accused, was elected as a councillor in Behror in 2020 after contesting on a BJP ticket.

With every passing year, as fresh newsmakers grabbed the headlines, calls to Pehlu's family from various journalists began waning. Khan's wife Jaibuna and their sons Irshad and Aarif are now almost forgotten and alone in their battle for justice* as media attention consistently shrinks. In 2017 alone, twenty-three cases of cow-related violence were reported across Rajasthan.[18] Since the death of Khan, other men from Mewat, including Umar Mohammad, Rakbar Khan,[19] Nasir and Junaid[20] died after being assaulted by cow vigilantes.

Churnings in the Communal Cauldron

When the Rajasthan assembly convened on a mid-February morning in 1973, then chief minister Barkatullah Khan made an emphatic

* In 2019, the Congress government at the time filed an appeal in the Rajasthan High Court against the acquittal of the accused by the trial court in Alwar. Six years later, the case is still being heard in the Rajasthan High Court. Source: Harsha Kumari Singh, 'Rajasthan Challenges Acquittal Of 6 Accused In Pehlu Khan's Mob Killing', NDTV, 18 October 2019. Available at: https://www.ndtv.com/india-news/pehlu-khan-case-rajasthan-government-challenges-in-high-court-acquittal-of-6-accused-in-pehlu-khans-2118713.

declaration: 'I have ordered that any government employee or officer, along with any employee of private institutions that get government aid, action will be taken if they are members of RSS or Jamaat-e-Islami.' Barkatullah Khan, who was a friend of Feroze Gandhi's and addressed Indira Gandhi as *Bhabhi*, spoke at length about the importance of maintaining harmony during a discussion on communal violence. 'We saw that [in 1939] when the Congress government had resigned, the day of deliverance was celebrated, and the Muslim League and Hindu Mahasabha were celebrating together. One was celebrating in temples, the other in mosques,' said Khan, taking on the radical elements of both communities.[21]

The only Muslim chief minister of Rajasthan, Khan was a statesman who was much more than a representative of a community that constitutes 9 per cent of the population of Rajasthan. Kamlesh Purohit, a former BJP councillor from Jodhpur, recalls how the Pushkarna Brahmin community in Jodhpur was so fond of Barkatullah Khan that people referred to them as 'Barkatiya Brahmins' during his tenure. Yet, by 2022, the communal fabric that once held Jodhpur, the city of Barkatullah Khan, together had been torn to pieces and the timing could not have been worse.

On the morning of 3 May 2022, the mood outside the heavily fortified bungalow number 8, Civil Lines – the Chief Minister's Residence – was celebratory. CM Ashok Gehlot was turning seventy-one, and posters of Congress leaders, ranging from election ticket aspirants to cabinet ministers, had sprung up all over Jaipur, wishing him a happy birthday. Many of these people owed their political careers to Gehlot, who has maintained an iron grip on the state for nearly five decades.

It was also Eid. Just a fortnight ago, the bungalow had played host to several hundred people for a grand *roza iftaar* party Gehlot had organized. The event had sent the message that the Congress cared about the issues impacting Muslims – an assertion which was much needed after several minority advocacy outfits had protested against the Gehlot government's neglect of them. Several Muslim leaders and social groups blamed the Congress government for weakening Urdu education and not appointing a Muslim mayor in Jaipur after the civic polls, despite the fact that a majority of the party's councillors who had fared well in the elections were Muslims. In addition to this, the All India Majlis-e-Ittehadul Muslimeen (AIMIM) had also recently announced its intent to contest in the upcoming assembly elections in Rajasthan, which was a matter of concern for the Congress. Its leaders had been publicly dismissive of the Hyderabad-based AIMIM's chances in the desert state, although they had privately expressed their worries about its potential for eating into the grand old party's vote share.

The iftaar party was part of a carefully planned social outreach drive by the chief minister in the run-up to his birthday. Gehlot had routinely met representatives of different communities to send out the message that he was a leader of '*chattis kaum* (all communities)'. He had often made it a point to say in public that he had been elected CM thrice in Rajasthan's caste-driven political climate, even though he belonged to the Mali community, a caste holding negligible clout in comparison to the Rajputs, Jats and Meenas.

Gehlot's birthday party was supposed to send a message to the faction-ridden Congress party and, more specifically, to his bête noire Sachin Pilot that the wily septuagenarian was still the most popular Congress leader in the state. The stage was all set, but the day did not turn out as it had been meticulously planned by the Chief Minister's Office (CMO) workers handpicked by Gehlot himself. By the afternoon, most of the visiting delegations returned without meeting the CM, who had had to cancel the celebrations abruptly. He was glued to his office chair monitoring the situation in his hometown of Jodhpur, where a communal clash had marred all his plans for the big day. It had caught the administration – stocked with bureaucrats personally picked by the CM – off guard.

To make things worse, it involved the Pushkarna Brahmins and Muslims. Both communities formed important voting blocs in Sardarpura – Gehlot's assembly constituency and the epicentre of the violence.

On the night before Eid, some Hindus stopped a group of Muslim youths from hoisting an Eid flag over the statue of freedom fighter Bal Mukund Bissa at Jalori Gate, a bustling spot situated at the heart of Jodhpur. Bissa, the late freedom fighter, was a Pushkarna Brahmin, a community that is predominantly confined to western Rajasthan and has extremely high literacy rates, resulting in its members occupying important positions as judges, doctors and bureaucrats. Violence broke out and eventually led to the Muslim side alleging that loudspeakers installed for the Eid *namaaz* had been damaged by the Hindus who had hoisted a saffron flag over the statue of Bissa. Later, on the day of Eid, the Muslim community made a sudden effort to remove the saffron flag, which led to further clashes involving the police.

Just days before the clash, the city had celebrated Parashuram Jayanti – a Hindu festival that has, in recent times, acquired importance for Brahmins as an occasion to display their strength with massive rallies hailing the mythological figure who has become a symbol of Brahmin assertion. During the celebrations, the district administration was on its toes to maintain law and order, and yet incidents of stone pelting and arson in the serpentine alleyways of old Jodhpur plunged the area into chaos.

This was not the first instance of communal violence in 2022, which had started with Gehlot proclaiming with great confidence that he would return as CM for a fourth term after the 2023 elections. The first sign that communal discord could derail Gehlot's desire to return to power based on 'good governance' came on 2 April, about a month before the incident in Jodhpur. Stone pelting and arson during a procession in Karauli district on the occasion of Hindu New Year, sent shockwaves right up to the highest echelons of the government. This incident also marked the end of the largely uneventful – from the communal tensions point of view – three years of the Gehlot administration. It made national headlines, with reporters rushing to the otherwise peaceful eastern Rajasthan district to interview the injured or take stock of the damage for themselves, as many predominantly Muslim-owned businesses had been torched by the rioters in retaliation to the stone-pelting.

Gehlot, who had been confident that he would retain power after the 2023 assembly elections despite the ruptures in the Congress and the state's tradition of voting out the incumbent government every five years, was now confronted with the biggest challenge of his political career. Retaining power in the 2023 elections was Gehlot's only bet at remaining the face of Congress in Rajasthan. Yet the prospect of that coming to pass was becoming less certain due to the constant threat posed by Pilot, the shrinking presence of the Congress in national politics, and a party high command that, in recent times, had been quick to point ageing regional satraps such as Captain Amarinder Singh to the exit.

Historically, communal riots in Rajasthan have been linked to the fall of the Congress's fortunes. Just like the incident in Karauli, thirty-two years ago, violence had gripped Kota following the passage of a Hindu religious procession through a Muslim locality on the occasion of the Anant Chaturdashi, the conclusion of a ten-day-long Ganesh Utsav celebration.[22] At least thirteen people were killed. While most of the Hindus had died from bullet injuries after the police opened fire to control the situation, the majority of Muslims who died had sustained injuries from sharp-edged weapons. Some had even been killed inside a mosque that had been stormed by Hindu rioters. A memorandum from the Muslim side had named, among others, BJP MLA Dau Dayal Joshi as one of the persons leading the rioters.

Five months after the riots, when the assembly elections were held in February 1990, the BJP, in a sweeping victory, won all five seats in the riot-affected Kota district. In the aftermath of the riots, the consolidation of votes in favour of the BJP could also be seen in other parts of the Kota division, comprising Kota, Bundi, Baran and Jhalawar districts. The BJP won fifteen out of the eighteen seats in the state, with its chief ministerial candidate Bhairon Singh Shekhawat choosing to contest from the Chhabra constituency in the Baran district. The Congress remained out of power for eight years after the 1989 Kota riots, its prospects worsened further by the loss of many lives in communal clashes in Jaipur in 1990, in the wake of Advani's arrest in Bihar during the Ram Temple rath yatra.

The churnings in the communal cauldron after the incidents in Karauli and Jodhpur were the omens that made Gehlot fear for the fate of the Congress in the 2023 assembly elections, which the grand old party subsequently lost.

A caricature shared by the Rajasthan BJP on its official social media handles in April 2022 showed a man slightly resembling Gehlot sitting on a throne, wearing a skull cap with his eyes blindfolded. Next to the cartoon was a newspaper clipping about an alleged rape case in the state, wherein the woman was Hindu and the accused was Muslim. As the communal clashes in Jodhpur, Karauli, Bhilwara and other places rocked Rajasthan, the BJP posted such cartoons regularly on its social media. Another such graphic was captioned: '*Betiyon ki asmat ho rahi taar-taar, Grahamantri* Gehlot *kar rahe* iftaar (The dignity of the nation's daughters is in shreds, Home Minister Gehlot is having iftaar parties)'.[23]

Much before Bhajan Lal Sharma became BJP's surprise choice for the top post of chief minister, during its time in the opposition between 2019 and 2023, the saffron party had been witnessing power struggles of its own between former CM Vasundhara Raje and more than half a dozen leaders with chief ministerial ambitions. It had found a new phrase to criticize Gehlot and his government with: 'appeasement politics'. The saffron party was trying to make the most gains in a battle of perceptions by slapping labels on its competitors, such as calling the Congress a 'minority-appeasing' party.[24] The BJP's strategy was not to let go of any chance where the state government could be portrayed to be partial to Muslims. When the Jodhpur electricity department issued an order in early April to ensure unabated electricity supply in Muslim-majority areas during Ramzan, the opposition leapt at the opportunity. Ultimately, the order had to be withdrawn.

It was also around this time that former CM Vasundhara Raje – widely considered to be among the more moderate crop of BJP leaders from the Atal Bihari Vajpayee era – underwent a noticeable shift in her stance towards the Congress. She, too, accused Gehlot of practising appeasement politics. The sudden change in Raje, who had hitherto refrained from openly playing the Hindutva card and included powerful Muslim figures such as Yunus Khan in her government, was a clear sign of the BJP's intentions to capitalize on religious leanings to win elections. This shift in the party's rhetoric before the 2023 assembly elections coincided with its return to power in Uttar Pradesh and a second consecutive term as the chief minister for Yogi Adityanath, the firebrand Hindu monk who was a surprise choice for the top post when the saffron party picked him in 2017 to be the CM of the country's most populous state.

By mid-2022, for the first time since the Congress came to power in 2018, Rajasthan was regularly in the news for incidents of communal violence. Between just April–May 2022, five such instances were recorded in various districts, including Karauli, Jodhpur, Bhilwara and Hanumangarh. After the 2 April incident during the procession in Karauli, incidents of communal tension emerged from other districts such as Bhilwara and Hanumangarh as well. The aftermath was the same in all cases: internet shutdowns, curfews in some places and the BJP carrying out protests.

In Hanumangarh, a member of the VHP was injured in a

confrontation with some Muslim men in May 2022. The district collector said that the Hindu groups were trying to distribute sticks and other weapons but were apprehended by the police before communal tensions could escalate further.[25] At this time, the BJP started bringing national leaders, such as Tejasvi Surya, to Rajasthan to protest against the alleged appeasement politics of the state government in general, and the Karauli violence in particular. In areas like Jodhpur that were already riddled with communal strife, BJP MLAs walked out of peace committee meetings.

In mid-April, a huge procession of men holding saffron flags made its way through Alwar, a district that traces its tryst with Hindutva back to the pre-Independence era and has been in the news in recent years for cow vigilantism. '*Pukaarti, pukaarti, pukaarti Maa Bharati, khoon se tilak karo, goliyon se aarti* (Mother India is calling you, adorn her forehead with blood and offer her your prayers through bullets),' chanted the men, accompanied by Alwar BJP MP Mahant Balak Nath. The immediate cause for the rally was the demolition of two ancient temples in Alwar, which had resulted in widespread criticism of the Congress government. After videos of the temple demolition went viral on social media, the state government went into damage-control mode. It promptly put out a rebuttal in the form of the district collector's statement pointing out that the demolition was carried out as part of an anti-encroachment drive approved by the Alwar Municipal Council, a civic body that was controlled by the BJP. State Congress president Govind Singh Dotasra organized a hurried press conference, attacking the BJP for its double standards and clarifying that the Congress government had nothing to do with the temple demolition as the administration was only carrying out the orders of the local municipal council.

But the tactic of passing the buck to the municipal council did not succeed and the BJP promptly launched a counterattack. It claimed that the anti-encroachment drive plan approved by the local body did not explicitly mention demolishing any temples – that was a deed the district administration had carried out unilaterally. Later, the party also cited the fact that the Congress had suspended two officials, including a sub-divisional magistrate, reaffirming that the government was at fault.

The campaign by the BJP to strengthen public perception that the Rajasthan government was acting against the interest of Hindus was multi-pronged. While its state leadership, including MPs and the union minister from Rajasthan, held daily press conferences to reassert their stance, on the party's social media pages – with over 1 million followers – cartoons and caricatures mocking CM Gehlot and the Gandhi family were being posted. One such cartoon showed the chief minister driving a bulldozer to demolish a temple.

Gehlot, the wily and battle-hardened son of a magician* who had outrun many Congress stalwarts in the race to be chief minister, understood very well that the rise in communal violence just before the elections did not bode well for his desire to retain power in 2023. To make a bad situation worse, shocking news of more killings followed.

A Tale of Two Killings

A short stretch of just over 60 kilometres separates Dhoinda, a small township nestled in the hilly and arid Rajsamand district in historic Mewar, from Maldas Street in Udaipur – a crowded market area with long rows of shops located near the periphery of the biggest city in southern Rajasthan. Giant trailers overloaded with marble blocks slither across the Rajsamand–Udaipur highway every day, resembling huge caterpillars whose deep rumble and ear-splitting horns constantly warn smaller vehicles to move out of their way. Within a span of five years, both these places made

* Gehlot's father Laxman Singh was a celebrated magician.

national news.

Citing religious reasons, assailants had brutally cut short the lives of Mohammad Afrazul and Kanhaiyalal Teli, sending shockwaves across the country and causing journalists and reporters from all quarters to flock to Rajasthan. The two victims had only been separated by a highway, but they had never met each other; and yet, their stories have much in common. Although the communal cauldron in Rajasthan has certainly seen stirrings from time to time in the seventy years since the state's formation, the two gruesome hate crimes which took place in December 2017 and June 2022 stand out. These killings are a true reflection of the increasingly polarized environment that has come to prevail in the region in the past decade, characterized by communally charged political rhetoric, curfews and internet shutdowns.

Mewar is a traditional stronghold of the BJP, and a part of the Chittorgarh *prant* (chapter) of the RSS – one of the three divisions of the Sangh in Rajasthan. It is also the backyard of the former leader of the opposition and ex-Udaipur MLA Gulab Chand Kataria, whose enviable grip on the party in the region has resulted in the BJP consistently performing well here.* Mewar's favour for the party was evidenced by the fact that in the 2018 assembly elections, even though the BJP lost to the Congress, it won sixteen of the twenty-four assembly seats in the districts of Rajsamand, Udaipur, Bhilwara and Chittorgarh – all part of this region. The Congress, always playing second fiddle in Mewar, has senior leader and former union minister C. P. Joshi as its face in the region. Although well-advised, this choice has restricted the party's appeal to Joshi's constituency, Nathdwara. But unlike Kataria, who was an eight-time MLA, five-time legislator Joshi hasn't been able

* Kataria retired from mainstream politics in 2023 after his elevation to the post of governor.

to win as consistently.

On the evening of 6 December 2017, a video shot on a mobile phone was circulated in various WhatsApp groups in Rajsamand before going viral on social media and being flashed across news channels. Its gory contents instantly caught the attention of the police. In the video, Shambhulal Regar, a tall, lanky man dressed in a red shirt could be seen hacking a middle-aged man to death with a shovel before dousing him with petrol and setting him on fire. The victim was Mohammad Afrazul, a migrant labour contractor from Malda, West Bengal. The video was filmed by Shambhulal's juvenile nephew, whose unsteady hands recorded his uncle ignoring Afrazul's pleas for mercy before violently lunging at him.

The day Shambhulal killed Afrazul marked the twenty-fifth anniversary of the Babri mosque demolition. Before his arrest on the following day, Shambhulal released video statements featuring an anti-Muslim diatribe and claims that he had murdered Afrazul to save a 'Hindu sister' who had been caught in the trap of 'love jihad'. However, journalistic investigations on the day after the killing revealed that the 'Hindu sister' in question had nothing to do with the victim; in fact, it was Shambhulal who had been troubling her.[26]

An unmade bed, half-peeled potatoes and a group of terrified migrant labourers greeted visitors at the small one-room accommodation in Dhoinda where Afrazul had lived. The area is home to a large population of migrant labourers, most of whom are Bengali Muslims from Malda and nearby areas. Mohammed Ziaul Haq, a resident of the area for the past decade, had been working hard to earn an income but felt his determination being snuffed out at the sight of Afrazul's half-charred body. Within a few days after Afrazul's death, Dhoinda was emptied of migrant labourers who fled, afraid for their lives.

Afrazul had chosen a life far away from his home state and his wife Gulbahar to ensure that his family did not have to worry about sustenance. After he managed to establish a successful business as a private contractor in Rajasthan, many of his acquaintances from his village arrived to join him. After his death, having lost their guardian, they were forced to return home. While Afrazul's family mourned him at Saiyadpur, a border village in Malda, saffron-clad men gathered at a huge rally in Udaipur, more than a thousand kilometres away, heralding his killer as a 'symbol of Hindu anger'. They also slammed the local Muslim community for taking out a procession to demand punishment for his assailant.

One of the most-discussed moments of the Hindu rally was when one of the protesters hoisted a saffron flag over the gate of the district and sessions court in Udaipur. Ganesh Vaishnav, a member of the Udaipur-based Shiv Sena, claimed that not cracking down hard on 'love jihad' by way of legal action was likely to give rise to more Shambhulals in the future as he was a symbol of what the entire Hindu community truly felt.[27]

In Rajsamand, the first signs of approval for Shambhulal's actions manifested in a WhatsApp group originally meant to streamline coordination between the district administration and citizens to further the goals of the Swachh Bharat Mission, the flagship scheme of the Narendra Modi-led BJP government to ensure improved standards of cleanliness and sanitation facilities in the country. A participant in the group – which also had then Rajsamand MP Hari Om Singh Rathore and MLA Kiran Maheshwari as members – posted messages applauding Shambhulal for his actions. After a news report on this WhatsApp group was published in *The Indian Express*,[28] it was picked up by other publications, resulting in a mass exodus of members from the group. In the end, Prem Mali, the admin of the group who claimed to be a BJP worker, deleted it.

Already bogged down by the nationwide outrage over cow-related lynchings in Rajasthan, Vasundhara Raje's government announced a compensation of ₹5 lakh for Afrazul's family, handing over the cheque to his son-in-law. But the support that poured in for the murderer from right-wing groups was telling. Days after the killing, Updesh Rana, a Hindutva supporter with more than 8 million followers on Facebook, vowed to come to Rajsamand to hold a rally in support of Shambhulal. While Rana was held by the local police in Jaipur, more than ₹3 lakh was collected in support of Shambhulal's wife, with over 500 people across India making donations.

A defining image of this polarized time in the aftermath of Afrazul's death is from March 2018, three months after the incident. A colourfully decorated tableau made its way through the city of Jodhpur as part of a procession to celebrate Ram Navami. A man dressed as Shambhulal from the infamous viral video sat atop the tableau clutching a shovel, a spitting image of the accused, who had been jailed by this time. A poster attached to the tableau read, '*Hinduon bhaiyon jaago, apni behan–beti bachao, love jihad se desh ko azad karana chahiye* (Hindu brothers, wake up, save your sisters and daughters. The country should be freed from the clutches of love jihad)'.

Nearly five years after the killing of Afrazul, Udaipur found itself turned into a fortress. It was June 2022 and mobile internet services across Rajasthan had been suspended; senior state police officials were camping day and night near a small tailor shop in Udaipur's usually crowded Maldas Street to ensure no one violated the curfew. The innocuous shop had become a centre of attraction for the press and bulletproof vest-clad policemen alike overnight. It was here that Kanhaiyalal Teli, the owner, had been attacked by two armed men carrying knives and cleavers, almost completely severing his neck from his body. A stream of blood drenched the street outside. The assailants had taken advantage of the bustling activity on the street to flee the scene in broad daylight.

The two assailants, Mohammed Riyaz and Ghouse Mohammed, had pretended to be customers looking to get a kurta stiched. While Kanhaiyalal's attention was on taking measurements, they attacked, plunging their weapons into his neck. Just as Shambhulal Regar had done five years ago, the murderers then released a video confessing to the killing and stating their reason: Kanhaiyalal had disrespected Prophet Muhammad. They claimed that they had murdered the forty-eight-year-old tailor for sharing a post on his social media in support of former BJP spokesperson Nupur Sharma's comments on Prophet Mohammad.[29] Sharma had made comments on the Prophet during a TV news debate, which had led to massive outrage that transcended national borders and caused several Gulf countries to register complaints with the Indian consulates there. The BJP had subsequently distanced itself from Sharma and suspended the leader. Kanhaiyalal's family, however, denied that he had ever shared any post related to the Prophet.[30]

The killing in Udaipur happened at a crucial juncture when Congress was already under fire over communal clashes that had become a regular occurrence in the state since April 2022. Much like Afrazul, Kanhaiyalal had worked hard to fend for his family since he had migrated to Udaipur from the nearby tribal district of Dungarpur, sometime in the mid-1990s. After working at local shops for several years, he had set up his own tailoring business on Maldas Street. While his two assailants were arrested on the same day as they were fleeing towards Ajmer, the Rajasthan government was deeply concerned about a Hindu backlash, causing them to promptly suspend internet connection all across the state in an unprecedented turn of events.

A day after the killing, the crowd assembled outside Kanhaiyalal's house in Udaipur was furious. As it slowly grew in size, a slogan began to emanate from its midst: '*Desh ke gaddaron ko, goli maaro saalon ko* (Shoot the bloody traitors to our country).' Inside the house, Kanhaiyalal's wife Yashoda collapsed as his body was readied for cremation. His two teenaged sons, Yash and Tarun, choked on their tears as they told the media that their family had lost its sole breadwinner. The Congress realized that the murder of Kanhaiyalal could snowball into anti-Congress sentiments in the state if its actions against the perpetrators were not strong. The Gehlot government sprang into action – the CM himself visited the bereaved family to pay his respects. Over the next few days, he announced other relief measures for them as well, including government jobs for both of Kanhaiyalal's sons, financial compensation and round-the-clock security to the family. The state government readily handed over the case to the National Investigation Agency (NIA), which arrested more people who were allegedly involved in the conspiracy. The two primary accused, Mohammad Riyaz and Ghouse Mohammad, were residents of Khanjipeer – a predominantly Muslim locality named after a seventeenth-century Dawoodi Bohra saint. Despite these steps taken by the state government, when Home Minister Amit Shah visited Jodhpur three months later, in September 2022, he criticized the Gehlot administration for the Udaipur killing.

When Kanhaiyalal's body was being carried to the crematorium, a huge crowd – dressed in jeans and saffron bandanas – assembled despite the curfew, following his funeral procession on bikes. The slogans soon turned into pejoratives directed at Muslims, with the crowd knocking over a signboard in front of a mosque next to the crematorium. A senior police official remarked that it was impossible for them to attempt to control a mob of this size without risking a bigger violent outbreak, so they had no choice but to overlook the hate speech and vandalism.[31] The next day, the police had to resort to a mild lathi charge to disperse a crowd after an episode of stone-pelting. What could have caused this, one might wonder? Turns out, the crowd was infuriated to see a hoarding featuring the Bollywood superstar Shah Rukh Khan.

For the second time in five years, the air of tension pervading Udaipur threatened to dismantle the communal fabric of this popular tourist spot.

While the political class in recent years has consistently tried to exploit the Hindu–Muslim fault lines in the state to reap electoral dividends, there have been instances when the hollowness of the rhetoric has risen to the surface. An apt example of this is the condition of Pakistani Hindu refugees in Rajasthan. A minority in the neighbouring Muslim-majority country, they fled Pakistan after suffering persecution and settled in refugee camps in Rajasthan. They routinely figure in election speeches in the state, particularly in those of the BJP leaders, who promise them relief.

However, despite the party having come to power in the state several times, even until 2021, around 10,000 Pakistani Hindus living in Rajasthan did not have access to even basic amenities such as water and electricity and were yet to be granted Indian citizenship. In 2021, when the COVID-19 pandemic struck, the Pakistani Hindu refugees in Jodhpur helplessly watched their family members die as they were not able to get vaccinated in the absence of an AADHAAR card.[32] It was only after the Rajasthan High Court pulled up the Congress-led state government over the issue that the administration arranged for the vaccination of these refugees.[33] Several refugees also chose to return to Pakistan after subsistence became impossible for them in India. In Jaipur, too, the Muslim Rohingya refugees from Myanmar suffered a similar fate initially, due to no arrangement for their vaccination being put in place.[34] The equally pitiable state of both Pakistani Hindu refugees – often courted in political speeches and yet left in the lurch without basic amenities – and Muslim Rohingya migrants – branded as infiltrators – reflects the opportunism in the communally-charged narrative peddled by politicos in the state.

After the ouster of the Gehlot government in 2023, the communally charged rhetoric of politicians and actions such as bulldozer demolitions and anti-conversion legislations chalked the trajectory of the new BJP government that came to power, as detailed at length in Chapter 11, reflecting the fact that the state's communal cauldron continues to simmer.

6

SHACKLES OF CASTE

Exploitation and Resistance

AN 11-FOOT-TALL STATUE HAS TOWERED OVER THE MANICURED LAWNS of the Rajasthan High Court since 1989. There is no plaque to indicate the name of this bearded figure with his hands in a blessing gesture immortalized in cement, but his identity is well known. He is the author of the *Manusmriti*, and the contentious history of the book and the statue are deeply entwined with the story of Rajasthan. Despite immense backlash and the historic burning of the controversial text by Dr B. R. Ambedkar nine decades ago, in 1927, the statue continues to be the first to greet all seekers of justice who flock to the Jaipur court.

The statue has invited the ire of activists and outfits for marginalized communities not only because of the anti-Constitutional values it represents, but because Rajasthan has consistently been ranked among the top three states in the country witnessing the highest number cases of Dalit atrocities. Despite vehement demands for its removal from the court premises and multiple unjust arrests for its defacement as a sign of protest, the statue ominously casts its shadow over the highest judicial authority in the state to this day. The petition for its removal is the oldest one pending at the court and is seldom listed for hearing. The last time it was listed made for sensational courtroom drama.

Lawyer A. K. Jain, representing the Dalit groups at the hearing, recalls that the court resembled a battleground. A large 300–400-strong crowd of Brahmin lawyers – including office bearers from different bar associations of Jaipur – broke out into protest when Jain started reciting the passages from the *Manusmriti* that are offensive to Dalits. 'We were hardly able to speak,' Jain said.[1]

The Only Dalit CM

Less than 50 metres from the contentious Manu statue is the sprawling compound of the state secretariat, which houses the CMO. Since Independence, only one Dalit has ever occupied this office – CM Jagannath Pahadia was at the helm for a little more than a year, although his short tenure and the circumstances under which he was made to leave the CM's residence further illustrate the deeply entrenched casteism in Rajasthan's politics.

When Pahadia was the CM between 1980–81, Congress leaders often referred to the chief minister's residence as 'Mohalla Khatikan',* a derogatory reference to Pahadia's Khatik caste, which is classified as SC. Former MLA and MP Pandit Ram Kishan is now over 100 years old and had preceded Pahadia by a decade as a legislator from Weir, Bharatpur. He was elected on an SSP ticket in 1962 and 1967 and recalls several instances when Pahadia was stopped from entering temples because of his caste, despite being a multiple-term MLA and a chief minister. For many people in his constituency, he was merely a Khatik and he confided in Kishan about his pain at this treatment.

Pahadia was made to abandon charge just a year after assuming office and never invited to hold the chief ministerial post again, even as other Congress CMs, such as Shiv Charan Mathur and Hari Dev Joshi, were given the opportunity to hold the top post multiple times, despite having had to resign for serious governance lapses.

---

* As learned from the authors' conversation with MLA Pandit Ram Kishan.

Dalit rights activist Bhanwar Meghwanshi describes how there have been no major resistance movements for the last 1,500 years in the state due to the inherently feudal nature of its society. In the shadow of this silence, the established political systems are no longer working to stop caste atrocities and discrimination has become an everyday occurrence.[2]

Bahujan Samaj Party

The only Ambedkarite party to have penetrated the social fabric is the Bahujan Samaj Party (BSP), which has been consistently bagging at least one seat in the assembly elections conducted in the past two decades. According to activist Kailash Mina, who had contested the 2004 Lok Sabha elections on a BSP ticket from Sawai Madhopur, when the party first arrived in Rajasthan just before the 2000s, the marginalized communities had a lot of hope from it as an outfit founded by the renowned social reformer Kanshi Ram.[3] However, as the BSP started giving out tickets to candidates who were known to hold starkly contrasting ideological stances, their supporters in the state became disillusioned. One such candidate had been Congress MLA Giriraj Singh Malinga, a Rajput, who publicly thanked BSP supremo Mayawati for launching his political career with a ticket to contest the assembly elections in 2008.[4] He later switched to the Congress. Ironically, in 2022, when he was the sitting Congress MLA from Bari, Malinga was arrested for assaulting Harshadhipati Valmiki, a Dalit engineer from the electricity department. Valmiki sustained multiple fractures and was admitted to Sawai Man Singh Hospital, Jaipur, in a serious condition. While the victim of the gruesome assault took almost a year to recover, lying in his hospital room, unable to walk and with his legs encased in braces, Malinga organized public meetings in his constituency, Bari, which were attended by CM Gehlot himself.

After sustained pressure from Dalit leaders and activists, the

Congress was forced to relent and denied Malinga a ticket to contest the 2023 assembly elections. This prompted him to switch parties and join the BJP, where he was welcomed with open arms, despite its earlier criticism of the Congress government for the growing number of Dalit atrocities in the state when Valmiki's assault had come to light.[5]

Malinga's political journey is an apt reflection of how the Kanshi Ram-founded party lost its mass appeal. A year after he was first elected on a BSP ticket in 2008, Malinga and five other BSP MLAs merged with the Congress. This was repeated in 2013 and 2018, when Malinga won the election from Bari in Dholpur on a Congress ticket. Months before the elections, Rajendra Singh Gudha – another Rajput MLA who had won on a BSP ticket – was heard asking the state assembly, 'In my party BSP, tickets are sold for money. If someone offers more money, then he will get the ticket. If a second person gives a still better price, then the first person's ticket is cut and given to the second one, and so on. What solution do you have for this?'[6] A month later, he switched to the Congress with five other MLAs who had won the election on a BSP ticket.

Party workers and supporters who had voted for these MLAs were disenchanted on seeing their votes laid to waste. They gathered in front of the BSP office in Jaipur on 22 October 2019 in anger. The faces of the party's then state president, Sitaram Meghwal, and national coordinator, Ramji Gautam, were blackened before they were garlanded with shoes and made to ride on donkeys. The video of this incident subsequently went viral on social media.[7]

Pushback from the Upper Castes

In April 2018, Hindaun, the largest town of the Karauli district in eastern Rajasthan, was hit by one of the worst caste conflicts in the history of Rajasthan. The houses of two Dalit politicians – sitting

BJP MLA Rajkumari Jatav and former MLA from the Congress, Bharosi Lal Jatav – had been set on fire by a mob of upper caste protesters. While the residents themselves had made a hasty retreat when the mob had entered their houses and vandalized their property before setting fire to the houses, the impunity of the act was shocking. The two charred houses were left abandoned in the curfewed city with several policemen patrolling the streets.

The immediate trigger for the upper caste backlash was the nationwide protests by Dalit outfits on 2 April 2018 in the wake of the Supreme Court's decision to change certain provisions of the SC/ST (Prevention of Atrocities Act), one of which enabled the accused in such cases to apply for anticipatory bail. Dalit outfits saw this as a clear dilution of the purpose of the law, which had been instituted to safeguard the weaker sections from atrocities. The 2 April protests shook Rajasthan as well, stretching from the eastern districts of Karauli, Alwar, Sawai Madhopur and Jaipur to the westernmost districts of Barmer and Jaisalmer, situated along the state borders. Worried that the Supreme Court's decision would empower the perpetrators of SC/ST atrocities, the protesters from Dalit and tribal communities went on a rampage, obstructing railway tracks and roads, while the police in the then BJP-ruled state scrambled to get the situation under control.

However, a counter-mobilization by the upper castes took the streets by storm soon after. The Karni Sena – a self-styled outfit positioned as protectors of the Rajput community – clashed with Dalit groups in the desert district of Barmer. The air, resonant with chants of 'Jai Bhim!', now rang with the counter-sloganeering from the Rajput side yelling 'Jai Bhawani!'. Lives were lost during these clashes, including that of twenty-seven-year-old Pawan Kumar Jatav, a Dalit man who had dreams of becoming a lecturer someday. He was killed in the police firing in Alwar's Khairthal and his father Jallaram Jatav alleged that the firing was deliberate. His son had been visiting Khairthal to meet his brother-in-law.[8]

The upper caste fury eventually reached Jatav Basti in Hindaun, 160 kilometres from Khairthal, where Dalits were threatening to convert to Islam. It was here that the upper caste mobs burned down the houses of the aforementioned Dalit politicians. According to Ashwini Jatav, a resident of the basti, upper caste men went around checking people's identity cards to make sure they were Dalits before assaulting them, not even sparing the women.[9]

Such backlash has become much more frequent in Rajasthan during recent years, when caste outfits such as the Karni Sena and the Brahmin Mahasabha – each with several factions led by self-styled heads – have started voicing concerns over the 'victimization' of upper castes.* Much before the BJP government at the centre introduced the 10 per cent reservation for economically weaker sections (EWS), people such as Pandit Suresh Mishra, Congress leader and president of the Sarv Brahmin Mahasabha who later switched to the BJP before the 2023 assembly elections, had been making demands for such a quota in Rajasthan.[10] In a viral video, former president of the Shree Rashtriya Rajput Karni Sena, Sukhdev Singh Gogamedi, was heard saying, 'If anybody frames you in a false case of SC/ST Act, go to the administration and give them proof of your innocence. If they still don't listen, cut off both the legs of the person who has filed the case.'[11] The crowd had cheered wildly in response. Gogamedi, who would later be shot dead in 2023 allegedly by assailants with links to organized criminal gangs, had a habit of issuing such sermons over social media.

The horrific scenes in Hindaun in the aftermath of the 2 April protests were proof of how Dalit leaders – whether they were from the Congress or the BJP – would not be spared in case of conflict. The BJP was already under fire from Rajput outfits over other

---

* For more detail on Brahmin assertion, the following report details a recent meet in Jaipur: Prem Narayan Meena, 'जयपुर में ब्राह्मण महापंचायत : ब्राह्मणों ने दिया एकजुटता का सन्देश, रेलमंत्री अश्विनी वैष्णव ने कही ये बात', *हिन्दुस्तान*, 19 March 2023.

issues, including the controversies stirred up by *Padmaavat* and the Anandpal Singh encounter, and so it refrained from outrightly condemning this fresh violent outbreak by upper caste protesters.

According to the 2011 census, the SC and ST communities form a collective 31.31 per cent of the population. While thirty-four assembly seats are reserved for the SCs, there are twenty-five constituencies reserved for STs. Despite the two communities being a decisive force for nearly sixty assembly seats, cases of Dalit and tribal atrocities have only increased, reflecting how deeply entrenched the caste fault lines are in the formerly feudal state. In recent years, however, Rajasthan has seen greater disillusionment with the established political order among the Dalit youth, evident in the rise of outfits such as the Bhim Army.

Anil Kumar Dhenwal, who was the Rajasthan state in-charge of the Bhim Army in 2022 remarked at how after being let down repeatedly by major parties such as the Congress and BJP, Dalit youth naturally gravitated towards the Bhim Army. With members and volunteers in all districts using all possible media available, including social media and WhatsApp groups, the outfit started highlighting cases of Dalit atrocities ignored by mainstream media.[12]

Ambedkarite movements in the state have been fuelled by the anger of Dalit youngsters who are allied with neither the Congress nor the BJP. Over the years, the statue of Manu mentioned at the beginning of this chapter has also become a symbol for rallying Dalit voices. Time and again, groups representing oppressed communities from across the country have called for the removal of the statue. In 2018, two Dalit women from Maharashtra's Aurangabad were arrested along with an associate for smearing the statue with black paint.

Apart from the rise of outfits such as the Bhim Army,

marginalized communities have also continued to express their grouse against the system electorally, through the power of the ballot. Dalit anger was palpable in the results of the 2018 assembly elections, when the BJP's tally suffered the most in SC/ST-dominated areas which had seen violence during the 2 April protests. The BJP could win only twenty of the fifty-nine reserved seats in the state. In 2023, as the Gehlot-led Congress government tenure had been seeing many cases of Dalit atrocities and had faced immense backlash from the community as a result, their hopes to get elected were dashed by the loss of the reserved seats they had secured in the previous elections. They could win in only twenty of the fifty-nine reserved constituencies – meeting the same fate as the BJP five years back.

Dalit Atrocities: A Constant Phenomenon

Rajasthan achieved a dubious distinction in mid-2022, when the National Crime Records Bureau released its annual crime data for the previous year. Earlier the third state to see the most number of Dalit atrocities cases, Rajasthan had now moved up to the second spot after Uttar Pradesh. In 2023, it retained its spot once again.[13]

While it is true that the state saw Dalit atrocities rise steadily even during the BJP regime between 2013–18, the administrative inaction and negligence during the Ashok Gehlot-led Congress government between 2018–23 drew significantly more criticism from both the opposition and activists. The first such instance which led to nationwide outrage occurred in April 2019, just four months after the Congress formed the government. A Dalit woman was travelling with her husband when she was waylaid and gangraped by a group of men in Alwar district, who filmed a video of the crime and later circulated it on social media. The horrific details of the case stunned the country and teams of media personnel rushed to her home in response.

The anger of the eighteen-year-old Dalit woman's relatives in Alwar's Thana Ghazi could be felt in the air. The woman's father told the media that for two days after the incident, the family promptly reported the whereabouts of the accused whenever they were in the vicinity of the local police, but no action was taken. To make matters worse, the family was instructed to wait until after the elections. Despite the gruesome nature of the case, statements of multiple family members and victims made it clear that there was no police action whatsoever for seven days until the Lok Sabha elections came to an end. Their repeated implorations for the accused to be arrested, as they feared that the video would be circulated on social media, were met with dismissal.

The incident was reminiscent of the 1992 Bhanwari Devi incident, when Devi, a Dalit woman working as a Saathin* with the Women Development Programme, was gangraped by a group of men who were angered by her attempts to stop child marriages.[14] The case eventually became the basis for the Supreme Court to formulate the landmark Vishakha Guidelines for prevention of sexual harassment at the workplace. Lad Kumari Jain, former chairperson of Rajasthan Women's Commission, who had spearheaded the massive protests by women activists after the Devi gangrape case, said that the government neither supported nor escalated the issue. If it were not for the sustained protests by women's rights groups, the case would have gone altogether unnoticed.[15]

In the case of the Thana Ghazi gangrape, the state government responded by removing the Superintendent of Police (SP) of Alwar and later dividing the district into two separate jurisdictions – Alwar and Bhiwadi – for better policing. When it was discovered

* Saathin, which translates to 'friend', is a female worker with the Department of Women and Child Development deputed to visit households in rural areas to spread awareness among the people about government's schemes and educating them on how to care for mother and child health. Their role is similar to those of Anganwadi workers.

during investigations that the victim had approached the SP's office but was told to go to the police station, the government created a provision for registering an FIR at the SP office as well. The case had exposed gaping loopholes in the system, but this was hardly the end and more issues continued to crop up every time a heinous crime against Dalits was committed over the course of the next four years.

The increasing instances of such atrocities have only proven that violence against Dalits, especially women, remains a constant to this day. According to Rajasthan Police data, there was a 7.23 per cent increase in cases of atrocities against SCs in 2021 as compared to 2020. During this time, one of the most common responses of the state government was to assert that the reason there was a perceptible increase in crime figures was because of their directions to the police to compulsorily register every complaint brought to them. They even claimed that more than 58 per cent cases of rape were found to be false.[16] The opposition and women activist groups refused to accept this argument.

Further, in a controversial statement in August 2022, CM Gehlot made an absurd attempt to explain the rise in rape-murders with 'Rapes are happening with girls. And since death penalty was introduced for accused, after Nirbhaya ... a lot of murders are happening of girls. The rapist feels that tomorrow she will become a witness against me.' This invited even more backlash and damaged his government's reputation.[17] A report by *The Indian Express* revealed that contrary to Gehlot's claims, rape-murder cases in Rajasthan constituted only 0.45 per cent cases in the last five years and have actually decreased over the years.[18] As demonstrated in the incident in Thana Ghazi, a lot of the cases could have been dealt with in a sensitive way by the police but due to administrative apathy, were not handled properly.

In June 2021, twenty-one-year-old Vinod Bamnia, a member of the Bhim Army in Hanumangarh, was brutally attacked and killed by people who had torn off posters that he had put up on the occasion of Ambedkar Jayanti. The victim was assailed and threatened with '*Aaj tumhe tumhara Ambedkarvad yaad dilwayenge* (Today we'll remind you of your Ambedkarite ideology),' as per the FIR registered in the case.[19] The Bhim Army also staged a protest over Bamniya's death, alleging police inaction.

In another instance, administrative negligence failed to avoid a preventable death. Despite the orders of Rajasthan High Court, eighteen-year-old Pinki Saini was honour killed by her father in March 2021 for marrying Roshan Mahawar, a Dalit. The tragic incident happened despite Mahawar repeatedly telling the police that Pinki's family had taken her away and there was a likelihood they might kill her. The police dismissed his fears and told him they were sure Pinki would be brought in for her next court hearing. 'I cried and pleaded with the police, but they did not take my concerns seriously,' recalls Mahawar, his voice breaking.[20] As with other cases of negligence, the government suspended or removed IPS officers in response to demands for action and instituted committees for better governance, but the cases continued unabated.

In March 2022, Jitendra Meghwal, a Dalit contractual health worker from Pali district, was allegedly murdered by upper caste men who had earlier threatened his family in 2020 because he had 'dared to look up' at them. After his murder, the victim's family members alleged that one of the reasons behind his killing was the accused's intolerance for a Dalit man sporting a moustache.[21] In the same year, Indra Kumar Meghwal, a nine-year-old Dalit boy from Jalore district died after being beaten by his schoolteacher, who had been infuriated at the sight of the Dalit boy drinking water from an earthen pot meant for him.[22]

Even as the Congress was voted out in December 2023 and the BJP government led by CM Bhajan Lal Sharma came to power, not much changed. Despite the state now having a Dalit deputy chief minister in Prem Chand Bairwa, in August 2024, Dalit activist groups once again had to take to the streets after Babu Lal Bairwa, a Dalit head constable in his mid-forties died by suicide, alleging harassment by his superiors.[23] Three months before his death, Rameshwar Valmiki, a Dalit sanitation worker, was beaten to death by the liquor mafia in Rajasthan's Jhunjhunu district. A video of the assault on Valmiki went viral on social media, wherein his assailants were seen assaulting him with sticks while he was tied up and hung upside down from a rod.[24]

Even as the Congress – now in opposition – took on the new state government over the issue of Dalit atrocities, new incidents continued to come to light, reflecting an unfortunate reality – while it may have shed its feudal past in name through its transition to a democracy, marginalized communities remained vulnerable as ever.

The corridors of power, too, did not offer shelter from caste discrimination. When Congress MLA Tika Ram Jully was appointed the leader of opposition in the Rajasthan assembly in early 2024, he became the first person from the Dalit community to hold the post. A year later, in April 2025, after Jully visited a temple in his home district of Alwar, former BJP MLA Gyan Dev Ahuja sprinkled Gangajal inside the temple to 'purify' it. The incident drew massive criticism and the state BJP decided to expel Ahuja under public pressure.[25]

Another incident that took place at the Rajasthan assembly in July 2024 served to reaffirm the lack of sensitivity among the political class in the state. When Harish Chaudhary, a Congress legislator, read out the famous poem 'Thakur ka Kuan' – which highlights the oppression faced by marginalized communities – written by poet Om Prakash Valmiki, he faced immediate opposition from other legislators, primarily Rajput MLAs, who said they were 'pained' by Chaudhary's recitation and even went on to pen counter poetry glorifying the valour and sacrifices of the Rajputs. His own fellow party leaders from the Rajput community objected to the recitation, which was ultimately expunged from the assembly records by speaker Vasudev Devnani.

The fact that even the work of a well-known poet such as Om Prakash Valmiki detailing the plight and inhumane living conditions of Dalits was denied a place in the records of the state assembly upon the insistence of lawmakers themselves is deplorable. Despite the state's considerable Dalit population and a long, consistent history of atrocities perpetrated against them, the reluctance of upper caste leaders to share the metaphorical dais with them shows that Rajasthan still has a long way to go to break the shackles of caste.

There are, however, stories of hope as well, which reaffirm the ability of social initiatives against caste discrimination to drive change. One such initiative was started by the Bundi district police in 2022. For several years now, policemen have become a common feature of Dalit wedding processions in Rajasthan. In January 2022, the Bundi Police launched Operation Samanta, an equality campaign that aims to fight against the long-established taboos relating to Dalit wedding processions, especially bridegrooms not being permitted to ride a mare. In Chadi, a small village in Bundi district, Dalits often avoid this Hindu wedding rite for fear of harassment and violence by upper caste vigilantes – a pitiful remnant of the state's feudal past. Just two months before Operation Samanta started, people pelted stones at a Dalit wedding procession in Jaipur despite police being present on the scene.

According to figures recorded by the Rajasthan police, in the previous decade, seventy-six cases had been registered across the state wherein Dalit grooms were stopped from riding mares.[26] This is the reason Shriram Meghwal's wedding procession was a radical break from tradition. The pure joy felt by his family members on the twenty-seven-year-old's wedding day in Chadi was infectious. The groom mounted the beautifully decorated mare, adjusted his *safa* (the Rajasthani turban) and clasped the hilt of the traditional sword before the procession began its journey through his village. Meghwal was overjoyed to be the first Dalit groom to ride a mare on those roads. He hoped that his act would definitively change the oppressive mentality of the upper castes. 'This is one step towards equality,' he said with pride.[27] The air reverberated with slogans of 'Jai Bhim!' as Meghwal's friends and family danced to the music. On the stage was a portrait of Dr Ambedkar next to the bridegroom, jubilant at having turned a new leaf in the history of his village which he hoped would be repeated without fear by other Dalits as well.

The Rise of Adivasi Parties and Meena Politics

'BTP *nek hai isiliye* Congress BJP *ek hai* (BTP is honest, so BJP and Congress have united),' Chhotubhai Vasava, the founder of the Gujarat-based Bharatiya Tribal Party (BTP), posted on X on 10 December 2020.[28] In a completely unforeseen move, arch rivals Congress and BJP had joined forces to defeat an independent candidate supported by the BTP in the Zila Pramukh elections. BTP was, at the time, supporting the Gehlot government and, despite having contested just one election so far, posed a formidable challenge to the political behemoths. In December 2018, in its very first electoral stint, the BTP won two seats in Dungarpur, defeating both Congress and BJP. This sent alarm bells ringing among the members of the Vanvasi Kalyan Parishad, an arm of the RSS that works to bring tribals into the Hindutva fold. Despite widespread discontent with the Gehlot government, the Vanvasi Kalyan Parishad considered BTP to be the bigger ideological threat compared to the Congress.

Tribal leaders and ideologues such as Kantilal Roat, who had contested the 2019 Lok Sabha elections as the BTP candidate from Banswara, had gained immense popularity for their stance that Hindutva proponents were trying to forcefully convert tribals, who were not Hindus. This narrative enabled the BTP to capture Chorasi and Sagwara – both seats in the tribal-dominated Dungarpur district reserved for candidates from the ST community, which comprises 13.48 per cent of the total population of Rajasthan.

The Udaipur division, a traditional stronghold of the BJP, is an important region for the Sangh-affiliated Vanvasi Kalyan Parishad and the organization enjoys considerable ideological influence on the ground. The former MP from Dungarpur, Kanak Mal Katara, has long been associated with the Parishad and his fierce opposition to the BTP's narrative of Adivasis not being Hindus and Christian missionaries working in the tribal belt has contributed to the turf war over this area.

In 2017, tribal leaders opposed to the RSS and Vanvasi Kalyan Parishad invited the Gujarat-based BTP to establish itself in the region to give them a platform for entering electoral politics. Thereafter, two BTP MLAs won elections and raised issues important to the tribal population in the two districts – classified as tribal sub-plan areas – in the state assembly, such as a separate religious code for tribals, issuing of land deeds and better employment opportunities. As the BTP support base expanded in the area, both the Congress and BJP grew uneasy.

Sure enough, tensions boiled over and violence erupted in Dungarpur in September 2020, when tribal youths demanding appointment to teaching posts reserved for STs clashed with the administration atop the Kakri Dungri hills, blocking a national highway. The already simmering discontent of the tribal community exploded during these protests, leading to the deaths of two persons and heavy damage to property. Rajkumar Roat, the BTP MLA from Chorasi at the time, alleged that the police implicated the local youth in a slew of false cases, which resulted in widespread persecution and harassment of innocent tribal youngsters in the wake of the protests.[29] The withdrawal of these cases became one of the foremost demands of the BTP thereafter, which revoked its support of the Congress, resulting in the BJP and Congress combining forces for the Zila Pramukh election.

Before the Rajya Sabha elections in June 2022, however, the two BTP MLAs Rajkumar Roat and Ramprasad Dindor announced their decision to support the Congress after CM Gehlot assured them that the withdrawal of the Kakri Dungri cases would be considered again.

What the BTP achieved in its short stint is remarkable for it has steered the political discourse in the state towards a subject that both the Congress and the BJP have long overlooked – the tribal identity. Its support of the demands for a separate Bheel Pradesh and a religious code for the tribal community has helped it gain immense popularity among the young tribals. It also forced other politicians to end their silence on these contentious issues. In March 2021, the Rajasthan assembly was left stunned when Ganesh Ghogra, the president of the state Youth Congress, reiterated the BTP's stance that Adivasis are not Hindus. The BJP was outraged at his statement where Ghoghra had said, 'We want a separate religious code and this is a special demand. Even today Adivasis don't have the right to sit on *khat* (cot), and they have to take off their slippers first. Are we not humans? Aren't Adivasis humans?'[30] The BJP even alleged at one point that they suspected that 'naxal elements' were behind the Kakri Dungri violence, a claim rejected by the state police.[31]

The Congress was equally eager to bury the issue. 'It will be in the interest of the Hindu samaj if we forget this debate. Otherwise it will damage the Hindu community,' remarked a senior Congress cabinet minister when his views on Ghogra's statement were requested.[32] Another party leader and minister, Pratap Singh Khachariyawas, also reiterated the belief, remarking,

'Tribals are also Hindus but they also have the right to express themselves.' However, he refrained from defending Ghogra from the BJP's onslaught, only remarking that everyone has the freedom of speech.[33]

Prior to the BTP's arrival, the ST Meena community held immense sway over the state's politics and welcomed the overtures of both the Congress and BJP for its support. But Meena leaders too avoided discussing issues like a separate religious code for Adivasis and the exploitation of tribals by larger parties, and largely acted as integral cogs in the political ecosystem. According to a former BTP MLA from Sagwara, Ramprasad Dindor, the tribal community needed to present a united front in order to safeguard their culture and seek political change.[34]

Thus, it came as a surprise when in mid-2022, two tribal MLAs and their supporters severed ties with the BTP over differences with its founder, the Gujarat-based Vasava. They were reportedly unhappy with the Gujarat BTP's repeated interference in Rajasthan's affairs. These leaders then formed their own party, the Bharat Adivasi Party (BAP), debuting in the 2023 assembly elections and presenting a new challenge to the Congress and BJP in Rajasthan's tribal belt. BAP won three seats in the 2023 assembly elections, while the BTP drew a blank after its cadre defected to the new outfit en masse. With the Gujarat-born BTP's journey coming to an end in Rajasthan, the state now had BAP as the party that claimed to represent the voices of tribals. The BAP also won in Banswara in the Lok Sabha elections in 2024 and an assembly by-election, establishing the tribal party as a significant force in southern Rajasthan.

In mid-July 2021, a video of a saffron flag being pulled down from the historic Amagarh fort in Jaipur went viral on social media. It was a crucial moment in tribal politics as the flag was taken down by members of the Rajasthan Adivasi Meena Sewa Sangh, led by an independent MLA from Gangapur City, Ramkesh Meena. For him, the installation of the saffron flag atop the fort was an effort by the Sangh ideologues to appropriate tribal icons as symbols of Hindutva. The Amagarh fort had been built by an ancient Meena King and was home to several tribal deities, including Amba Mata and Bhairu ji. The removal of the flag was welcomed by the BTP as well, which was already raising a clamour for a separate religious code for Adivasis.

It was around this time that the most well-recognized Meena leader from Rajasthan made an entry: Kirodi Lal Meena. Owing to his clout in his community, Meena, during the course of his five-decade-long political career has helped the BJP several times to win in constituencies with significant number of tribal voters. Meena was born in a small village in Dausa back in the 1950s. A firm believer in the Hindutva ideology of the RSS, he is the most influential Meena leader in Rajasthan. The consolidation of Meena votes has borne rich political dividends for Kirodi Lal Meena, who had left the BJP in 2008 over differences with CM Raje, but was brought back by the party in 2018 to capitalize on his immense popularity with his community. However, even when he did not contest on a BJP ticket, he was able to win elections and become an independent MP from Dausa, a Meena-dominated constituency, in 2009. In 2013, he and his supporters won the assembly elections by joining the National People's Party founded by P. A. Sangma and helping the party – hitherto unknown in Rajasthan – win four seats, a reflection of his clout.[35]

Kirodi Lal Meena never loses an opportunity to proclaim that he is proud to be a Hindu. Days after the saffron flag was removed, Meena marched in Jaipur with hundreds of tribal youngsters holding placards saying '*Hum Hindu the, Hindu hain, Hindu rahenge* (We were Hindu, are Hindu and will always remain Hindu)'. He defied the Jaipur police to raise a white flag at Amagarh fort as a symbol of his community, while also demanding the arrest of independent MLA Ramkesh Meena, who had asserted that tribals are not Hindus.

In December 2022, Kirodi Lal Meena brought a private bill demanding that a nation-wide Uniform Civil Code be introduced before the parliament. In recent years, despite his differences with other BJP leaders, Meena has emerged as an invaluable support for the saffron party for his ability to at once garner Meena votes and propagate the RSS narrative among his tribal followers. He kept this up in the 2023 assembly elections as well, mobilizing tribal support for the BJP in eastern Rajasthan and winning with a thumping majority himself from Sawai Madhopur. Compared to 2018, when the BJP could win in only one assembly constituency in eastern Rajasthan, across Bharatpur, Dausa, Dholpur, Karauli and Sawai Madhopur districts, it won thirteen seats in 2023, with the Congress winning in just eight constituencies across the region.

The long feudal past of Rajasthan has ensured that the state perpetuated its inherited legacy of the oppression of marginalized communities. In the seventy-eight years since Independence, it is true that steps have been taken for the upliftment of Dalits and tribals in the state, supported by affirmative measures such as reservation and government policies aimed towards social justice. In a similar vein, political representation from the hitherto oppressed castes has also increased – in all parties – with some of the leaders going on to hold important ministerial posts. And yet, as the examples in this chapter make abundantly clear, caste-based discrimination remains ingrained within the state's story – past and present. It regularly manifests as gruesome crimes against the weaker and vulnerable sections of the society and the constant anti-Dalit political rhetoric that grabs national headlines. What is commendable, however, is the incredible resilience shown by the oppressed communities in pushing back against caste oppression, be it through sustained movements, protests or electoral contests to ensure that their voices are not ignored.

7

A WILY SURVIVOR

Ashok Gehlot's Political Craft

IN THE EARLY 1970S, IT WASN'T UNCOMMON TO SEE A TALL, LANKY young man with a wide forehead riding a Yezdi motorcycle near Jalori Gate in Jodhpur, on his way to or from Solanki Tea Stall. Ashok Gehlot's favourite hangout in the city, this tea stall was owned by a man known as Kaka, and is an important landmark in his history as one of Rajasthan's longest-serving chief ministers. According to his college friend, Mahesh Bora, he and Gehlot would order three cups of tea to share among four of them, and Gehlot would then discuss politics for several hours. Bora himself was the former general secretary of the Jodhpur Youth Congress and recalls how they would sometimes be joined at their haunt by well-known intellectuals of the time, including noted author Vijaydan Detha and folk artist Komal Kothari.

Ashok Gehlot's father was the celebrated magician Laxman Singh, who had also served as the chairman of the Jodhpur Municipal Council. While Gehlot was doing his LLB at Jodhpur University in the late 1960s, he would occasionally borrow a leaf from his father's book and perform magic tricks for his classmates. The popularity he won enabled him to foray into student politics. However, Gehlot's initial years in politics were entirely forgettable – he faced a string of defeats in the student elections. BJP leader

Shambhu Singh Khetasar, his contemporary, still takes great pride in having defeated Gehlot in their first student elections.*[1] When the National Student Union of India (NSUI), the student wing of the Congress, was formed in 1971, Gehlot became its first Rajasthan president.[2]

The Indo-Pak war and subsequent independence of Bangladesh in 1971 coincided with a massive refugee crisis. Gehlot was one of the hundreds of volunteers who participated in the relief efforts during this time and this laid the foundation for his full-time political career in the Congress. From his usual hangouts near Jalori and Sojati Gate to a tin shed at Indira Gandhi Bhawan – the Congress party's state headquarters in Jaipur – and finally to the spotless corridors of the CMO in the state secretariat, Gehlot's political magic has lasted for more than fifty years. In these five decades, he has been elected CM of India's geographically largest state thrice between 1998 and 2023 and, despite his government's loss in the 2023 assembly elections, remains an immensely powerful force in the state's politics to this day. His tenure is second only to Mohan Lal Sukhadia's, who had held office consecutively for seventeen years throughout the 1950–60s.

The story of Gehlot's political career is replete with anecdotes of ingenuity, marked by a ruthless will to outsmart his rivals and an exceptional ability to foretell their moves, paired with remarkable strategic acumen.

The Gandhi Connection

Mahesh Bora reveals how Gehlot developed a knack for Gandhian values – an important feature of his political identity. While in

* But it was Gehlot who emerged victorious in all subsequent electoral contests. Khetasar, who was fielded by the BJP against Gehlot from the Sardarpura assembly constituency in both 2013 and 2018, has not been able to replicate his success from his student days and lost both elections to the veteran leader by a huge margin.

Jodhpur, he regularly visited the Gandhi Shanti Pratishthan and was heavily influenced by the centre's director at the time, Nemi Chand Jain. Gehlot became something of a disciple of Jain's, emulating his ways by wearing khadi and staying away from confrontations. He was very hardworking and took great pains to strengthen the NSUI's organization in the state. In line with his tenet of simplicity, he often appeared in the same black *achkan* on every public or social event that he attended.[3]

Much like his first student elections, Gehlot lost his first assembly elections in 1977 as well, which he had contested from Sardarpura. By the mid-1970s, however, Gehlot had been able to expand his influence enough to shuffle between Jodhpur and Jaipur. Veteran Congress leader Mumtaz Masih* – a firsthand witness to Gehlot's rise within the party – recalls that he, as a representative of the Congress Sewa Dal, Janardan Singh Gehlot† from the Youth Congress and Ashok Gehlot from the NSUI occupied the three tin sheds at the RPCC office in Jaipur together. Until the 1980s – when he became a die-hard loyalist of Rajiv Gandhi's – Gehlot was among the group of young leaders in Congress who drew their strength from being in the good books of Sanjay Gandhi.

In the 1970s and '80s, the political sphere in Jodhpur and its adjacent districts was dominated by Paras Ram Maderna and family – one of the most influential Jat clans in the state alongside the Mirdhas. As elaborated in Chapters 2 and 3, the anti-jagirdar movement from the early twentieth century had left in its wake powerful Jat political dynasties, who were as influential as the feudal

---

* Masih, now seventy-seven years old, was the Congress Sewa Dal Chief of Rajasthan from 1978–86 and remains a staunch loyalist of Gehlot to this day.

† Apart from Gehlot, the third occupant of the tin shade at the PCC office, Janardan Singh Gehlot was a close aide of Sanjay Gandhi's, and had famously defeated former CM Bhairon Singh Shekhawat from the Gandhinagar seat in Jaipur in the 1972 assembly elections. He went on to become the president of the International Kabaddi Federation and passed away in 2021.

lords had been. Hence, it comes as no surprise that when Gehlot was taking his first steps in politics, no election in Jodhpur could be won without the support of Paras Ram Maderna. Before the 1980 Lok Sabha elections, Maderna took Gehlot under his wing and helped him gain a foothold. The young leader, too, acknowledged Maderna as his political guru.[4]

The 1980 Lok Sabha election changed Gehlot's life, catapulting the young man from Jodhpur into the power corridors of Delhi. As Indira Gandhi returned to power after being dethroned in 1977 after the Emergency, twenty-nine-year-old Gehlot was comfortably elected to the Lok Sabha, buoyed by Maderna and Jat support. As Paras Ram Maderna stated in an interview for *Mahanagar*, he had fielded Gehlot from Jodhpur in the 1980 Lok Sabha elections and had even accompanied him to the constituency's villages to formally introduce him to the public. Two years later, Gehlot was inducted as a junior minister in the Indira Gandhi government, setting the stage for his entry into the big leagues, as detailed later in this section.

Initially, it appeared that in the context of Rajasthan's caste-driven politics, Gehlot was a misfit with a clear disadvantage. Since he belonged to the Mali community, he had OBC status, but the community is so widespread throughout the state that it lacks a unified political front and, as a result, does not hold much influence as an en masse voting block unlike other communities such as the Jats and Meenas. For decades, Gehlot has been among only a handful of leaders from the Mali community to be elected to the Parliament and state assembly. The tag of 'magician' has been passed down from father to son for his seemingly impossible feats in the political arena. In December 2018, after being elected as CM for the third time, Gehlot jokingly acquiesced to the nickname: '*Jaadu karte karte main yahan tak pahuncha hun. Mali community ka aadmi, koi jaati ka base nahin, 200 mein se khaali ek vidhayak Mali jeetke aata hai, toh bhi mukhyamantri aap mujhe banate ho baar baar. Toh jaadu nahi hai kya ye*? (Magic might just be the reason I have got this far. A Mali community man with no caste base to support him, when out of 200 MLAs, only one is usually Mali and yet, you elect me as the chief minister time and again. Isn't this magic?)'. [5]

In September 2022, Divya Maderna, first-time MLA, was seen reminding reporters about incidents that took place twenty-four years ago. She was furious and did not mince her words while criticizing her own party leaders. 'My grandfather Parasram Maderna ... said the party high command decision was paramount. It never happened in Congress in the past that there were conditional resolutions,' she said, slamming Mahesh Joshi and Shanti Dhariwal, the right- and left-hand men of CM Ashok Gehlot, her grandfather's protégé.[6] The immediate cause of Maderna's anger was the near-rebellion led by Dhariwal and Joshi, wherein Gehlot's supporter MLAs had taken the liberty to skip a meeting called by the Congress high command, hold a parallel meeting of their own and, thereafter, submit their resignations to assembly speaker C. P. Joshi in a bid to stop the party leadership from replacing Gehlot and appointing Sachin Pilot as the CM instead.

The year 1998 was a sore spot for the Maderna family. It was the year when Gehlot finally inched past his mentor to win the electoral race to become the Rajasthan CM. It is worth examining how Gehlot, a relatively fresh entrant, managed to outshine several established leaders and former chief ministers, such as Hari Dev Joshi, Shiv Charan Mathur, Heera Lal Devpura and Paras Ram Maderna. The answer lies in Gehlot's strategic ties with the Gandhi family for over three generations, beginning with Indira Gandhi herself, followed by Sanjay, Rajiv and Sonia, and now with Rahul and Priyanka. 'My relationship with the Gandhi family is beyond any argument,' Gehlot declared in October 2022, dismissing all speculations that he may be replaced by Sachin Pilot and expressing anger at the actions of his supporters, who had defied the orders of the high command and skipped the CLP meeting called for the crowning of Pilot, as per anonymous sources.

Whenever he makes a public appearance and takes to the dais, Gehlot never fails to state that India won the 1971 Bangladesh war thanks to the leadership of Indira Gandhi, and that it was Rajiv Gandhi who introduced information technology and computers to the country, and how both the PMs sacrificed their lives in the nation's service. He also regularly names government schemes after them as a token of his respect. While an unflinching loyalty towards the Gandhi family is not uncommon among Congress leaders – in fact, it is the convention – Gehlot stands out from his peers in that he has never once gone against the Gandhi clan. As Masih recalls, when Rahul and Priyanka were young, Gehlot would often entertain them with magic tricks he had learned from his father.

One of the first indications that Gehlot had managed to enter the good books of the Gandhi family came in 1982 when, despite being a first-term MP, he was elevated to the post of deputy minister for Tourism. Three years later, at the age of thirty-four, he became the state president of the Rajasthan Congress, stepping into the shoes of senior Congress leader Nawal Kishore Sharma. This was a time when PM Rajiv Gandhi had laid great emphasis on younger leaders taking on bigger roles in the party and changed many other PCC presidents across the country as well. Gehlot became the youngest-ever PCC president in Rajasthan, a record he holds to this day. Even as the Congress high command drove Rajasthan CMs out of office before they could complete a term, Gehlot consolidated his influence in the party as PCC president.

In December 1988, PM Rajiv Gandhi publicly rebuked Hari Dev Joshi for defying his orders of organizing a low-profile meeting with his council of ministers in Sariska. CM Joshi had instead brought hundreds of cars and government officials to accompany him, which had left Gandhi seething. Many within the Rajasthan Congress attribute it to Gehlot's magic that the fact of Joshi's defiance was uncovered. Within a month, CM Joshi was made to put in his papers and Shiv Charan Mathur was appointed in his place. Yet another high point in Gehlot's career arrived in 1989, when at the age of merely thirty-eight, he was invited by PM Gandhi to join Mathur's government as home minister.

At the time, Gehlot was an MP from Jodhpur. He was set to be elected to the state assembly within six months but, sensing the impending defeat of the Congress, Gehlot resigned in November 1989, months before the Rajasthan Congress was pushed out of power by the BJP for eight years. Gehlot was defeated by senior BJP leader Jaswant Singh from his home constituency. In May 1991, Rajiv Gandhi's assassination dealt yet another blow to Gehlot's career and he lost an important pillar of support within the party high command. He recovered within two years, however, and won back the seat to become MoS for Textiles in the union government led by P. V. Narsimha Rao.

Nestled comfortably in the top rungs of Rajasthan Congress, Gehlot now shifted his focus to the top post. He became the PCC president once again in the mid-1990s and dedicated all his time to taking on the Bhairon Singh Shekhawat-led BJP government in the state. It was at this time that his ambitions clashed with that of his mentor's. Paras Ram Maderna was appointed the leader of opposition in 1993, after Shekhawat was elected for a second term – the first instance in the state's history when non-Congress parties formed the government for two consecutive terms. Riding the post-Babri demolition Hindutva wave, the BJP under Shekhawat looked comfortably poised to rule for the next five years.

However, after eight years of being in office, anti-incumbency against the Shekhawat government began piling up. This meant that the Congress, despite its diminished stature in the national politics, had a realistic chance of ousting the BJP from power. For Maderna and the Jat community, this seemed like the perfect opportunity for the Congress to show its gratitude to its largest voter base. While a heavyweight like Maderna was sure to achieve this objective as well as rake in the votes, he was denied the opportunity as the high command had a different preference: Ashok Gehlot.

Rohit Parihar, deputy editor at *India Today*, has covered Rajasthan for over three decades and observed how PCC president Gehlot emerged as a distinct leader compared to his peers. Gehlot was disciplined and meticulous in crafting press statements, ensuring consistent media visibility and worked relentlessly as PCC chief. He travelled the length and breadth of Rajasthan during electoral campaigns and was prescient in his assessment that the BJP government led by Bhairon Singh Shekhawat was on its way out. While Maderna was often projected as a strong contender for the chief ministership, the ground reality was different. Gehlot's energy, youth and visibility gave him an edge over the veteran leader and his media-savvy personality was compelling in its consistent criticism of the BJP government's policies in his press notes. It was this steady presence and unrelenting effort that Parihar attributes to Gehlot's political relevance at the time, even as the state's politics were dominated by towering figures like Shekhawat and Maderna. Gehlot's humble mannerisms and background were also unusual – he neither belonged to a powerful caste or a wealthy family, nor was he fluent in English. He compensated for what he lacked in terms of a caste backing by maintaining simplicity in line with his Gandhian values. He was always warm in his interactions, dressed in plain khadi and remained accessible to all who came seeking him, presenting himself as a grounded politician with no arrogance. He was especially friendly towards the media, carefully nurturing ties that would bolster his political image, Parihar adds.[7]

When the Congress won a thumping victory in the 1998 elections with more than three-fourths of the total seats in the state assembly, the question on everyone's mind was: who would become the chief minister? 'I remember ringing up senior Congress leader Natwar Singh to ask if he was going to be the one. He told me, "Rohit, I am not the one becoming the CM, but whoever it will be, it will be a young person,"' recalls Parihar.[8] He also confirmed that Maderna had a chance since he had a strong support base in his community, but the Congress high command had already indicated its preference for a younger face. Soon, the names of Gehlot and Girija Vyas began circulating in Delhi's political corridors. Eventually, Gehlot was picked, edging out both Maderna and Vyas.

Months before the 1998 assembly elections, Sonia Gandhi had taken charge as the national president of the party. To her, Gehlot, the state unit president at the time – who had been a five-time MP by then – appeared a more suitable choice for CM as the existing state unit president; more in sync with her late husband's vision of a youth-centric Congress. Gehlot was dynamic and shared a good rapport with Sonia Gandhi. Meanwhile, Maderna and his supporters could only watch helplessly as the crown that they felt was rightfully theirs was bestowed upon Gehlot. This act drove a permanent wedge between Gehlot and certain sections of the Jat community loyal to their representative veteran leader. The magician had hexed his own mentor.

Even after being appointed as the CM, Gehlot maintained his mild-mannered, modest demeanour and spoke about upholding democratic traditions and the importance of listening to the issues raised by the opposition. He said during one of his earliest speeches in the state assembly, in January 1999:

> We are about to enter the twenty-first century. In democracy, there are victories and defeats, as the honourable Leader of the Opposition said, and for this reason, I would like to say that

> whenever the Congress could not win the elections, it accepted the mandate with humility and modesty and always tried to raise issues of public interest while sitting in the opposition.[9]

He immediately followed with, 'Although I am definitely saddened by the fact that when the Bharatiya Janata Party was in power, these democratic traditions were not followed. This is my complaint,' proceeding on a long diatribe against the BJP over issues of corruption, unfulfilled promises and misgovernance, while the leader of opposition, Bhairon Singh Shekhawat, sat listening. Gehlot established clearly in this first speech as the CM that his brand of politics was going to be relentless towards his rivals, but not bereft of humility.

Able Administrator and an Organization Man

Ashok Gehlot has painstakingly and artfully cultivated the very brand of politics he had first established in 1999. He has maintained a clean image and reputation for delivering good governance with a special focus on welfare schemes. Despite having spent five decades in politics and served as CM thrice, Gehlot has never been embroiled in any major controversies, which has further cemented his salt of the earth reputation. This is not to say, however, that he lacked shrewdness or political acumen, as was evident from the constant tussles he has been involved in since the beginning of his career to retain power. Yet, it is notable that the public perception of him as a leader has been largely positive.

In his first term from 1998–2003, Gehlot moulded his identity as an administrator. Unlike his softer approach during his later tenures, his first stint as CM was characterized by his favouring discipline over populism. According to Parihar, the CM introduced strict measures such as the 'No Work, No Pay' rule, which was meant to deter government employees from boycotting work or going on strikes by penalizing them with no pay. He also directed bureaucrats to pay for use of official vehicles for personal purposes. An employees' protest organized in December 1999 demanding payment of bonus and dearness allowances and involving multiple government employees' unions lasted for sixty-four days until it was finally called off in February 2000. This became a thorn in Gehlot's side, who believes it was one of the main reasons his government was voted out in the following elections.[10]

Gehlot was widely accepted within the Congress. He kept his loyalists, including Raghu Sharma, Mahesh Joshi and Rajiv Arora,* close and his contemporaries too remained supportive. In Delhi, he was backed by powerful Congress leaders, such as Ahmed Patel and Digvijay Singh. Even after the Congress was ousted in 2003, he managed to retain his stature as the most well-known leader of the Rajasthan Congress, despite the fact that senior leaders – B. D. Kalla†

---

* Raghu Sharma and Mahesh Joshi have served as MPs and ministers in the past. Rajiv Arora is a well-known businessman and Congress leader, also considered to be close to Gehlot.

† In fact, when it seemed as if Kalla might become a major power centre in his own right, with some of his loyalists portraying him as a Brahmin leader who can helm the top post, controversy derailed his ascent. As the president of the state Congress, Kalla released a book titled *Sonia Gandhi and Indian Politics*, written by Manchand Khandela, a former member of the RPCC. When it was discovered that the book was critical of both Indira Gandhi and Sonia Gandhi, even accusing the former of promoting corruption, Kalla had to face the outrage of his party. He maintained that the manuscript he was shown prior to the launch was different from the published book, but Sonia Gandhi persisted in her demands for a formal explanation from him. Kalla lost the high command's favour after this and then went on to lose two consecutive assembly elections in 2008 and 2013. He was re-elected in 2018, when Gehlot graced him with a ministerial portfolio. See also PTI, 'Congress expels writer for Sonia remarks', Rediff, 28 September 2005. Available at: https://www.rediff.com/news/report/sonia/20050928.htm.

and C. P. Joshi* – were PCC presidents after his government lost the elections.

Gehlot was then made the party's general secretary, Delhi, under the chief ministership of Sheila Dikshit. This only served to strengthen his influence even further as he began to frequent the corridors of power in Delhi, while still participating in Rajasthan's state matters in his capacity as former CM. He successfully parried a challenge from senior Jat leaders, including Paras Ram Maderna, union minister Sis Ram Ola and Sona Ram Choudhary, who had openly demanded in 2008 for the Congress to give someone from the peasant community – that is, Jats – the chance to become the new chief minister. Since the party did not win a clear majority in the 2008 elections, winning ninety-six seats – four short of the halfway mark – Gehlot was once again entrusted with the chief ministership.[11] He comfortably secured the support of legislators

---

* Kalla's successor as the PCC president, Joshi was among the most powerful challengers that Gehlot had encountered at the time. He had led the Congress to victory in the 2008 assembly elections and been a frontrunner for the post of CM. His fate had been sealed by a single vote, due to which he had lost the election even as his party won. The Rajasthan High Court later declared the election void, rubbing salt in his wounds, and eventually, the Supreme Court ruled the contest a tie. This made no significant difference, however, as Joshi's ambitions had been dealt a fatal blow. While he maintains that he does not regret being denied the opportunity and is content knowing that he was able to see the job entrusted to him through, state Congress insiders often remark at how close he had been to the chair. Source: Interview with anonymous Congress leader, 2018.

A senior Congress leader shared that Joshi had Rahul Gandhi's backing – who was gathering a group of his own loyalists within the party at the time – and was immensely powerful. Gehlot himself had hinted to his supporters in 2008 that he was unsure if he would become CM ever again, considering how rapidly Joshi had been rising through the ranks. A former union railway minister, Joshi was appointed the speaker of the Rajasthan assembly in 2018 after Gehlot became the CM for the third time. Source: 'C.P. Joshi new Rajasthan Speaker', *The Hindu*, 16 January 2019. Available at: https://www.thehindu.com/news/national/other-states/cp-joshi-new-rajasthan-speaker/article26007144.ece.

from the BSP and independents to ensure that the Congress had the numbers it needed to form the government – a testament to his political prowess.

Due to his ability to consistently deliver the results expected of him, Gehlot remained ahead of his peers in both the chief ministerial race as well as other organizational matters when he was not in office. The best example of this was during the 2017 Gujarat assembly elections, when the Congress performed better than it had in the previous years and increased its tally from sixty-one to seventy-seven seats under the leadership of Gehlot, who had been appointed the general secretary in-charge of Gujarat. While it had been unable to form the government, its improved performance in the home state of PM Narendra Modi boosted the morale of the party.[12]

After this feat, the party decided to entrust Gehlot with even more power as the general secretary in-charge of organization and training of the AICC, a post he held until he became CM of Rajasthan for a third time. While he was not the loudest voice, nor the most charismatic or caste-backed leader by conventional standards, Gehlot was a steady, reliable and low-profile leader whose quiet organization, accessibility and sheer persistence, along with an aversion to courting controversy, made him stand out.

The Gehlot Brand: Welfare Schemes and Realpolitik

CM Ashok Gehlot's brand of politics had been clearly established by the time his second tenure began: good governance and Gandhian values. He launched the Chief Minister Free Medicine Scheme in 2019, which provided essential medicines to all in- and out-patients in government hospitals and health centres across the state.[13] He further bolstered this scheme during his third term as CM, introducing the idea of universal health insurance, which also won the appreciation of public health experts across the board.

Gehlot maintained a cordial relationship with civil society organizations (CSOs) throughout his career, obliging representatives with appointments, holding meetings on policy matters and inviting activists from across the country to participate in various state government conferences. His government passed two bills against mob lynching and honour killing,[14] as a nod to the efforts of CSOs, although the bills could not get the necessary presidential approval to be written into law.[15] Nevertheless, they strengthened public perception of Gehlot as a progressive leader with an ear to the ground.

In May 2021, Gehlot launched the Chiranjeevi Swasthya Beema Yojana, a universal health insurance scheme that offered an annual cashless insurance cover of ₹5 lakh to every family in the state. The main highlight was that while previous such initiatives were meant for below poverty line (BPL) families, this scheme offered coverage to anyone who wished to invest a nominal yearly premium, amounting to a little more than ₹800. Later, the insurance amount was increased from ₹5 lakh to ₹10 lakh and by the time the 2023 Rajasthan assembly elections arrived, Gehlot had increased the annual health insurance limit of the Chiranjeevi scheme to a whooping ₹25 lakh.[16]

Other welfare measures implemented by Gehlot include the Jan Soochna Portal, a platform that improved transparency by providing information about schemes, beneficiaries and workings of the government on the lines of the Right to Information (RTI) Act,[17] increasing the number of working days in the Mahatma Gandhi National Rural Employment Guarantee Scheme (MGNREGS) from 100 to 125[18] and introducing a bill for the welfare of gig workers.[19] The fact that Gehlot spoke about the plight of gig workers signed up with various service delivery platforms and decided to pass a legislation to protect their interests set him apart. When his administration became the first state government to pass the Right to Health Bill in 2023, despite pushback from the medical community,[20] it further bolstered his image as an empathetic leader.

Gehlot earned the monicker 'Marwar ka Gandhi' for his championing of Gandhian values and routine invocation of the Mahatma in his speeches. His government regularly organized seminars and conferences on Gandhi's teaching and in his third term, he even built Gandhi Vatika, a museum in Jaipur dedicated to Gandhi's philosophy. As one of the most experienced politicians in the country, Gehlot mastered the art of juggling his various hats without letting it tarnish his overall image as a conscientious leader. Even as he remained the picture of philanthropy on most days in the state's political arena, he was also unafraid of ruffling feathers for either ethical reasons or political rivalries. The following examples illustrate these two qualities.

On the heel of the pub attacks in Mangalore, Karnataka, wherein a group of young men and women were assaulted and humiliated by a Hindu right-wing group at a bar, CM Gehlot came under fire for making a careless statement unbecoming of his stature. He said that he did not like boys and girls holding hands in malls or sitting in bars, exposing a narrow-mindedness that had not been associated with him until then. He tried to retract his comment and plead ignorance of the incident later in the day – correctly gauging that his words were incongruent with his image as a progressive and pro-democracy politician – while reaffirming his support for personal freedom and requesting that his remarks not be linked to the Mangalore attacks.[21] This instance showed that Gehlot did not just understand his brand, but the responsibility, upkeep and care required to maintain it and retain his partymen's favour. Perhaps it was this awareness that prompted him to drop Mahipal Maderna from his cabinet when he was alleged to be connected to the Bhanwari Devi conspiracy, even as it invited the ire of the Jat community, worsening his relationship with them.[22]

While Gehlot has an impeccable record when it comes to leaving behind his opponents through his shrewd political manoeuvring, his Achilles heel has persisted despite his best efforts. The three-time chief minister of Rajasthan may be swift to grab the top post whenever his party comes to power, but he has never been able to retain this power at the end of the term. After his first term ended in 2003, Gehlot's government was ousted by the BJP, then led by the enigmatic Vasundhara Raje. The Congress's tally was reduced from 150 seats to just fifty-six. After his second term ended in 2013, the defeat was even more dramatic as the Congress won only twenty-one seats compared to the BJP's 163 – its highest tally so far in the history of the state. A decade later, in 2023, despite leaving no stone unturned to see his government re-elected, announcing a flurry of welfare schemes and a prolonged publicity campaign, Gehlot was once again ousted from power after the Congress lost the assembly elections.

A major reason for this has to do with the lack of a caste support base of his own. As a result, with every anti-incumbency wave and the opposition's constant efforts to regain public loyalties, Gehlot loses his grip around the armrest of the CM's chair. An example of this was seen as early as 1999. Between the 1960s and '80s, the presence of larger-than-life Jat leaders in the Congress and the Jat–Rajput rivalry won the party the majority of the Jat vote – a major factor for its ability to remain in power from 1952 to 1990 almost consecutively, barring the three years immediately after the Emergency. But when Atal Bihari Vajpayee announced in a rally in Sikar on 30 August 1999 that his government will provide reservation to the Jats of Rajasthan,[23] the community shifted its loyalties to the BJP. Four years later, when BJP's chief ministerial candidate Vasundhara Raje portrayed herself as a daughter-in-law of Jats before the 2003 assembly elections, there was no reason for the community to stick with Gehlot – a large section blamed him for sidelining Maderna. Gehlot's three tenures as CM did see some prominent Jat leaders – such as Govind Singh Dotasra, Harish Chaudhary and Dr Chandrabhan Singh – hold important posts, including that of the PCC president, but they were unable to match the stature and influence of their more powerful predecessors such as the Mirdhas and Madernas.

In 2013 as well, the Gehlot government's loss was owed to a resurgent BJP, which had declared Gujarat CM Narendra Modi as its prime ministerial candidate. The image of the UPA government at the centre riddled with allegations of graft and cornered by the India Against Corruption movement led by Anna Hazare further sealed the fate of the Congress in Rajasthan. In later years, between 2018 and 2023, Sachin Pilot and his supporters constantly brought up Gehlot's inability to retain power, and placed the blame for the Congress's meagre twenty-one-seat tally in 2013 at the senior leader's door. As Congress MLA P. R. Meena said in 2019,

> Ashok Gehlot ji doesn't have influence now … There's no public backing, Jats, Meenas and Gurjars are angry … who will vote? … It should be seen why he is being made the CM. The party should also see that such a person is made the CM who can fetch votes and the public can expect something from him. If he has already failed before, then what's the use of making him the CM again?[24]

The Leader Who Cannot Be Written Off

'*Mujhe ab kuch hone wala nahin hai. Ab pandrah saal se bees saal mujhe kuch nahin hone wala. Ab dukhi hona ho to ho dukhi, mere bas ki baat nahin hai. Mujhe kuch nahin hoga.* (Nothing can stop me now. For the next fifteen to twenty years, nothing is going to affect me. If that upsets you, let it; there's not much I can do about that. I'm not going anywhere).'[25]

Gehlot's voice echoed across the gathering at a government function in October 2021 as he sent a message to his rivals, particularly Sachin Pilot, that he intended to tower over the Rajasthan Congress for at least a decade or two more, after his angioplasty procedure. The next assembly elections were to be held in 2023, still two years away. At the same event, Gehlot not only declared he was going to lead his party to victory a second time – a feat he had not been able to achieve thus far – but also that he will become CM and he had people in mind for the various portfolios in his future government. He announced his intention to allocate the important ministerial portfolio of Urban Development and Housing (UDH) to incumbent UDH minister and his close aide, Shanti Dhariwal. He then went on to reiterate these convictions several times over the following months. 'When we had formed the government in 1998, we won 156 seats. I was the president of the Pradesh Congress Committee back then. I would want to go forward with Mission 156.* We are working towards it. The opposition hasn't been able to raise issues in four years,' he repeated in early 2023, months before the next elections.

However, it is worth considering what made Gehlot feel so certain of his re-election between 2021–23. His third stint of chief ministership stood out from his previous two terms because of one crucial fact: the constant power tussle between him and Pilot since the government was formed. The chance to become CM had nearly slipped out of Gehlot's hands after the Congress high command expressed its desire for him to contest the elections for the national president in October 2022 and for Pilot to replace him in the state. In a shocking turn of events, more than eighty party MLAs chose to stand with him, rebelling against Pilot's appointment to the top post and defying the high command. A seasoned politician, Gehlot knew that this was going to definitively alter his equation with the

* In the run-up to the 2023 elections, then CM Gehlot often referred to the Congress's victory in the 1998 elections and talked about repeating the feat. 'Mission 156' was the target he set for his party before the 2023 assembly elections, a clear sign of his confidence.

Gandhi family. Although he distanced himself from the MLAs' acts of rebellion – including submitting their resignations and rejecting Pilot as their candidate for chief minister – the fact that they were openly loyal to him did not help his case. Eventually, Gehlot pulled out of the Congress presidential race and apologized to Sonia Gandhi, but the fact that the Rajasthan unit of the Congress had defied the high command had fogged up his prospects in the party.[26] He was also aware that age was not on his side.

The rebellion of the Gehlot camp had invited the disapproval of party leaders such as Ajay Maken, the former in-charge of the Rajasthan Congress, who termed it 'indiscipline'.[27] The party leaders also issued show cause notices to three of Gehlot's most trusted loyalists – Shanti Dhariwal, Mahesh Joshi and Dharmendra Rathore – while several Congress leaders such as MLA Preeti Shaktawat, whose late husband was a follower of Pilot, said that they were kept in the dark about the parallel meeting at Dhariwal's house. Joshi was subsequently denied a ticket in the 2023 assembly elections. The strict action served as an effective deterrent for the rebels, who knew that it was unlikely they would be able to stall Pilot's crowning a second time. However, Gehlot had succeeded in his larger objective as he continued to be the chief minister who would lead the Congress into the elections.

Gehlot tried every trick in the book to ensure he remained in office after the elections. Wary of facing the anger of government employees as he had during his first term, as mentioned earlier in the chapter, he also announced the decision to revert to the old pension scheme to gain their support. In just the span of one year, he held meetings, launched new schemes and toured across the state.[28] He also hoped that the division of camps within the BJP – due to multiple leaders nursing chief ministerial ambitions – would somehow improve the Congress's – and his own – prospects for a fourth time.[29]

However, the results of the 2023 assembly turned out to be

humbling – the Congress had managed to perform better than in 2003 and 2013 but was restricted to seventy seats, which meant that Gehlot would not be able to break the hex and retain power for another five years. As before, he took the loss in his stride and his campaign efforts and welfare schemes were hailed as the primary factor behind Congress's improved performance in the 2023 elections. The septuagenarian leader enthusiastically set about taking on the Bhajan Lal Sharma-led BJP government in the state, touring across its expanse and meeting supporters, showing no intention of retire. In a video from 2025 widely circulated on social media, Gehlot was seen smiling as a supporter urged him, 'Next time when you become CM, please change the car.' He was alluding to the fact that Gehlot has been spotted in the same vehicle for fifteen years.[30] The casual reference to the 'next time' he became CM is a reiteration of the fact that as far as the public is concerned, Gehlot is very much still likely to return to power.

By the time the 2028 assembly elections arrive, Gehlot would have turned seventy-seven. The question remains whether he would be considered for the post of CM for the fourth time if the Congress wins. Considering there is no dearth of instances where the grand old party has selected septuagenarians to hold chief ministerial and even prime ministerial offices, Gehlot has a fair chance at bagging the post again. It is equally likely that in case his own candidature is vetoed, Gehlot might decide to put his weight behind a candidate of his choosing so the brand may continue and evolve.

Whatever the case may be, one thing is evident: the larger-than-life influence of Gehlot in the Rajasthan Congress is not likely to be upstaged anytime in the foreseeable future.

8

THE GAME CHANGER

Vasundhara Raje's Raj

TWO STONE ELEPHANT SCULPTURES FLANK THE GATES OF THE ANCIENT temple of Lord Charbhuja Nath – an avatar of Lord Krishna – which is one of the foremost pilgrimage destinations in Rajasthan. One can see the red turbans of its Gurjar priests in the distance approaching the temple through the serpentine roads of Garbhor, a village in the mountainous district of Rajsamand. In August 2018, however, there was also a sea of government officials and BJP workers milling through the narrow streets, making last-minute repairs and renovations, ensuring the roads were clean and pothole-free in preparation for the chief minister's visit. The Charbhuja Nath temple has been tied inextricably to Vasundhara Raje's political career – she has visited the sacred spot to seek the presiding deity's blessings before every election. This particular visit, however, had sent the local administration into a tizzy since BJP President Amit Shah was also slated to share the stage with Raje to flag off the grand launch of the Rajasthan Gaurav Yatra.

For the locals of this temple town, seeing hundreds of vehicles as part of Raje's cavalcade halt at Charbhuja with supporters in tow was hardly unusual. Local shopkeeper Nand Kishore Sharma recalled the scenes from 2003 and 2013, when L. K. Advani and Rajnath Singh, respectively, had come to flag off yatras in a similar fashion. He glanced at the hundreds of BJP flags strewn all over the village, right up to the temple, and said fondly, 'Madam considers this place to be lucky for her'.* Raje had good reason for this – after all, fifteen years ago, she did emerge victorious in the elections, beating all odds. The story of her ascent to the top post is replete with many first-time feats – from becoming the first woman CM of Rajasthan to ruthlessly quelling opposition within her party.

In less than five months, Rajasthan was headed for the 2018 assembly elections and Vasundhara Raje hoped that the deity would bless her for a third time. After all, a lot had changed since 2003.

Early Days and Raje's First Yatras

Raje's tryst with the Charbhuja temple began in 2003, when she took out the Parivartan Yatra with an intention to connect with the masses. Looking back, she admitted that it had proven to be the perfect avenue for gaining an understanding of the workings of Rajasthan and mobilizing the party cadre. In 2013, her Suraj Sankalp Yatra had played a major role in the ouster of the Congress government with the biggest-ever mandate seen in Rajasthan politics for her party, the BJP. This time, in August 2018, towards the end of her second term as CM, Raje decided to launch the Rajasthan Gaurav Yatra to see how the government schemes had impacted the lives of people.[1]

It must be apparent by now that Raje's yatras were, in fact, immensely popular, but her larger-than-life presence did not always dominate the political terrain of Rajasthan unchallenged. She was the union MoS for Small Scale Industries in September 2002 with no known chief ministerial ambitions, while the BJP was under the influence of its best-known face and three-time Rajasthan CM Bhairon Singh Shekhawat. Shekhawat had retired from state

* Raje had been nicknamed 'Madam' since her first term as CM.

politics to become the country's vice president in August 2002, leaving the state unit of the party with a leadership vacuum for the first time in its history. It was not that the BJP had no options, but most of Shekhawat's rivals – such as Ramdas Agarwal, Lalit Kishore Chaturvedi, Hari Shankar Bhabhra and Raghuveer Singh Kaushal – were in their seventies and lacked the public appeal or backing required to pull the party out of its funk after its disastrous 1998 defeat. The party had won only thirty-three seats at the end of Shekhawat's eight-year-long tenure.

Ramdas Agarwal of the old guard was the national treasurer of the BJP when Shekhawat was elected as the vice president and the primary driver of the anti-Shekhawat lobby within the state unit. He came with the support of the powerful merchant community, which comprised the core of BJP voters, although its leaders could hardly hope to compete with Shekhawat's popularity, as evidenced by his three-time chief ministership. Even the unrelenting support of the RSS could not compare. Some other leaders such as Hari Shankar Bhabhra managed to rise to the office of Deputy CM, but they were merely powerful in name – it was still always Shekhawat who called the shots. There was a group of younger leaders such as Gulab Chand Kataria and Ghanshyam Tiwari – the second generation of the Jan Sangh and BJP in Rajasthan – who had past ministerial experience and enviable clout in the party, as well as chief ministerial ambitions. All these contenders saw the veteran Rajput leader's appointment to the post of vice president as a fresh opportunity to jump back in the fray.

It should come as no surprise then that when the party's national president M. Venkaiah Naidu announced Vasundhara Raje as the next state party president and, by extension, its next chief ministerial candidate, it ruffled some feathers. Raje's non-involvement in state politics was a well-known fact, even though she was a union MoS at the time. She had been elected as an MP from Jhalawar, a constituency from which she has been elected to the parliament constantly since 1989. Raje belongs to the Scindia royal family of Gwalior, Madhya Pradesh and her mother Vijaya Raje Scindia was a founding member of the BJP;* a towering figure who was jailed during the Emergency. Her sister Yashodhara Raje too had a well-established political career. These crucial connections have contributed to smoothening the path of Raje's own career in politics, the high point of her journey arriving in 1998, when she was appointed the MoS for external affairs.

Once again, the agent of change had been 'Babosa' Shekhawat himself. He may have relocated to New Delhi, but his influence in the Rajasthan BJP had evidently persisted. He recommended Raje for the job of the state party president to his close friend, PM Atal Bihari Vajpayee, who agreed that there was a need for a fresh face to lead the party in the 2003 assembly elections. When it became clear that Raje was the one being backed by the BJP top brass – Shekhawat, Vajpayee, L. K. Advani and Pramod Mahajan – some of the senior leaders such as Lalit Kishore Chaturvedi and power centres such as Gulab Chand Kataria and Ghanshyam Tiwari thought it better to toe the party line and swallow their resentment. They decided to lie in wait for the opportune moment to assert themselves.

There is no denying that Raje's entry into Rajasthan politics has been the biggest game changer for the state. In a society marked by gender disparity and feudal traditions, a woman has rarely ever been allowed to wield authority as Raje has managed to do. She admitted to feeling daunted at first as she had not been involved in the state's politics at all until her appointment as the state party president,[2] although she had been active in national politics, having served as a five-time MP and union minister. She had contested and

---

* The Scindias were among those royal families of princely states that laid the foundations of anti-Congress politics in the country when democracy curtailed their influence, as elaborated in Chapter 1.

won an assembly election from Dholpur in 1985,* but thereafter focused solely on national politics. She made her second attempt to enter the state's politics in the 1993 assembly elections from Dholpur, but was defeated by Congress leader Banwari Lal from the same constituency.

On the occasion of Raje accepting the charge of BJP state president in late 2002, it was visible that new life had been infused into the party workers, who had been demoralized by the stinging 1998 electoral defeat. As her cavalcade entered Jaipur, it was greeted by several leaders of the Rajasthan BJP and thousands of party workers shouting slogans in her support. In the next few months, Raje was everywhere – attending public events and candidly speaking with the media, not shying away from answering tough questions or accepting the areas of improvement for her party. She had also devised plans for mass outreach so she could meet and interact directly with the public, which culminated in the state's first political yatras.

In April 2003, Advani flagged off Raje's first yatra, the aforementioned Parivartan Yatra from Charbhuja Nath temple, eight months before the assembly elections. The yatra and Raje's campaign against the Congress were closely managed by the dynamic leader Pramod Mahajan. In that pre-social media era, the BJP had to rely on the Bharat Sanchar Nigam Limited (BSNL) telecom networks to propagate its campaign messages recorded in Raje's voice. Advertisements ridiculing Gehlot's government sprung up everywhere in the state. On the eve of the elections, full-page advertisements saying 'Alvida Gehlot (Goodbye Gehlot)' were carried in regional newspapers.[3] While Mahajan worked behind the scenes to ensure the success of this ingenious campaign, Raje did a commendable job of being the face of the party.

---

* She married Maharaj Rana Hemant Singh of the erstwhile royal family of Dholpur in 1972. The couple separated but her ties to Dholpur persist to this day.

According to Suman Sharma,* Raje's rise to power was remarkable because of how disruptive it was to prevailing preconceptions and beliefs. Her own party workers had inhibitions about how a royal would ever manage to engage with and appeal to the rural public of Rajasthan. However, contrary to their expectations, Raje 'Rajasthan *ke rang mein dhal gayi* (she embraced the colours of Rajasthan)'. In a luxury rath designed specifically for her yatra, over a period of more than 100 days, she ventured into the remotest villages in the state, holding public rallies, smilingly embracing rural women and asking them to vote for 'parivartan' or change. Recalling scenes from the yatra, Sharma shared how Raje had once stopped her car near a field to pluck mooli (radish) from a field and then savoured it with the villagers, sitting on a charpoy.[4]

The sight of a powerful woman leader especially appealed to the women voters, who had never before been viewed as a homogenous voting bloc in the traditionally patriarchal desert state. Raje's promises of efficient governance and her approachability, paired with her painstaking efforts to appear in the traditional attire of the region she was visiting, only endeared her to them further. She dressed in the manner of Sahariya women in the Hadoti region or Bhil women in other tribal regions and in traditional Rajputi *poshak* in Chittorgarh; she was met with great enthusiasm by the local women.

She leveraged her unique position as a royal and thus an ally of the Rajputs by default, the daughter-in-law of Jat royalty† and the mother-in-law to her son's Gurjar wife to win the favour of all three communities. However, she maintained her secular stance

---

* Sharma has been a BJP worker for decades. She has also served as the president of the party's Mahila Morcha in the state and the chairperson of the Rajasthan State Women's Commission.

† The Jats, resentful of the Congress not appointing a CM from their community despite constituting their biggest voting base and bringing the party into power in 1998, were amenable to settling for the next best option – Jaton ki bahu Raje.

and steered clear of any saffron agenda, especially when making public statements or appearances. When the Gehlot-led Congress government arrested VHP leader Pravin Togadia in April 2003[5] after the latter defied a ban on distributing tridents as part of the VHP's 'trishul deeksha' programme* in Rajasthan, Raje chose to avoid commenting on the instance.[6] This became a bone of contention between the leader and the RSS and pitted her against fellow party leaders who drew their strength from the Sangh Parivar, as detailed later in this chapter.

Raje's BJP chose to address local issues while in opposition, conducting surveys to corner the Gehlot government over a long drought, atrocities against women and the rising prices of electricity. The BJP eventually propped Raje up as its chief ministerial candidate in the 2003 elections and all her efforts bore fruit at the December 2003 polls. She clinched a resounding win, stunning both the Congress and the BJP old guard, who regarded Raje as a novice. The BJP had won 120 seats, while the Congress was left with just fifty-six MLAs in the 200-member house.

Madam had arrived.

First Term and Initial Political Challenges

In early 2004, a few months after becoming CM, Raje began to understand the sheer magnitude of the responsibility entrusted to her. The state had more than thirty districts and her role thus far had been restricted merely to her own parliamentary constituency

---

* In 2003, the VHP launched a controversial programme to distribute tridents to the youth. By 2024, the programme was revived with the outfit talking about distributing tridents, training and deploying youths across Rajasthan to convey to the people the 'dangers of love jihad and conversions'. See also 'The rise of hate through Trishul Deeksha events: A dangerous trend in India', Citizens for Justice and Peace, 27 December 2024. Available at: https://cjp.org.in/the-rise-of-hate-through-trishul-deeksha-events-a-dangerous-trend-in-india/.

of Jhalawar. Two years into her first term, however, it was evident that she had found her footing. Her government passed the Rajasthan Sports (Registration, Recognition and Regulation of Associations) Act in 2005, a provision of which stated that no individual member would have the right to cast a vote to elect the executive body of a district-level or state-level sports association.[7] This had been preceded by an ordinance brought a year ago by the state government, which was now being formalized into law. While it had no apparent implications for administrative matters, the passing of the Act significantly improved the prospects of a close family friend of Raje's, Lalit Kumar Modi.

This was long before Modi became the cricket czar who transformed the sport's landscape in India forever with the establishment of the Indian Premier League (IPL). If not for the Raje government's swift action in passing the 2005 Act, Modi would not have been able to strengthen his influence in the Board of Control for Cricket in India (BCCI) or head the Rajasthan Cricket Association (RCA) as its president – his seat of power for several years. Only once the new law divested the individual members of the RCA of their voting rights did Modi finally gain the numbers required to challenge the monopoly of the powerful Rungta family, who had ruled over RCA for decades.* By 2005, Modi had become the new president of the RCA and a separate power centre outside of Raje's council of ministers. While their association would become a contentious issue for the CM a decade later – when Modi would become embroiled in controversy† – he enjoyed considerable

* A well-known family of Marwari businessmen, the Rungtas had the last word over every matter related to the RCA, which they had governed like their personal fiefdom since 1972. It was unthinkable that their power could be challenged until the colourful maverick Lalit Modi burst onto the scene with help from the newly crowned CM Raje.

† In 2015, the Congress had accused Raje of signing a document backing Lalit Modi's immigration application to the UK. Modi, who had left the country, allegedly having

say in the state's matters, much to the frustration of other leaders in the administration. It is not an exaggeration to say that Modi would not have been able to create the Indian Premier League (IPL) if he had not established a firm foothold in the RCA, and subsequently BCCI.

Some other major initiatives of Raje's government include investing ₹7,000 crores towards the improvement of the roads network in the state and laying greater emphasis on public–private partnership (PPP) in various sectors. As a result of this, organizations such as Genpact were able to open offices and call centres in Rajasthan, establishing it as a hub for Business Process Outsourcing (BPO). The entry of private players in the state has been a constant phenomenon ever since, with subsequent legislations further facilitating private investment, for instance, the Rajasthan Private Universities Act, 2005, which opened up avenues in the education sector.

Raje was widely known to be a tough taskmaster and commanded great respect for her determination to get things done. She was referred to simply as 'Madam' by her supporters and bureaucrats alike, who understood well that 'she wanted results'[8] and would not tolerate any delays or pendencies within the machinery. Despite all her popularity, however, Raje struggled to endear herself to fellow party leaders who nursed their own chief ministerial ambitions – she had to be strategic in the distribution of ministerial portfolios. It did not help that the new president of the state BJP, Lalit Kishore Chaturvedi, did not see eye to eye

---

Raje's backing, and was being investigated by agencies such as the Enforcement Directorate (ED) became a key issue for the opposition to corner the BJP and Raje, even demanding her resignation. However, Raje remained in power. Source: PTI, 'Opp guns for Raje after fresh document shows she backed Lalit Modi's plea', *Deccan Herald*, 24 June 2015. Available at: https://www.deccanherald.com/india/opp-guns-raje-fresh-document-2136053.

with Raje. He was openly critical of Raje's new excise policy* and wanted greater say in administrative matters. Chaturvedi's successors, Mahesh Chandra Sharma and Om Prakash Mathur, were also close to the RSS and shared a tumultuous relationship with Raje, who naturally wanted the party president to support her. Sharma was a staunch saffron ideologue and remained unmoved by Raje's overtures to make peace with him on her visits to the RSS office.

To the CM's credit, she made considerable attempts to appease the RSS. After some initial hesitation, her administration lifted the ban imposed by the previous Congress government on the trishul diksha programmes of the VHP in July 2004, seven months after forming the government. They also passed an anti-conversion law in the assembly.† Yet, the discontent among the RSS-loyalist leaders showed no signs of abating. The increased interference of Lalit Modi in governance matters further alienated Raje from these leaders.

---

* Introduced in 2005, Raje's excise policy proposed an increase in liquor shops from 7,000 to 11,000. While the government had claimed this would result in an increase in state revenue, Chaturvedi had disagreed, arguing that the move will allow more non-locals to enter the liquor business in the state, thus benefiting outsiders more. Source: Rohit Parihar, 'VHP names Vasundhara Raje as potential BJP chief, surprises Rajasthan CM', *India Today*, 2 May 2005. Available at: https://www.indiatoday.in/magazine/states/story/20050502-vhp-names-vasundhara-raje-as-potential-bjp-chief-surprises-rajasthan-cm-787791-2005-05-01.

† In her first tenure, the Raje government had brought the Rajasthan Freedom of Religion Bill, 2006, which was passed in the state assembly but could not get the assent of then president Pratibha Patil, following opposition by human rights organizations and minority groups, who alleged that the bill was aimed at appeasing Hindu groups. The bill was meant to check forcible or fraudulent religious conversions. Later, in 2008, an amended version of the bill was introduced as well, but was not passed into law by the centre. See also 'The Rajasthan Prohibition of Unlawful Conversion of Religion Bill, 2025', PRS Legislative Research. Available at: https://prsindia.org/bills/states/the-rajasthan-prohibition-of-unlawful-conversion-of-religion-bill-2025#:~:text=The%20Rajasthan%20Legislative%20assembly%20had,in%20case%20of%20repeated%20contravention.

Apart from the infighting, the Gurjar agitation of 2007–08 struck a serious blow to the party's fortunes and lost them a loyal voter base in the Gurjar community. To make matters worse, the biggest Meena leader in the state, Food and Civil Supplies Minister Kirodi Lal Meena parted ways with Raje's government after its response to the agitation. The Gurjars were demanding reservation under the ST category and in protest, had disrupted road and train traffic, especially in eastern Rajasthan districts such as Dausa and Bharatpur. More than seventy protesters were killed in police firing during this time. A few days later, the Meena community began counter-agitations, sensing the possibility that their share of reserved seats would be reduced if the demands of the Gurjar community were accepted by the Raje government.[9] By mid-2007, Gurjar–Meena clashes were rocking eastern Rajasthan, resulting in several casualties.[10] In a show of solidarity, sitting minister Kirodi Lal Meena chose to side with his caste over his party and resigned from the state assembly.

Although the government managed to reach a shaky truce with the agitating Gurjars by the time the elections arrived, the BJP's fortunes had already dwindled and the divided house was ousted from power in 2008. Its 120-seat tally from 2003 was reduced to seventy-eight, while the Congress emerged as the single largest party with ninety-six seats and formed the government with the support of independents and the BSP. The window awaited by the anti-Raje camp had arrived and they promptly sprang into action.

The Years Out of Power: 2008–13

Between December 2008 and 2013, the five years when Raje was out of power after serving her first term as the Rajasthan chief minister from 2003 to 2008, the voices of dissent within the party picked up a clamour, getting strength from her election defeat to the Congress. These loyal lieutenants of the RSS felt that in Raje's ascent, the party chose a person who had not been active in the state's politics over many of them who helped the Jan Sangh and the BJP gain a foothold in Rajasthan.

One of the first persons to target Raje was the very man who had helped her become the BJP's chief ministerial face in 2003. After his stint as vice president, Bhairon Singh Shekhawat, now in his late eighties, was miffed to see Raje function independently and pay little heed to his suggestions. Her treatment of his son-in-law Narpat Singh Rajvi, who was initially made a cabinet minister but was gradually sidelined in party matters, left Shekhawat fuming. Raje made some attempts to reach out to Shekhawat, including meeting him and later appointing IAS officer Sunil Arora as her secretary. Arora had been a secretary in the Shekhawat administration as well. But the inner circle of the Raje camp now consisted of leaders such as Rajendra Rathore and Yunus Khan, which left leaders such as Rajvi, who was a general secretary of the BJP during his father-in-law's tenure as chief minister, devoid of power.

In January 2009, a month after Raje was ousted from power, Shekhawat told the media that he had written a letter to newly crowned chief minister Ashok Gehlot, asking him to immediately constitute a committee to investigate the allegations of corruption to the tune of ₹22,000 crore against Raje. Raje also had to face the anger of another founding member of the BJP, former foreign minister Jaswant Singh, who, after being ignored in state affairs despite supporting Raje initially, now closed ranks with Shekhawat.

One of the seniormost leaders of the BJP, Jaswant Singh, was furious when the court ordered the registration of an FIR against him and several other Raje detractors who had met at his residence in 2007 for a function. Singh took it as a personal insult that he had been accused of serving opium-mixed drinks to his guests on the occasion – a long-established tradition of Rajputs – in the FIR.

In the same year, Jaswant Singh's family filed a police complaint against a local man for a poster where Raje had been portrayed as goddess Annapurna. Other senior BJP leaders, such as Harishankar Bhabhra, held Raje responsible for the 2008 election loss, alleging that projecting her as the only chief ministerial face had cost the party dearly. Five months later, the BJP would be further embarrassed by its performance in the 2009 Lok Sabha elections, when it could win only four of the twenty-one parliamentary seats from the state. One of these four seats where the BJP could win was the Jhalawar-Baran Lok Sabha constituency, represented by Raje's son, Dushyant Singh, since 2004. When state BJP president Om Mathur tendered his resignation in June 2009, the leader was terse in his suggestion that 'other leaders' should also show courage and accept responsibility for the party's poor performance. There was little doubt about the identity of this other leader.

However, despite being ousted from power, Raje refused to bow down to the party's diktat of resigning from the post of the leader of opposition in the assembly and held onto it for months. She finally resigned in October 2009, although this was no indication that the 'maharani' – as many of her detractors in the party called her as a sarcastic reference to her erstwhile royal roots – was about to back down. In an audacious display of strength, days after resigning, Raje returned to Jaipur to be greeted by thousands of party workers, addressing them and pledging her intention to serve the state for the rest of her life. Her loyalists were vocal in their support, not even sparing the BJP central leadership. Rohitash Sharma, who was a BJP MLA at the time, had claimed that the 'so-called' high command had sunk its own fortunes by forcing Raje to resign as leader of opposition. He reiterated his and other party workers' intent to erase the party at the state level, where it owed its strength to their efforts.

It is worth examining how Raje managed to become the BJP's official candidate once again in the 2013 assembly elections despite having senior party leaders among her detractors. The sheer command she exercised over the party's legislators was made visible in August 2009, when around sixty of the seventy-eight BJP MLAs in the assembly presented themselves in Delhi before the national party president Rajnath Singh in a barely disguised show of strength.

The party appointed Arun Chaturvedi – a leader with strong ties to the RSS but relatively lower stature than that of his predecessor Om Mathur – as the state president. Raje stayed abroad for long stretches even as her MLAs lobbied firmly for her between 2008 and 2013. The ruling Congress often targeted her party over her absence. In a rare instance, she even lost her temper in the assembly in July 2009, when Congress MLAs Raghu Sharma and Ashok Bairwa took a jibe at the BJP over this, claiming that during Raje's term between 2003–08, it was well known that there will be 'no CM after 8 p.m.' The party targeted Raje, alleging that while she was the chief minister, she became inaccessible to the public after 8 p.m. Congress MLA Bairwa brought this up in the assembly, causing a seething Raje to rush to the well of the House to register her protest. The former chief minister expressed her shock, terming the language of the Congress legislators as 'disgusting', and demanded an apology.

Journalists who had reported this episode for various media outlets say that the fact of its coverage led to Raje developing a deep distrust of scribes, which became even more evident during her second term. *Rajasthan Patrika*, one of the largest and most widely read newspapers in the state, actually moved the Supreme Court in 2016, claiming that public advertisements to the daily had been cut severely during Raje's second tenure.[11] It also became rather common for news reporters and editors to get calls from her press attaché, Mahendra Bhardwaj – and on rare occasions, from Raje herself – complaining about reports that 'portrayed the government in a negative light'.[12] During her first tenure, Raje was extremely amicable towards journalists and would always be ready to answer any questions. She would even talk about subjects other than politics, on occasion. However, after she was voted out of power in 2008 – and more specifically, following the 8 p.m. episode – her guard went up for good.

Despite spending a substantial amount of time abroad between 2008–13, Raje had managed to keep an iron grip on party matters through her loyalist MLAs. In 2012, when her former home minister Gulab Chand Kataria decided to embark on a Jan Jagran Yatra to highlight the failures of the Congress government, Raje and her supporters put their foot down until the programme stood cancelled. Kataria's yatra – since he was a strongman from Mewar with chief ministerial ambitions and experience of serving as a minister under both Shekhawat and Raje – was seen as the senior leader's attempt to present himself as the face of the BJP before the 2013 assembly elections. By putting a stop to it, Raje had once again established her authority. The BJP was cautious not to repeat its mistakes, even with Raje being presented as its chief ministerial candidate for a second time. In its election manifesto, the party announced that it would provide 5 per cent reservation to the Gurjar community, hoping to win back its support after the 2007–08 agitation.

Raje was back at Charbhuja's doors to launch her Suraj Sankalp Yatra in 2013, ten years since she had first embarked on the Parivartan Yatra in 2003 and become CM. She was rewarded and enabled to lead the BJP to victory with a record tally of 163 seats. Despite an ongoing internal tussle with the national party president Rajnath Singh and multiple detractors who were ever eager to replace her, Raje seemed invincible. This election was crucial for the party also because it set the stage for the 2014 Lok Sabha elections, wherein Gujarat CM Narendra Modi was presented as the saffron party's prime ministerial candidate for the first time in a historic moment that was going to shift the course of national politics.

While Raje and Modi may have been compatriots, being

chief ministers of neighbouring states, there had been no record whatsoever of the two having shared a close bond. However, given the fact that the 2013 polls were but an interlude before the climactic Lok Sabha elections the following year, Modi toured alongside Raje extensively across the state to support her campaign for a second term. A few months later, after the BJP's landslide victory, Raje returned the favour and exerted all her might to ensure that all twenty-five Lok Sabha seats from Rajasthan went to her party, contributing to Modi's victory as the prime minister.

Raje 2.0 (2013–2018)

On a sunny afternoon in early 2018, the most sought-after destination in Jaipur's Civil Lines was abuzz. It was the annual lunch thrown for journalists by Chief Minister Vasundhara Raje at her residence. Not known to be one who addressed many press conferences, apart from her speeches at government events, Raje's interviews were mostly restricted to those during the anniversaries of her government. Even in these rare instances, journalists were told to ask only a fixed set of questions which were handed over to them by the CM's media attaché.

But on this day, Raje was playing the host to absolute perfection, moving across the sprawling lawn, courteously enquiring after the well-being of scribes and photojournalists, some of whom had been covering Rajasthan for decades. The chief minister spoke jovially, nodding at the ones who greeted her with folded hands. The arrangements for the lunch were perfect, uniformed waiters passed water bottles to the guests. But the mediapersons were not ready to witness a rare outburst from the chief minister.

Shortly after the pleasantries, as the journalists were sitting around Raje at one of the lunch tables, the chief minister had sharply expressed her displeasure with some of the reporters, particularly those from the print media, over what she thought was 'malicious' reporting of lynchings and incidents of hate crimes in Rajasthan. For a moment, there was pin drop silence at the table, where a hearty, informal chat had suddenly turned into a rather uncomfortable situation. Raje glowered at the reporters, who tried to politely reason with her by pointing out that they had only reported facts about the deaths of Pehlu Khan and Umar Mohammed in Alwar district along with that of Zafar Khan in Pratapgarh.*

By the time this conversation took place, Raje was at the end of her second term as chief minister. Not known to publicly lose her temper like this, the sudden outburst had stunned those present. The awkwardness was finally allayed by the arrival of a local media baron, heaping praises on Madam.

A few months before the get-together, Raje's government had completed four years in power after she led the party in the 2013 assembly elections to a victory the scale of which was unheard of in the state – 163 seats in the 200-member Rajasthan assembly. Nobody had achieved the feat of getting more than 160 seats until then. Not Shekhawat, the BJP's only other chief minister in Rajasthan; not even Congress when the party was an election-winning machine in the country from the 1960s to '80s.

In the Raje government's second tenure, Rajasthan also witnessed an increased tilt towards saffronization at the administration level. It became the first government in the country to have a separate ministry for the welfare of cows; school textbooks were revised to rewrite the outcome of the battle of Haldighati[13] while omitting references to key historical figures, such as India's first prime minister and Congress leader Jawaharlal Nehru, while giving greater exposure to Hindutva ideologues.[14] Some of these moves

* While Pehlu and Umar had lost their lives in Alwar while transporting cattle, Zafar Khan, a member of the CPI (ML), had died after an alleged scuffle between him and members of the local municipal council over the latter's drive to spread awareness about Swachh Bharat Abhiyan.

served to appease the RSS. Raje continued sidelining her rivals after coming to power. Among these were senior BJP leader Jaswant Singh, who was denied a ticket to contest the 2014 Lok Sabha elections from Barmer, and replaced with senior Congress leader Colonel Sonaram Choudhary, who was especially brought into the BJP fold and then fielded from Singh's seat. Singh contested the elections as an independent and lost, despite getting more votes than the Congress candidate and coming second in the electoral contest.

Manvendra Singh, former MP and son of Jaswant Singh says that the friction with Raje did not happen overnight.[15] Manvendra was a BJP MLA between 2013 and 2018, who left the party, joined the Congress and unsuccessfully contested against Raje in 2018 from her constituency of Jhalrapatan to make a statement for the sidelining of his father – an endeavour in which Rajput community leaders supported him. He returned to BJP only after the end of the Raje era in the party.

As 2018 arrived, more issues reared their heads as Ashok Parnami – a close aide of Raje's who had been made state party president after the 2013 assembly election win – was left with no choice but to resign following the bypoll losses in Ajmer, Alwar and Mandalgarh. This led to a stand-off between Raje and the national BJP president Amit Shah, over the appointment of the new state in-charge. Gajendra Singh Shekhawat had seen a meteoric rise in his political career ever since he defeated Chandresh Kumari Katoch, the daughter of erstwhile king of Jodhpur, in the 2014 Lok Sabha elections and was an important pillar of the Amit Shah camp.

A first-time MP, Shekhawat was soon made MoS and the Rajasthan assembly elections being right around the corner presented an opportune moment to project him as the new face of the party. A Rajput, he would serve to appease his community, which had turned its back on the Raje administration after the Anandpal Singh encounter.

Raje, however, put her foot down. The impasse between her and Shah lasted for more than two months and saw Raje coming to Delhi with her loyal group of MLAs on several occasions to lobby against Shekhawat's appointment to state president. All this while, the vigilant Congress was watching and its president Sachin Pilot pointed out how for seventy-five days, the state BJP had been without a president.[16] Days turned into weeks into months, but a consensus was nowhere on the horizon. Finally, in July 2018, the BJP leadership at the centre gave its nod to the appointment of senior leader Madan Lal Saini as the Rajasthan president. Saini, a septuagenarian who had maintained a low profile throughout his career, was agreeable to both the party organization and Raje. When he first assumed charge, he was quoted as saying '*Ye kaanto ka taj hai* (This is a crown of thorns).' Saini's statement, describing thus the post of the state BJP president at a time when the assembly elections were just round the corner, reflected the party's awareness of the anti-incumbency wave and rising dissatisfaction of the masses. Nevertheless, despite the concerns about BJP's electoral fortunes in the 2018 polls, Raje, one of the last remaining leaders from the Vajpayee era of the BJP, had once again established her clout. Wary of challenging her influence again, the BJP under Shah allowed her to lead the state unit into the 2018 elections.

In early 2018, Raje also brought back Kirodi Lal Meena, who had left the party in 2008 after differences with the CM on the Gurjar reservation issue. Well known as a critic of Raje's, Meena's reinduction into the party fold was a move to secure Meena votes in eastern Rajasthan. It was a step backwards for Raje, who rarely reached out to her detractors, most often choosing to sideline them instead. 'Somewhere along the way, she knew being a woman and holding a top post will offend several people,' says BJP's Suman Sharma.[17]

In August 2018, the Rajasthan Gaurav Yatra passed through villages in the tribal belt of rural Dungarpur, where public meetings were organized to tell the residents about the work done by the government. Raje was at her charismatic best, stopping at small, lesser-known hamlets and greeting people in her trademark style. Gulab Chand Kataria, a known rival of Raje's who once hoped to take out his own yatra, was sitting in the front seat of the luxury bus that was designed as the Vijay Rath for the yatra. '*Matayein behenein dhyaan de* (Mothers, sisters, please pay attention),' Kataria spoke into a microphone, urging the public to give Raje a chance for another term. Quelling opposition within the BJP was an art that Raje had impeccably mastered over the years, as was indicated by the presence of Kataria. But her biggest feat till date is ensuring that then BJP president Amit Shah announced her name as the chief ministerial candidate in July 2018. The central leadership had gauged the mood of the public, which was angry at the Raje government over a number of issues and, despite her government's efforts to make a dent through widely publicized welfare schemes, it appeared this was not about to change.* For this reason, Shah's BJP decided against projecting a fresh face knowing they would be at a disadvantage. If Raje was the official candidate of the party, the entire responsibility of the impending electoral defeat was also hers to shoulder.

The saffron party had, just few months ago, witnessed the Raje camp successfully resist the appointment of Gajendra Singh

* One of the flagship initiatives of the second Raje government was the Bhamashah Swasthya Bima Yojana, a free health insurance scheme. To appeal to women voters, Raje had mandated that each family had to open a single bank account in the name of a woman relative to avail the benefits offered under the scheme. She followed this up with another populist scheme, opening Annapurna Rasois across the state, which were roadside canteens modelled after the Amma canteens of Tamil Nadu, providing meals for ₹5 and ₹8 to the public.

Shekhawat – the central leadership's choice – as the state party president. It was wary of the potential repercussions of not renominating Raje as the CM candidate before the 2018 elections, lest a divided front be projected to the voters so close to the polls. Any further tussles were bound to damage the public image of the BJP as a being fully under the command of the Modi–Shah duo.

One of the biggest factors that contributed to her subsequent defeat in December 2018 was her government's handling of gangster Anandpal Singh, who was killed in a police encounter in 2017. The resulting backlash from the Rajput community – a traditional support base of the BJP – had an adverse impact on her government's image. Outfits such as the Karni Sena alleged that the encounter was 'fake' and demanded a CBI inquiry into the matter. A massive protest was organized in Anandpal's village Sanvrad in Nagaur district, which turned violent and resulted in the death of one person. While the Raje government finally relented to a CBI investigation, the entire episode left Rajput groups effectively disenchanted with the administration.[18] Before long, the Rajputs were pledging support to Congress in their effort to oust Raje.

As a final effort to fight anti-incumbency, in her last budget in early 2018, Raje announced farm loan waivers for short-term agricultural loans availed from state cooperative banks. But by this time, the tide had turned against her. 'Modi *tujhse bair nahin*, Vasundhara *teri khair nahin* (Modi, we don't have enmity with you, but we won't spare Vasundhara),' chanted hordes of contractual health workers at a rally in Jhunjhunu district in 2018, angry at their demands being ignored, when Raje stood on the stage alongside Prime Minister Narendra Modi himself, who had been invited to launch the National Nutrition Mission and expand the Beti Bachao Beti Padhao Abhiyan. The dissatisfaction among the public had spilled out into the open.

It was around this time that Raje once again looked towards Charbhuja, from where she launched the Rajasthan Gaurav Yatra in August 2018, hoping to get lucky a third time. 'I have worked very hard, will not use Congress as benchmark,' Raje had said at the commencement of the yatra.[19] But the charm of Charbhuja did not work this time. A resurgent Congress under the leadership of Sachin Pilot ousted Raje from power in December 2018, leaving the BJP with just seventy-three seats. Just before the assembly elections, the central leadership sent Raje a firm message by denying her right-hand man, cabinet minister Yunus Khan, a ticket to contest from his constituency of Deedwana. He was made to contest from Tonk against Sachin Pilot instead, where he lost by a margin of over 50,000 votes. After the BJP lost the 2018 elections, the anti-Raje group was reinvigorated and Satish Poonia was crowned the new BJP president in 2019, after Madan Lal Saini passed away.

'Madam' in the Modi–Shah Era and an Enduring Legacy

A luxury Mercedes sedan stopped a bit short of the porch at C-51, Sardar Patel Marg, Jaipur – the Rajasthan BJP office. An SUV was already parked there, its driver nowhere to be seen. A crowd of journalists was gathered outside, watching the scene unfold. One of them asked, '*Ye gaadi kiski hai*? (Whose car is this?)', pointing at the SUV. '*Adhyaksh ji ki hai* (The state president's)', someone responded promptly. Over the next few minutes, BJP workers started gathering and kept a keen watch to see whether the SUV would move to make space for the Mercedes, but the larger car didn't budge. Finally, the Mercedes parked at a corner and someone rushed to let out its VIP passenger – Vasundhara Raje.

This was in February 2021, when the elections were still three years away. Days ago, however, the tussle between the new state president Satish Poonia and Raje's old associates had entered the public sphere. A group of around twenty MLAs loyal to Raje had written a letter to Poonia alleging that the assembly proceedings were subject to bias and that the voices of several senior MLAs were being deliberately ignored. The message was targeted at the leader of opposition, Gulab Chand Kataria, with whom Raje's differences were well known. Leading the assault on Kataria was the trump card in Raje's pack – eighty-seven-year-old Kailash Chandra Meghwal, former speaker of the Rajasthan assembly and the most senior member present therein.* A few months later, in September 2021, Meghwal wrote another letter threatening to bring a censure motion against Kataria, his political rival from Mewar. He also levelled several other allegations against him, including placing the blame for the BJP's dwindling electoral fortunes squarely on Kataria's statements.

In the twilight of his political career, Meghwal was scathing in his criticism of Kataria and his grievances dated back to the 1960s and '70s. His stature and valuable experience in politics had made him the most potent weapon in Raje's arsenal to secure her influence in the party. After winning the 2018 assembly elections by the highest margin in the state, Meghwal first made it to the headlines when, in July 2020, he slammed 'horse-trading', criticizing the practice of MLAs switching parties,[20] but this backfired. His statement happened to coincide with the rebellion of then Deputy Chief Minister Sachin Pilot against Ashok Gehlot, but was used by the Congress to criticize the BJP, which had remained in denial about any horse-trading whatsoever thus far.[21]

Speculation was rife that Pilot had plans to defect to the BJP and Raje was staunchly opposed to the possibility, even as her detractors – including Gajendra Singh Shekhawat – openly extended an invitation to Pilot.[22] The young leader himself maintained that he had no intentions of joining the BJP, but the developments exposed

---

* Meghwal held various enviable portfolios over the course of his long career, including MP, MLA, state minister and union minister, to name a few. His allegiances to the saffron ideology predated the BJP itself and he was jailed during Emergency, cementing his clout in the party.

Raje's stance on the emerging leader, who she knew would then be poised to be made the chief minister.

Some leaders such as Hanuman Beniwal, a known fierce critic of Raje's and the founder of the RLP was a leader of the ruling BJP alliance, who openly accused Raje of being hand in glove with Gehlot for twenty-two years.[23] Raje's fellow party leaders at odds with her stance continued to publicly voice their disagreements with her in the years following 2018, once she was no longer CM.

Despite these developments, Raje's loyalists maintained a determined front. 'Vasundhara ji was the leader accepted by all of us, she still is and will remain so. The elections will be contested under her leadership and for sure she will become the chief minister,' claimed seven-time-MLA and former minister Kali Charan Saraf in February 2021,[24] even as alarm bells were ringing in the Raje camp. Her influence was systematically dismantled under the leadership of Satish Poonia, who took over the reins of the party in September 2019 after the death of Madan Lal Saini. One of the biggest gripes of Raje's supporters was that the BJP state executive committee in Rajasthan was comprised mainly of Raje detractors such as Madan Dilawar and her friend-turned-rival Diya Kumari, mirroring the change unfolding within – the anti-Raje group was now in the majority. The animosity between the two camps meant that there was now a clear divide in the party.

Some of Raje's supporters continued to remain in denial of the change in the status, such as former Kota MLA Bhawani Singh Rajawat, who maintained that Raje's stature in state politics could not be matched and merely holding portfolios in the state executive did not guarantee success.[25] Raje now faced the most important battle of her career: staying relevant in a party where power was now fully centralized and the mission of the reigning Modi–Shah duo being to ensure that the days of regional satraps were over.

In December 2020, a huge blow was dealt to Raje when Poonia inducted senior leader and six-time MLA Ghanshyam Tiwari back into the BJP. Tiwari, one of the earliest contenders for the CM's office after Bhairon Singh Shekhawat, was known to have his differences with Raje. The senior leader was close to the RSS and had served in Raje's cabinet during her first term, but had been staunchly critical of her ever since. He sat on dharnas outside her bungalow, wrote letters accusing her government of corruption and finally left the BJP in 2018 to float his own party, citing the state of affairs as 'undeclared Emergency'.[26] When his party failed to win a single seat and he himself lost the 2018 assembly elections, he dabbled in the Congress briefly and shared the stage with Rahul Gandhi before returning to the BJP.

Tiwari's reinstatement in the BJP bore clear indications of favouritism by the RSS, since he had been a loyal member throughout his life. Poonia said that Tiwari's return to BJP had been made possible only by the approval of the central leadership[27] and to rub salt on the wounds of the Raje faction, the party sent the senior leader to the Rajya Sabha in 2022. When Raje posted a picture with Tiwari taken after his Rajya Sabha appointment on her Facebook,[28] the suspicions of her shrinking influence were confirmed – she had had to yield to the wishes of the party high command.

The wave of resentment that Raje now faced was brutal, with senior leaders making statements such as, '*Humein toh kachre ke dher mein patak diya tha* (We had been discarded like garbage in a dumpyard).'[29] When reporters questioned Raje about the chief ministerial ambitions of many of her party colleagues in Rajasthan, she was guarded yet clear in her response that merely wishing for the post could not make one the CM of India's largest state.[30] Between 2018 and 2023, despite all the indications that the winds were not blowing in her favour, Raje remained optimistic about making a comeback.

At this time, the Congress – affected by its own infighting between Gehlot and Pilot – started mocking the BJP for having too many contenders for the CM post – nearly a dozen leaders, including Raje, Kataria, Poonia, Gajendra Singh Shekhawat, Rajendra Rathore, Arjun Ram Meghwal and Om Mathur were possible candidates. While Raje, the national vice president of the BJP in the wake of the 2018 election loss, refrained from going against the party's decisions, the skirmishes between her followers and the state party leadership had claimed quite a few political casualties.

This included former minister Rohitash Sharma, a staunch loyalist of Raje's, who was expelled from the party for six years in July 2021. His expulsion came days after he said that there was no state-level leader who had knowledge about Rajasthan, targeting Poonia.

Adapting to the needs of the times as they change is a mainstay of surviving in politics. This fact is highlighted each time seasoned politicians change parties after spending decades in a different ideological fold, or when rivals become comrades-in-arms to suit the needs of realpolitik. In the years preceding the 2023 assembly elections, as the BJP took a more hardline Hindutva stance and continuously accused the Ashok Gehlot-led Congress government of 'appeasement politics', Raje followed suit.

The change in her rhetoric was significant as Raje had consciously avoided speaking on Hindutva during the 2003 Parivartan Yatra and instead named development as her area of focus. For the first time in her career, however, she started targeting the Congress over its 'appeasement politics'. This was so unexpected a turn in her rhetoric that even her former colleagues were surprised. In 2022, after communal clashes in Karauli, Raje had been prompt to visit the riot-hit area and meet Hindu victims. She had also accused the Gehlot government of trying to impose restrictions on Hindu festivals through administrative orders. 'I have never heard her talk so openly about Hindus and appeasement,' a former member of Raje's cabinet had remarked. The reactions of her colleagues were not unwarranted. Raje had a reputation to uphold as a leader who had avoided adopting the Hindutva rhetoric and instead focused on development and good governance. Her closest confidante, Yunus Khan, was one of the handful of Muslim BJP politicians to be made a minister and this was a remarkable feat for a leader of her standing in the party ranks.

Her move towards Hindutva simply cemented the fact that Raje was hardly hesitant to go down roads she may have avoided if it helped her stay afloat in the political culture of the times. By the 2023 assembly elections, the BJP had become an unabashedly Hindutva party nationally and an election-winning juggernaut. It shed its secular appearances, as it had done during the era of Vajpayee, and Raje – a protégé of the veteran leader – was once again present to bear witness to this evolution firsthand.

The political journey of Raje, who steered the state for a decade in the early and mid-2000s, is a story of many firsts in the history of Rajasthan. From its first woman chief minister even as it ranked among the top Indian states in female infanticide and foeticide,[31] Raje not only contributed to the state's development but also carved out a niche for herself as an iconic woman leader, who served to unite and then establish the strength of women as a voter group. She presented an exceptionally powerful and influential figure in the staunchly male-dominated arena of politics. In addition to effective representation, Raje also foregrounded women in her government's welfare schemes, including the Bhamashah Swasthya Beema Yojana, where it was a requirement to present a woman as the head of the family in order to avail benefits under the scheme.

Under Raje's leadership, Rajasthan also adopted the public–private partnership (PPP) model for the first time and opened its doors to multi-national companies, which greatly enhanced the employment prospects of young people in the state. Her tenure also saw greater adoption of technology to ease the process of delivering welfare scheme benefits to the people. Initiatives such as the aforementioned Annapurna Rasoi highlighted a focus on better nutrition for the population as well.

Harsha Kumari Singh, the resident editor of NDTV in Jaipur, who has been covering Rajasthan for the last three decades, claims that it was Raje's strength and charisma as a leader that enabled a huge fraction of the population to connect with her. 'Apart from having a very sharp political mind, Raje is also very adept in matters of governance and has a no-nonsense style of operating which never allowed the bureaucracy to get the better of her. Raje would not hesitate to take expert opinions and herself has a very good understanding of issues,' said Singh. She also emphasized that Raje's understanding of visual symbols and the importance of optics in politics is what played a crucial role in expanding her reach among the women in remote villages she met on her yatras. With a natural instinct for politics, Raje has managed to outmanoeuvre her rivals in the party and is still one of the strongest politicians ever to lead the desert state, according to Singh.[32]

Raje chose against being a mere figurehead and never hesitated to differ with senior party leaders when it came to matters of governance. She was a bold and tough administrator and invited widespread and fierce loyalty from her supporters. Even the remotest corners of the state felt seen and included under Raje's administration, rushing in huge hordes to catch a glimpse of the leader on her yatras and during campaign rallies – regardless of whether or not she was in office as CM. Her charisma and popularity are undeniable and her role as an important pillar of the BJP in Rajasthan remains unchanged even after the outcome of the 2023 assembly elections, as shall be detailed in subsequent chapters.

9

THE ASCENT OF THE CHALLENGER

Sachin Pilot's Rise

A Fresh Challenger

MUSTARD FIELDS DOTTED BOTH SIDES OF THE ROAD LEADING TO TONK, located 100 kilometres south of Jaipur. It was a mid-November morning in 2018 and one could see cattle in the distance, strolling on the dry, silt-covered riverbed of a seasonal river in what used to be the sole Muslim-ruled princely state in the days of the Rajputana. Farther away, tractor-trolleys were extracting sand from the riverbed. In just a few months, the green fields would be blanketed in yellow and by the time the Rabi harvest season rolled around, Rajasthan would have a new government.

A huge poster of RPCC president Sachin Pilot beamed at visitors just as they entered the Tonk city limit. It was the first of many more to come along that road. On this particular day, the many small villages strewn in the path of the Banas river flowing into Tonk from Sawai Madhopur were buzzing with activity. In Khareda, for instance, a DJ system had been set up and was blaring songs in Rajasthani, heaping praises upon Pilot during the last leg of campaigns before the upcoming assembly elections. A chariot pulled by a white horse stood waiting for the VIP guest to arrive. Before long, Pilot's SUV, leading a long caravan of cars, could be seen entering the village, sending the crowd into renewed frenzy. The guest of honour had arrived wearing his signature smile, his face showing no signs of exhaustion from the relentless campaigning across the state over the last few months.

The crowd was waving Congress flags and rushed to hoist Pilot onto the chariot decorated for him, mirroring the enthusiasm of the party workers – a far departure from 21 January 2014 – the day the young leader had assumed charge as the state party president. Congress had been reduced to just twenty-one seats in the assembly after facing a crushing defeat in the 2013 elections and its workers were extremely demoralized. No senior party leader even bothered to visit the Congress headquarters in Jaipur after his appointment, Pilot recalls.[1] It was the worst rout the party had faced in the history of the state and it had come at the hands of a resurgent BJP, riding the wave of Narendra Modi's skyrocketing popularity, and under the leadership of its formidable stalwart, Vasundhara Raje.

On that fateful day, 8 December 2013, TV screens flashed images of a saffron sweep across the desert state and the mood inside Indira Gandhi Bhawan turned grim. The congested lane outside the party headquarters was deserted as Congress workers left one after the other in dejection. The members of the Congress Sewa Dal lingered inside the damp rooms of the PCC office, avoiding the journalists gathered outside since that morning. Gandhi cap-clad stalwart party leaders looked down from within dusty frames on the walls of the PCC office as PCC president Dr Chandrabhan* typed out his resignation letter, stung by the humiliation of defeat.[2] CM Ashok Gehlot too was prompt to tender his resignation once

* Twenty years ago, Dr Chandrabhan, a member of the powerful Jat community, had been part of the erstwhile Janata Dal and had scored a thumping victory against the Congress candidate in Mandawa in the 1990 assembly elections. Now, as head of the state Congress, he stood fourth in the same constituency, even losing his deposit.

the magnitude of the loss became evident: BJP had won 163 seats in the 200-member assembly.

It was the end of an era that began with Mohan Lal Sukhadia in the 1950s and '60s. Govind Singh Dotasra was made the chief whip of the Congress in the assembly, but the party faced a peculiar problem. It could not afford to remain headless for long and needed to crown a new PCC president, although there were no seasoned leaders to choose from.

A recent rising star in the party, Sachin Pilot had achieved an amazing feat earlier in the year, in August 2013 – the passage of the new Companies Bill in parliament under his leadership as independent in-charge of the Corporate Affairs Ministry. The new law was aimed at replacing or updating most provisions of the Companies Act 1956. As the thirty-seven-year-old leader himself put it, this was a 'historic' feat, one that was sure to 'enhance transparency and ensure fewer regulations, self reporting and disclosure'.[3] The Confederation of Indian Industry heaped praise upon the move as well, cementing Pilot's image as a promising new political talent.

Before he turned forty, Pilot had already earned the distinction of being a two-term MP from Dausa and Ajmer constituencies, respectively. Back in 2004, he had become the youngest MP after winning the Dausa seat – from where his father Rajesh Pilot had also won – at just twenty-six years old as had his mother Rama Pilot in a by-election in 2000, months after Rajesh Pilot's death.[4] Five years later, he defeated seasoned BJP leader Kiran Maheshwari from Ajmer, expanding his influence even beyond his family stronghold.

He also shared a comfortable relationship with the Congress high command and the Gandhi family, who had known Pilot since he was a child when his father had been a union minister loyal to the Congress. Taking a cue from his accomplishments, then national Congress president Sonia Gandhi appointed Pilot to the important office of the Rajasthan Congress president at a time when the party was struggling to find the right candidate for the job in the wake of its humiliating electoral defeat. Less than six months after his speech in the parliament, Pilot was headed to Jaipur as the Rajasthan Congress president.

Slogans of '*Chhodh Kamal ka phool, haath pe button daba denge, abke badlenge sarkar, Sachin CM bana denge* (We will abandon the lotus and vote for the hand, this time when the government changes, Sachin Pilot will be CM)' echoed through the air in Tonk. A colourfully painted mini-truck styled as a DJ blared paeans for Pilot, who his supporters hoped would become the fourteenth CM of Rajasthan. Crowds were spilling out of the narrow, serpentine alleyways inside Tonk city to catch a glimpse of Pilot as he made his way to every house to seek votes. He waved to the people with one hand while using his other to pass on the garlands they were placing around his neck to the local Congress workers. It was a reassuring sight.

Since he had taken over as state party president in 2014, he had managed to attract an impressive following whose loyalty to Pilot was unwavering. The groundwork for this was laid by former CM Gehlot, who had jostled past many a contender to retain power, leaving in his wake a trail of discontented families. Take for instance Shiv Charan Mathur's* granddaughter, Vibha Mathur, who was among those whose clans had been Congress loyalists for generations and were approached by Pilot to rejoin the fold.[5] As a younger member in her thirties, she was assigned the task of improving the party's social media presence. This gave

* As a former chief minister, Shiv Charan Mathur was once again among the contenders for the top post when Congress won a landslide victory in the 1998 assembly elections. After Gehlot beat Mathur and other leaders to the post, the senior Congress leader had gradually faded into oblivion before his death in 2009.

her the opportunity to rebuild her family's legacy in the party. Similarly, Congress MLA Brijendra Singh Ola had not forgotten how his father, former union minister and stalwart Jat leader Sis Ram Ola, had been left out of the CM race in 2008. As a gesture of his support, Ola gave up his official residence in Jaipur's Jalupura so Pilot could set up his residence cum office there, in addition to the party president's office designated for him at the PCC.

Pilot not only steadily stitched up alliances with the younger generation of established political families and other youth leaders* who had been active in student politics, but also older leaders whose foray into full-fledged electoral politics had been hindered by the Congress old guard supporting Gehlot. In Pilot, they all found a new messiah, one who could facilitate their transition from reserve batters to main strikers or make it to the pitch at all. Some of them even made public proclamations of the fact of their pledged loyalty, such as Rakesh Pareek, a third-generation Congressman from Ajmer, who was overjoyed at being made the president of the Congress Seva Dal. He was quoted as saying 'I am ready to give every drop of my blood for Sachin Pilot.'[6]

The impact of this fresh crop of recruits was palpable, according to Mathur, who coordinated with different districts to create the Congress IT cell. Soon, there were Congress volunteers at the state, district, constituency and block levels, who were actively observing and highlighting BJP's misgovernance on social media.[7]

Not many people have had the fortune of going from delivering milk to the VIP bungalows on Delhi's Rakab Ganj Road to occupying

* These included young NSUI leaders, such as Mukesh Bhakar and Anil Chopra, who were first-generation politicians who had built their influence in the student politics circuit and had MLA ambitions. Chopra was the 2014 president of the Rajasthan University Student Union.

one of these grand old houses as parliamentarians. A man who flipped his fortunes on their head is Rajeshwar Prasad Bidhuri, later known as Rajesh Pilot, whose ancestral village Vaidpura is situated in present-day Greater Noida, Uttar Pradesh. Rajesh Pilot once recounted in an interview with journalist and future politician Rajeev Shukla, that between the 1960–80s, while he was staying at a dairy at Rakab Ganj Road, he would deliver milk on a bicycle to some of the bungalows of the parliamentarians as well as to the parliament canteen.[8] While Rajesh Pilot's roots were in Uttar Pradesh, Rajasthan would become his, his wife Rama's and later his son's centre of political power. When he was first elected to the parliament in 1980, Bidhuri officially changed his name to Rajesh Pilot by popular demand as a nod to his time in the air force. Rajesh Pilot's political journey is a tale of hard work and grit which enabled the son of a farmer to be elected to the Parliament and later become a union minister, emerging as one of the most charismatic politicians in the country until his untimely death in an accident in 2001.

His son Sachin Pilot's connection to Tonk was forged over six decades ago, when a young, lanky man, slated to become a multiple-time CM of Jammu and Kashmir, arrived in Jaipur. Farooq Abdullah was a student of medicine at the SMS Medical College, where he instantly hit it off with a fellow student, Ajmal Saidi, the scion of an influential family in Tonk. Their friendship lasted a lifetime and even after becoming CM, Abdullah regularly visited Saidi. Rajesh Pilot, too, grew close to Abdullah, since he was the Congress's troubleshooter on Kashmir issues during the 1980s and later as the union minister for internal security.

His son, Sachin Pilot, eventually married Abdullah's daughter Sara and found his way to Tonk with the support of Saidi's son, Saud, a youth Congress leader and his foremost ally in the constituency, becoming the first non-Muslim candidate to be fielded by the Congress in forty-six years.[9] In 2013, Saidi contested as an independent and stood third in the electoral contest. By 2018, he was supporting Pilot as the latter took to Tonk, with its substantial Muslim and Gurjar population, as a safe seat for him to enter the assembly. During his campaign, the audience had erupted into applause as he expressed his desire to win Tonk by the biggest possible margin in the 2018 assembly elections.

Locking Horns with Vasundhara Raje

Mahaveer Dhakad's brick house in Khairali village, Baran district, was enveloped in a melancholic silence as his family mourned the loss of the forty-four-year-old garlic farmer, who had hanged himself from a tree after his crops had failed to sell at a reasonable price. The wiry farmer had toiled night and day in his fields, braving the scorching heat, waking up early to ensure he did not miss the odd timings of irrigation water supply and using his own house to store the produce. Days after his death, his twenty-year-old son Anil loaded all the garlic in the house into his father's old tractor, drove to the Baran Krishi Mandi and had to sell it at the throwaway price of ₹400 per quintal at a time when the MSP was ₹3,257 per quintal. Despite the MSP set by the government being much higher, private players at agricultural markets offered a much lower price and the volume of government's procurement at the MSP was not adequate to accommodate all farmers. As a result, farmers were forced to sell their crops at throwaway prices, sustaining massive losses in the process. With a loan of ₹5 lakh to repay and one less working member, the family was left staring at an uncertain future.

At least ten garlic farmers in the Hadoti region suffered a similar fate between 2017–18.[10] Even as cash-strapped and debt-ridden farmers are routinely driven out of government offices, their requests either ignored or rejected, farmer suicides are unfortunately seen as golden opportunities for opposition parties to attack the government. With just one Congress MLA in the

Hadoti region, Sachin Pilot came with a rather audacious idea to put 'pressure on the government for a complete loan-waiver for farmers, GST exemption on agriculture equipment and raising the minimum support price for their produce'.[11] The Congress was to take out a 100 kilometre long padyatra through the constituencies of chief minister Vasundhara Raje and her son Dushyant Singh, named the 'Kisan Nyay Yatra', from 3–6 October 2017.

If CM Raje was the queen, Jhalawar was her bejewelled throne. Raje had been undefeated in Jhalawar since 1989, as was her son, Dushyant Singh, who is the present MP from Jhalawar-Baran. Fourteen years before Pilot planned his yatra, his mother Rama Pilot had contested the 2003 assembly elections against Raje from Jhalrapatan in Jhalawar.[12] His father Rajesh Pilot too had challenged Sitaram Kesri for the Congress president elections in 1997.[13] Both contests had ended badly for the proverbial Davids from the Pilot clan. Raje defeated Rama Pilot by a margin of nearly 30,000 votes. Rajesh Pilot had got only 354 votes out of 7,460 valid votes contesting against Kesri. Nevertheless, they managed to leave an impression on the public for their sheer courage to challenge the powerful in their own territory. Now it was their son's turn to take on Raje, who had been CM twice by this time and had the last word on all matters pertaining to Jhalawar's politics. He hoped to change the family trend and unseat Raje and her government this time.

According to Pilot, the idea of challenging CM Vasundhara Raje in her own backyard charged up the party cadre on the ground and the Kisan Nyay Yatra further contributed to build momentum against the ruling BJP before the 2018 elections.[14] Dressed in his signature white kurta-pyjama and flanked by fellow party leaders, Pilot walked across garlic fields, stopping at minuscule hamlets and obliging selfie requests from eager supporters. The change in the demeanour of the Congress was evident by this time – the party had clearly overcome the humiliation of the 2013 defeat and a new crop of leaders were now stepping up to wrest power from the incumbent BJP.

When Pilot entered Jhalawar on the morning of 6 October 2017, he was greeted with great adulation by the public and local Congress leaders, who had put up huge posters that said '*Ab ki baar* Sachin *sarkar* (This time, Sachin will form the government),' a clear reference to his chief ministerial ambitions. The Congress president made his way to the dais to deliver a scathing speech against the Raje government and stated the demands of their movement. Unlike the posters, Pilot was not wearing his trademark red safa. 'I won't wear Rajasthani safa until Congress forms government again in the state,' he said,[15] taking a leaf from Raje's book and making a dramatic declaration to capture the public's imagination effectively.

Pilot was invariably scathing in his criticism of Raje, sparing no opportunity to hold her personally responsible for the state government's failures or on charges of corruption.[16] A nondescript village in the middle of the Thar desert would soon become the stage for a massive protest, putting Raje's administration under pressure and giving political mileage to Congress and Pilot.

Trimohi is one of the last villages in western India short of the Indo–Pak border. A small settlement of Dalit families, its thatched huts are strewn across the arid landscape of the westernmost Barmer district. Delta Meghwal, a young resident of the area, was only seventeen and aspired to become the first woman from her village to pursue higher education. Her dreams were abruptly crushed in early 2016, when her lifeless body was discovered inside a water tank at the teacher training school in Bikaner, where she had been studying.* The alleged rape and murder of Delta shook

* Delta was a beacon of hope for her friends – other girls who hoped to follow her on the path of higher education. After her horrific death, other villagers refused to send their daughters to school. Her father Mahendra Meghwal, a schoolteacher, regretted sending his daughter to study further. 'I should not have educated her … she might

the country and as the hashtag #JusticeforDeltaMeghwal started to trend on X, in a rare instance, Rahul Gandhi himself made his way to Trimohi, flanked by Pilot.[17]

The image of Gandhi and Pilot walking side-by-side sent a clear message to other Congress leaders – with a robust direct line connecting him to the Gandhi family, Pilot had a clear advantage over the previous PCC presidents, whose sole point of contact had been Ashok Gehlot. CM Raje maintained a silence over Delta's death and her government refused to heed to demands of handing the case to CBI. Pilot said that the protests by the Congress party after the death of Delta Meghwal made the people see that even with just twenty-one MLAs in the assembly, Congress could take to the streets for the sake of issues that mattered to the public.[18] The Dalits were seething with anger. With a population of 17.83 per cent in Rajasthan, the community was rethinking its decision in 2013 to switch their votes to the BJP from Congress, the party for which they voted traditionally.

As anti-incumbency feeling steadily built up against the BJP, Pilot now realized that all he had to do was latch on to the momentum built up by the protests. This was a game he was determined to win at all costs. In mid-2015, Congress workers in every district of Rajasthan made their way towards the district collectorate, holding party flags and raising slogans against Raje.[19] Their source of anger was a man living on a different continent, inside his comfortable five-storey mansion on Sloane Street, London.

Lalit Modi, a friend of Raje's, had founded the IPL by this

have been alive,' he told the media. Source: 'Bikaner rape: Shouldn't have sent her to school, says father', *Hindustan Times*, 6 April 2016. Available at: https://www.hindustantimes.com/jaipur/dalit-father-rues-sending-girl-to-college-where-she-was-raped-killed/story-6wJgkNsyBcPBZmYJYk9T6H.html.

time and was wanted by the ED on various charges in 2015. As mentioned in Chapter 8, Modi was a regular at the CMO during Raje's first term. According to a former senior bureaucrat, IAS and IPS officers and even ministers were always on their toes around Modi as he was unpredictable, brash and did not hesitate to rebuke them publicly.

Back in 2015, Modi, who was living abroad while being investigated by Indian agencies, said that he had received help from then External Affairs Minister Sushma Swaraj and Rajasthan CM Raje. Pilot spearheaded a movement demanding Raje's ouster, organizing protests across the state, claiming the CM had helped Modi stay in the UK despite 'knowing well that he had siphoned off hundreds of crores of rupees and was wanted by law', terming her involvement criminal.[20]

When the BJP scrambled and whipped up counter-allegations of financial irregularities against Gehlot's son Vaibhav, who had earlier demanded the resignation of Raje, Gehlot went silent on Lalitgate.[21] This was a boon in disguise for Pilot, who leveraged the protests and the opposition's pushback over Lalitgate to bolster his political image. Ashok Gehlot's weakness turned out to be Pilot's strength.

A cluster of police barricades remains stationed permanently near the Civil Lines railway crossing, the road leading to the chief minister's house in Jaipur, to stop protestors from reaching the CM's residence. Between 2014–18, Pilot and his followers frequented this spot several times, jostling to get past the cops in an effort to gherao Raje's bungalow, climbing over barricades and enduring lathi charges. He once joked during an informal meeting with journalists in Jaipur, 'I went to jail while protesting for you guys', a reference to how often he could be seen leading protests against the administration. He was flanked by prominent leaders such as Pratap Singh Khachariyawas, the nephew of former vice president Bhairon Singh Shekhawat and Jaipur district

Congress committee president, who had accompanied Pilot on a bullock cart during protests against price rise[22] and demanded further investigation into an alleged mining scam.[23] He was also accompanied by his loyalists while he courted arrest over the passage of the Criminal Laws (Rajasthan Amendment) Bill, 2017, forcing the Raje administration to withdraw the bill that aimed to protect public servants from graft probes and barred the media from reporting on such cases. The bill was dubbed a gag order and '*kala kanoon* (unjust law)'. Such was the backlash against the bill that leading daily *Rajasthan Patrika* announced that it would not publish any news about CM Raje or her government's activities until the bill was withdrawn.[24]

The consistent flurry of protests organized under Pilot's leadership laid the groundwork for the Congress's revival in Rajasthan from the sorry state it had been left in after the 2013 election results. As Pilot toured the state, he also gathered loyalists in each district – Congress leaders holding various posts within the party ranks. They were primarily young men and women with backgrounds in student politics and older leaders who sided with Pilot after being ignored by the party. Pilot also personally supervised the 'Mera Booth Mera Gaurav' campaign* to enhance the party organization at the booth level, which boosted the morale of the cadre on the ground.

The sustained campaigns against her government had left Raje fuming. At first, she tried to ignore Pilot and would not even acknowledge his presence. But as his attacks became more incisive,

---

* The 'Mera Booth Mera Gaurav' campaign was launched by the Rajasthan Congress before the 2018 assembly elections to galvanize booth-level workers in all 200 assembly constituencies. As part of this, senior leaders – including then PCC chief Sachin Pilot – toured the state and interacted with party workers on the ground to rejuvenate them ahead of the polls. The exercise was meant to ensure that party workers felt encouraged to work round the clock, campaigning and helping voters feel connected to the Congress.

she was compelled to strike back. As part of its strategy, the BJP had tried to sideline Pilot by calling him an 'outsider' – a close aide of Raje's and a minister, Rajendra Rathore, reminded the public that Pilot's family is from Uttar Pradesh and not Rajasthan. This distinction backfired, however, when Pilot reminded them that Raje too was an outsider and had first come to Rajasthan only in her early twenties when she got married. 'My *doli* (bridal palanquin) came to Rajasthan and only my *arthi* (funeral cortège) will leave from here, and I will continue to serve the people of Rajasthan till then,' an acerbic Raje retorted later, in October 2018.[25] When a reporter tried to bring up the 'outsider' allegation yet again in an attempt to get a response out of Pilot at a press conference, he laughed off the issue altogether, unwilling to drag the matter any further. '*Aise kaise mukhyamantri banenge aap?* (How will you become CM like this?),' the reporter had asked tersely. Pilot had replied, '*Aise hi hanste hanste ban jayenge* (I'll just smile my way there).'

The Caste Factor

At the height of Gurjar–Meena clashes over reservation in the wake of delimitation, the Dausa parliamentary constituency was reserved for STs, which gave Meena leaders the upper hand as the dominant community in the category. However, the Gurjars were staunchly opposed to voting for Meena candidates and since they were not categorized as ST themselves, they could not contest elections from the constituency. In an unprecedented move, the community roped in Qamar Rabbani Chechi, a Muslim Gurjar from distant Jammu and Kashmir, simply because he belonged to the ST category.*[26] The caste divides ran so deep that the Gurjars

* Chechi contested the Lok Sabha polls as an independent candidate under the symbol of a gas cylinder and emerged second with about 2 lakh votes, ahead of both the

chose to vote for an outsider from a different state rather than for a local Meena candidate.

In an enviable feat, Rajesh Pilot, a Gurjar, had managed to be voted into the parliament five times from this Meena-dominated seat, starting from 1984 until his death in 2000. He managed to forge a unique alliance between the Gurjar and Meena communities. Despite clashes over issues of reservation in the mid-2000s, Sachin Pilot took steps to further strengthen this alliance between the Gurjars and Meenas in Dausa. Before the 2018 assembly election, Pilot gave the ticket from Dausa to a close aide of his, Murari Lal Meena. Umashankar Meena, a social media manager during Pilot's tenure, added that Dausa's Meenas visit Rajesh Pilot's statue every year since his sudden demise in June 2000 to pay their respects – a testament to their reverence for the family.[27]

As for the traditionally pastoral Gurjar community, classified among the Most Backward Classes (MBC) in Rajasthan, Sachin Pilot is viewed as a role model by the community's youth. Their shared caste identity with the foreign-educated, fluent English-speaking, safa-adorning young leader, who ended all his speeches with '*Ram Ram sa*', a traditional Rajasthani greeting, has endeared the young leader to them unlike any other.

Pilot himself, however, understood that brandishing his caste identity was a two-edged sword in the Rajasthani political arena. Being the most well-known politician from the Gurjar community, which constituted 7–8 per cent of the state's population, was a clear advantage in a society where caste was so central to electoral politics, but it could also prove to be limiting and risk alienating other social groups. An influential Gurjar leader from Dausa shared how, during his initial days as the state Congress president, Pilot would decline being captured in the same frame as Gurjar youngsters insistent on getting selfies clicked with him.

Congress and BJP; both parties had fielded Meena candidates.

He was apprehensive of being boxed in as a Gurjar leader and his fears are not entirely unfounded.[28] Rajasthan's seventy-year-long political history has indicated that the person elected to the chief minister's post needs to be acceptable to the chattis kaum, or all communities. Take for instance Kirodi Lal Meena, Hanuman Beniwal or Lokendra Singh Kalvi, who were all tall leaders of their respective caste communities but could never get close to the CM's chair. Despite being the founder of the Karni Sena and an influential Rajput leader, Kalvi was never able to win an election.

Rajesh Pilot is credited with putting the Gurjar community on the national political map and the same trust and unconditional support is extended by the community to his son, according to former Congress MLA Indraj Gurjar, a Pilot group insider.[29] 'Their support for Pilot is unconditional,' Himmat Singh Gurjar, a leader who has been involved in the Gurjar reservation agitation for years, reiterates.[30] All efforts of the Ashok Gehlot faction within the Congress to nurture other Gurjar politicians as alternatives to Pilot have been met with tremendous hostility from the community. Gurjar youth in Pushkar once hurled shoes at Ashok Chandna – a Gurjar MLA, minister and Gehlot loyalist – while chanting 'Sachin Pilot *zindabad* (Long live Sachin Pilot)'.[31]

In a rare instance of acknowledgement, three months before the 2018 assembly elections, Pilot was accompanied by his young son to the Lakkhi Mela at the Dev Dham Jodhpuriya temple, Tonk, a popular pilgrimage spot for Gurjars. Around midnight, Pilot made his way through the ecstatic crowd to reach the stage, even as his supporters rushed to click photos with him, constantly chanting his name. Elderly men clad in dhotis let go of their hookahs and arched their necks in the hopes of catching a glimpse of their beloved leader. He refrained from directly asking his community members to vote for him as it did not seem appropriate to the occasion, but sought their blessings nevertheless. '*Samaaj ka ashirwaad raha toh akele hi kabaddi khel jaaunga* (With the blessings of my community, I can win the [electoral] kabaddi match by myself),' he announced, his words drowning in the loud applause.[32]

One morning in March 2018, factory workers in the industrial town of Bhiwadi were taking a rare day off from their daily shifts at the local stockyards and manufacturing units. It was Holi and the slight winter chill still hung in the air that was usually cloaked in billowing smoke from the chimneys of industrial units. Neeraj Jatav, a ninth-class student, was finally able to join his friends in the festival celebrations, happy to get a break from his post-school shift at a neighbourhood clothing store. The young boys had arranged for a DJ for their settlement, Jatav Basti, situated at the edge of the town. However, the joy of festivities was short-lived. Later in the day, Neeraj's lifeless body was discovered close to the DJ stand. His family and friends registered an FIR alleging that the Dalit boy had been assaulted and killed by Gurjars, who were seen arguing and hurling casteist slurs at him for playing songs of his choice during the festivities.[33]

The Jatav community was horrified at the killing and their anger was palpable at a *mahapanchayat* meeting held later, comprising representatives from eighteen nearby villages. The attendees vowed to protest against the killing and cut off ties with the accused's community. '*Pagdi unke bandhte ho, samman unka karte ho, sab chodh do* (You tie the turban of upper caste people, give them respect, stop doing all this),' former BSP leader Omprakash Jatav was heard saying to the gathering, urging them not to tolerate atrocities and stop mingling with the Gurjar community.[34] Mere days later, the Jatav Basti was shrouded in gloom yet again as the charred body of fourteen-year-old Ajay Jatav, a friend of Neeraj's, was discovered by locals.[35] Family members demanded justice, alleging that Ajay had been killed because he had borne witness to Neeraj's murder. Although the authorities could not attest to the veracity of these claims or that the two cases were linked, protests broke out against the Vasundhara Raje-led BJP government.[36] The National Commission for Scheduled Castes, too, sent a notice to the Rajasthan government.

Ambedkarite groups were also angered by the opposition party's lack of promptness in taking up the issue, despite the fact that its Alwar district president, Tika Ram Jully, was himself a Dalit. Pilot decided to send a delegation from the Congress party to Bhiwadi the next day, headed by former union minister Bhanwar Jitendra Singh, according to local sources. He also issued a statement attacking the Raje government over the deaths: 'Atrocities against Dalits and the underprivileged in the society is on the increase. It cannot be without the tacit support of the present administration.'[37] The leader also did not hesitate to point out the fact that despite the accused in the case being from his community, he was not going to shy away from raising the issue in a non-partisan way.[38] The episode reflected the state Congress president's consciousness about his own caste identity and its possible repercussions on his chief ministerial ambitions and served as a clear rebuttal to his detractors within the state party who had been trying to portray him as a Gurjar leader.

None of Pilot's endeavours went to waste, as was evident from the results of the 2018 assembly elections. In a hitherto unprecedented phenomenon, BJP – the party Gurjars traditionally voted for – did not have a single Gurjar MLA elected to the state assembly; they were all swept away by the overwhelming support for Pilot. At the same time, many other candidates backed by Pilot from other communities, such as Meenas and Jats, emerged victorious as well, signalling his all-round popularity.

A Generational War Brews Within

A large crowd of villagers, wearing cheap, mill-made sweaters and covering their heads with white cloth to shield themselves from the December chill, surrounded a large cutout of a pair of scissors – the election symbol of an independent candidate, Mahadeo Singh Khandela. It was the last day of campaigning for the 2018 assembly elections and Khandela, a small town nestled in Sikar district at the heart of the Shekhawati region, became one of many sites of electoral contests that reflected the generational war brewing within the Congress.

Overlooked by his 'mother', the Congress party which he had served for four decades by then, Mahadeo Singh Khandela was in the twilight of his political career at seventy-five years of age. The former union minister was forced to contest elections as an independent under the symbol of scissors. In his stead, the Congress had chosen to field Subhash Meel, district president of the Youth Congress in Khandela and a part of the Sachin Pilot camp. Sixty kilometres away, Alok Beniwal, the son of former Gujarat governor Kamla Beniwal, walked around in the main market of Shahpura, soliciting shopkeepers for their votes. His election symbol was a sewing machine. He too had been associated with the party for a long time – his mother had served as a member for more than fifty years – and had recently been expelled. He decided to contest as an independent against the party's official candidate, Manish Yadav, who had been a student leader from the ABVP.[39]

Sachin Pilot played his biggest gamble yet. More than a dozen Congress leaders – including former ministers and senior MLAs who were part of the old guard and loyal to Ashok Gehlot – were denied tickets and replaced with younger leaders whose allegiances were pledged to Pilot. This was no reckless manoeuvre on his part, but rather a strategic move based on the party's recent winning streak in the by-elections under his state presidentship. The

Rajasthan Congress under Pilot focused on smaller-scale elections, such as the Krishi Mandi, Panchayat Raj and municipal elections, among others, and had performed well.[40]

The young leader recognized the necessity of backing up grand claims with tangible electoral successes shortly after taking charge of the crumbling party in 2014. There was no other way to renew the enthusiasm of party workers. He switched out the old ways for a whole new approach wherein he ensured his party remained in campaign mode throughout the length of his tenure, rather than reserving all such activity to six months before the polls.[41] His efforts bore fruit that year. Congress workers exchanged ladoos with journalists and Pilot's supporters enthusiastically surrounded him as the results for the by-elections in four assembly seats – Surajgarh, Weir, Nasirabad and Kota South – were declared. Congress had won three seats – one short of a clean sweep.[42]

Pilot had ticked all the boxes – extensively toured the state, relentlessly attacked the BJP for every act of misgovernance and even bitten the bullet to address joint rallies with future bête noire Ashok Gehlot – to ensure victory for the Congress in the by-elections and it had worked. Despite having lost the 2014 Lok Sabha elections from Ajmer himself in the wake of the Modi wave sweeping across the nation, he had ensured victory for his fellow party member, Raghu Sharma, and reclaimed the Ajmer seat. The writing on the wall was clear: the anti-incumbency wave against Raje's government offered a clear advantage to the Congress. Buoyed by the victory, Pilot installed a digital clock at the PCC headquarters in Jaipur that showed a countdown to December 2018, when he was confident the Raje government would be voted out of power.

February 2018 gave the biggest boost yet to Pilot's promising career – this time, Congress won all sixteen assembly segments in the by-elections for the two parliamentary constituencies of Alwar and Ajmer. His conviction strengthened by the unanimity of all voter bases in two major constituencies, Pilot finally set about purging the old guard – the Gehlot camp – for good. Congress leaders who were once the uncrowned kings of their constituencies were stunned into silence by the party's newly announced list of candidates. While leaders such as Mahadeo Singh Khandela prepared to go into battle against their own party, others were able to rely on substantial support from their respective constituencies even in the absence of a formal election symbol. One of these leaders was former Congress MLA and minister Babulal Nagar, who claimed that he had been denied a ticket for the 2018 assembly election because he was a supporter of Gehlot's, even as, in his own words, 'In my constituency (Dudu, in Jaipur district), I am Congress party'.[43]

The bugle was sounded and the generational war between Pilot's young Turks and Gehlot's old guard had begun. While on the face of it, everything had seemed normal thus far – with Pilot and Gehlot even riding on the same motorcycle for a photo op, attending Sankalp rallies organized by the party's national president, Rahul Gandhi, together and embarking on their campaign trail in the same helicopter – this final move had opened a rift between them. To remain on top of the numbers game, Pilot had begun gathering his loyalist MLAs to back him in the assembly. He turned up the campaign heat by appearing in person to address rallies alongside them in their respective constituencies.

As the countdown timer at the Congress headquarters entered its final phase, Sachin Pilot's intent to occupy the chief minister's chair resulted in a long-drawn political chess match. The ensuing decade saw Pilot become the deputy chief minister in 2018, take on the old guard in a no-holds-barred political sparring in 2020, play an active part in the government and then, even in the absence of a portfolio, continue to be a force to reckon with. He commanded the loyalty of a formidable group of Congress leaders and was subsequently also be inducted to the Congress Working Committee (CWC) in 2023, the party's highest decision-making body, while being entrusted with the duty of overseeing the party's affairs in other states as well – a show of trust by the Congress high command. He was also reelected to the Tonk assembly constituency in 2023 with a huge margin and till date continues to be one of the most popular leaders of Rajasthan.

While Pilot's quest for the topmost post in the state is ongoing at the time of writing, it is an undeniable fact that the tall, bespectacled second-generation Congress leader who prefers to dress in all white, has carved a niche for himself in Rajasthan politics, attracting supporters, fanfare and rivalries in equal measure. In recent times, such outpouring of popular support and the occasional criticism for any leader have become far rarer. The story of Pilot's ascent is a story of the aspirations of Rajasthan's younger demographic that are finally posing a serious challenge to age-old systems and traditions in the political milieu. One may love or hate the charismatic leader – the face of this historic youth-led movement – but, as an integral thread in this grand tapestry, he cannot be ignored.

10

OLD GUARD VS YOUNG TURK

Games for the Gaddi

A PECULIAR ANOMALY HAD NOT GONE UNNOTICED BY THOSE gathered near the majestic Albert Hall Museum in Jaipur on a cold December morning in 2018. Long rows of seats had been reserved for Congress leaders, former MLAs and their families to get a peek at the preparations for the swearing-in of the new government. After a long gap of five years, the Congress once again had another shot at power.

Albert Hall, built in the nineteenth century and named after British royalty, looked picturesque as hundreds of pigeons flapped above their home. Soon, VIP vehicles started lining up. Once the stage was occupied, Ashok Gehlot and Sachin Pilot could be seen seated on either side of then governor Kalyan Singh, who was to administer the chief ministerial and deputy chief ministerial oaths to them. Sixty-seven-year-old Gehlot was being sworn in as the Chief Minister of Rajasthan for the third time in his five-decade-long political career – it was a historic moment. 'As the Chief Minister of Rajasthan, I will execute my duties respectfully and with a clear heart,' he said, dressed in his trademark black kurta.

Then came the turn of the deputy chief minister to repeat the words. What followed cast a shadow over the faces of hundreds of Pilot supporters who were chanting slogans for their leader in the crowd. To their disappointment, they never heard the words that would distinguish him from the other cabinet ministers. 'As a minister of an Indian state,' Pilot read aloud, 'I will execute my duties respectfully and with a clear heart.' Unlike chief minister or assembly speaker, deputy chief minister was not a constitutional post – and hence does not come with a special oath – and it is commonly understood that political parties elevate leaders to the post of deputy chief minister merely for appeasement or optics' sake. Even though the Congress high command had managed to convince Pilot to accept the post despite his reluctance, it was obvious that the real power rested with Gehlot. Having had his eyes firmly set on the chair of the chief minister for the longest time, Pilot may have settled for the role of the deputy chief minister on paper, but in practice, everything – right from the swearing-in oath to his powers – were the same as that of any cabinet minister.

Three days before the swearing-in ceremony, the then Congress president Rahul Gandhi had tweeted a photo of a smiling Gehlot and Pilot standing on either side of him, with the caption, 'The united colours of Rajasthan!'[1] This was a much-needed photo op to counter the ridicule that was coming the Congress's way because of an apparent impasse about who would come to occupy the chief minister's post. While the decision had been relatively easy in the case of Madhya Pradesh, after Jyotiraditya Scindia had agreed to bow out of the CM race to make way for Kamal Nath, Pilot and Gehlot had been camping in New Delhi ever since the results of the 2018 assembly elections had been announced, and neither was in the mood to let go of the opportunity to bag the top post.[2]

A CLP meeting was held in Jaipur to gauge the opinions of various party MLAs on the chief ministerial candidate, but it came to nought, with the MLAs passing a resolution to authorize the Congress president to make a decision. Halfway through the meeting held at the Indira Gandhi Bhawan, Pilot emerged from his office and hastily bypassed the journalists waiting for his comments

– a departure from his usually media-friendly demeanour. A high-stakes game was afoot for the chief minister's chair and the pressure was clearly mounting.

Ramkesh Meena, an independent MLA from Gangapur City, did not mince his words in conveying who his choice for CM was. 'We independents are ready to support the Congress if Ashok Gehlot sahab is made the chief minister. There will be no negotiation on this condition,' Meena declared, still fuming over the Pilot-led Congress denying him a ticket to contest the elections.[3] The voices of independent MLAs like Meena had grown in relevance after the Congress had won ninety-nine seats in the assembly of 200 members, emerging one short of the halfway mark. At least ten of the thirteen independent MLAs expressed that they would support Congress only if Gehlot was made CM. Apart from their unflinching loyalty to Gehlot, they also had another reason for being opposed to Pilot. Despite spending decades in the party, they had been denied tickets under the leadership of Pilot, and later, when they had filed their nominations as independents, the Congress had expelled them.

It was at this point of time that the two-term CM Gehlot edged out the younger leader from the competition. Where had Pilot gone wrong after leading the party for four years in the state? A senior incumbent MLA remarked at Pilot not being able to convert the Gehlot loyalists. He had hoped that denying them tickets and replacing them with favourable candidates of his own would help turn the tide in his favour, but such was the groundswell of support for these leaders from the old guard that the public chose to vote for the Congress rebels over the official candidates of the party.[4] This made the Congress realize that it needed the support of the independents to form the government and sustain its regime, as they clearly offered an edge to Gehlot. These newly independent candidates were senior Congress leaders, after all, who understood that the public in their constituencies voted for the party because of them and would readily do so again if they were denied tickets and contested independently. Murlidhar Palsaniya, a former Congress block president, reiterated that he was confident of the victory of the independent since nobody in his constituency knew the Congress candidate. He was among the Congressmen from Shahpura who had resigned after Alok Beniwal was denied a ticket by Pilot. Beniwal had rebelled thereafter, contesting and winning the elections as an independent after defeating the Pilot-loyalist Manish Yadav, who was the Congress candidate. Election results showed that the young leaders Pilot had relied on to win the assembly elections had lost to the Congress-rebel candidates. Five years later, Yadav won the constituency in the 2023 assembly elections, but by then, Congress was again in the opposition.

As the results of the 2018 assembly elections came in, with the support of independent MLAs now decisively in his favour, Gehlot knew that even though the Gandhi family trusted Pilot, its primary concern was to install a stable government in Rajasthan. The grand old party had lost too many states to the BJP in recent times and was now focused on holding on to the ones it had won. In Madhya Pradesh, the Congress already had a paper-thin majority over the BJP. Knowing that rubbing the independent MLAs the wrong way in Rajasthan could further delay government formation, it did not persist in its preference for Pilot. What could have been the grand coronation of Pilot as CM was thus reduced to a show of tokenism, with him being assigned to the post of deputy chief minister as a consolation prize.

The wily, battle-hardened Gehlot had set the ball rolling in his favour a year in advance of the 2018 elections after the Congress's by-election win. His supporters, including former MP and later minister in Gehlot's cabinet Lal Chand Katariya, began making open declarations that Congress could form the government only under the leadership of Gehlot, who was then Congress General Secretary (Organization). He began setting time aside from attending to his responsibilities in New Delhi to visit the state frequently to assure his loyalists of his support. '*Main thansu door koni* (I am not far from you),' he would tell them, alluding to the fact that Pilot may be running the party in the state, but he, the old war horse, was still very much in the electoral race for the CM office. The swearing-in ceremony on the chilly December morning was but a display of having stood by his word to his supporters. He had successfully retained the number one spot.

A Divided Government

On Christmas Eve 2019, daily wage labourer Deepak Kushwaha could be seen frantically running down the corridors adjacent to the neo-natal intensive care unit (NICU) of the J. K. Lone government hospital in Kota, the biggest state-run medical facility for children. Despite Kushwaha's best efforts, his one-and-a-half-month-old infant daughter Mishti died tragically. The last forty-eight hours had left parents of ten children grief-stricken and the dismal situation and lack of facilities at the hospital were to blame for the mishap. The paediatrics department mentioned in its report that of the total 533 pieces of equipment at the hospital, 320 did not function.[5]

A heartbroken Kushwaha lamented how it had been a wasted effort rushing their child there as the doctors had rarely graced patients with a visit and people were allowed to enter the NICU without any restrictions or regard for medical protocol. Despite voicing these concerns, the authorities did not extend any further assistance to the patients or their attendants. Most of the distraught families who had gone to J. K. Lone could not afford private hospital expenses and were compelled to turn to the biggest government hospital in the area. Their hopes of providing their children with the best care the state had to offer were brutally dashed, leaving them to grieve the loss of precious lives instead. The one-year-old

Gehlot government received severe criticism for the deaths of the infants, and Health Minister Raghu Sharma blamed the previous BJP government for the lack of infrastructure at the hospital. The rebuttal to Sharma's statement, however, came from unexpected quarters.

'Our response to the entire episode could have been more sensitive, I think we should have been more compassionate. I feel that after 13 months of being in government, it may not serve any purpose to keep pointing to the previous government's misdeeds or wrongdoings,' said Deputy Chief Minister Sachin Pilot, after visiting the hospital and taking stock of the situation.[6] Pilot invited appreciation from then Rajasthan BJP president Satish Poonia, who lauded Pilot for being a 'mature leader'. This marked the beginning of a trend that came to characterize the seventeen-month period of Pilot's deputy chief ministership. Public suspicion that all was not well within the state government was reaffirmed when Pilot openly expressed his disagreement with the government on several important issues, his statements often sounding even more scathing than that of the opposition.

There were clearly two factions forming within the government: one that was loyal to Gehlot, who had an iron grip over even the smallest matters of every department, and the other that favoured Pilot, who may have held an important title, but had little power in practice. The first signs that the deputy chief minister's office would be of little importance emerged when Gehlot chose his council of ministers. Despite repeated lobbying by the Pilot camp, the three-time chief minister refused to part with his finance or home portfolios and, after forming the government, took the excise, general administration and agricultural marketing portfolios into his fold as well. The three ministers from Pilot's faction were put in charge of Tourism, Food and Civil Supplies, and Transport.

Among the departments under Pilot's care were the public works department (PWD) and the ministries of Panchayati Raj and rural development, apart from portfolios such as statistics and science and technology. But Pilot soon realized that despite this, his authority was limited. After he disagreed with Health Minister Raghu Sharma – once a close associate of Pilot's, who switched loyalties after Gehlot became CM – refusing to accept his argument that the previous BJP government was to be blamed for the J. K. Lone tragedy, Pilot was indirectly attacked when Sharma told the media that the maintenance of Kota hospital's facilities was the PWD's responsibility. A close aide of Pilot's confirmed that the deputy CM had tried reaching out to the department's secretary in the wake of the Kota hospital tragedy but had been met with indifference. The bureaucrat had not answered Pilot's calls at all, sending the clear message: CM Gehlot was in charge.[7] Once Pilot resigned to his fate and accepted that there was little he could do to influence policy or governance decisions, he assumed the role of a voice of conscience for the party, often putting the state government on the dock.

In 2019, Rajasthan Urban Development and Housing (UDH) Minister Shanti Dhariwal declared that his government had decided to adopt a 'hybrid' model for the election of mayoral candidates under local bodies. The new system was to enable a person to contest mayoral elections even without having been elected a councillor in the past, thus opening the doors for virtually anyone to hold the office as long as they were voted in by councillors. Pilot vehemently opposed the move: 'I want that the election should happen with the vote of the public,' adding that he felt the system may result in horse-trading.[8] Despite Dhariwal being Gehlot's right-hand man and not directly answerable to Pilot since UDH was not under the deputy CM, the government was compelled to heed to the clamour raised by Pilot's remarks and ultimately withdrew the order. This was a major victory for the deputy CM, who had demonstrated that even if he was denied direct influence in the government, he still held considerable sway over public opinion.

Pilot's actions as deputy CM to Gehlot were not much different from his actions as the leader of the opposition during the reign of former CM Raje. As the state president of the party, he toured across Rajasthan to meet with supporters and attended assembly sessions, but had little say in matters of governance. The response to a Right to Information (RTI) application revealed that the state government had spent over ₹25 crore on newspaper advertisements, but none of them featured Pilot's photograph; only CM Gehlot's picture was used.[9]

Another public incident from Pilot's deputy chief minister and party president era further underlined the unease between him and Gehlot. In 2019, when the media asked a question pertaining to the Gurjar community's threats of protest, Gehlot smiled and pointed towards Pilot, who was seated beside him during the press conference, asking the younger leader to answer. Pilot was annoyed by the redirection, owing to the well-known fact within the Rajasthan Congress circles that he detested being portrayed as a Gurjar leader, as the image restricted his appeal and boxed him in as merely a representative of his caste. 'Do you want your answer from the government or the party?' a visibly irritated Pilot retorted while Gehlot continued to smile. This instance exposed the dichotomy between the government and the party, which had grave implications for important political appointments which hung in the balance for more than two years after the Congress came to power. Since the two factions were perpetually at odds, supplying different lists of names to the party's high command for the appointments, important boards and commissions such as the women's commission, the minority commission and scheduled caste commission were forced to function without heads. The National Commission for Women (NCW) came down heavily on the Gehlot government in 2020 for not appointing a chairperson to its state counterpart despite repeated reminders. Pilot also chimed in routinely to point out that these posts were yet to be filled, emphasizing how crucial it was to make the party's supporters – its voters and workers – stakeholders in the government.[10] This was a stand that he was quite vocal about, publicly denouncing the state government's non-fulfilment of its promises to the Congress workers. The frequency of such statements was consistently increasing.

Throughout 2019 and early 2020, Pilot criticized the government over atrocities against Dalits and its various policy decisions, repeatedly reminding them to make good on the promises made in the party's election manifesto. With the bad blood between the deputy chief minister and chief minister rising with each passing day, the hostilities were bound to come to a head.

All-out War

'*Hum jaante the ye nikamma hai, nakara hai, kuch kaam nahi kar raha hai, khali logon ko ladwa raha hai* (We knew he was useless and worthless, and has nothing else to do but merely incite people to fight).'

It was unusual for the soft-spoken Ashok Gehlot to use such strong language, especially for his deputy chief minister – a man who had taken him pillion on a motorcycle during an election campaign. However, the full-blown political crisis that engulfed Rajasthan in July–August 2020 led to many firsts in the state's political history. It started with a notice under sections 124A (sedition) and 120B (criminal conspiracy) sent to Pilot by the special operations group (SOG) of the Rajasthan Police in early July 2020. The state police had lodged the FIR on its own, stating that they had tapped the phones of some unnamed accused persons who were discussing 'toppling' the Gehlot government and had mentioned that the 'Chief Minister and Deputy Chief Minister are having a fight ... Deputy CM says that he will be the CM'. While Pilot was not mentioned explicitly as an accused in the FIR, he and

CM Gehlot were both sent a notice under section 124A (sedition) to record their statements.[11]

For the police, which comes under the CM-controlled Home Department, sending a notice under the section pertaining to sedition to the deputy chief minister was an unprecedented move, never before witnessed in the history of the desert state. With it, the Gehlot–Pilot tussle that had been simmering over the last several years was definitively flung into the public view.

Pilot's faction had long been discontented over him being sidelined. His deputy chief ministerial powers curbed, Pilot had been reduced to a sitting duck in his party's government. His supporters, who had hoped to be rewarded after the Congress came to power, were growing impatient and enraged by the centralization of power in Gehlot's grip. Pilot feared that by accepting the status quo, he might end up losing supporters and his concern was not unfounded. The notice was the last straw and triggered a rebellion both as a tactic of putting pressure on the party to take Pilot seriously and to safeguard his supporters from further attacks by the Gehlot camp.

Transport minister and Jaipur district Congress president Pratap Singh Khachariyawas, former CM Bhairon Singh Shekhawat's nephew, had been Pilot's closest aide. 'How can Ashok Gehlot decide who will be the chief minister of Rajasthan?' he was heard saying in a leaked audio clip before the 2018 assembly elections.[12] In February 2020, the state anti-corruption bureau (ACB), which was under Gehlot, raided Khachariyawas's department to bust a bribery scam. After the incident came to light, while some MLAs raised a clamour against Gehlot, Khachariyawas switched loyalties to become Gehlot's steadfast supporter, and distanced himself from the Pilot-loyalist MLAs during the tussle between the two leaders. He was furious when MLA Mukesh Bhakar reminded him that he owed his career ascent to the Transport Department to Pilot. 'When Sachin Pilot ji used to wear knickers, I had already become the president of the Rajasthan University in 1992,' he retorted.[13] Avinash Pandey, the then Congress General Secretary in-charge for Rajasthan, also attracted the ire of the Pilot camp for being perceived as a Gehlot supporter.

The sedition notice sent to Pilot rang more alarm bells in his camp, as his supporters now began to fear they might be dragged into legal cases, hampering their prospects in politics for good. They felt that they needed to send a message to the Congress that Pilot's cooperation was not to be taken for granted. One group stood firmly with Pilot, with MLAs Vishvendra Singh, Ramesh Meena and Deependra Singh releasing a formal statement reiterating their support.

> For years, we have worked with dedication, devotion and service towards the party. And we are taking a stand to protect our dignity and self-respect at a time when our leader is threatened with notices from the SOG under the charges of sedition and criminal conspiracy. ... This is unprecedented in Indian democracy and the Congress party, for whom we have toiled with sweat and blood.[14]

Singh and Meena were sitting cabinet ministers at the time, while Shekhawat was a former assembly speaker. Pilot himself left Jaipur, along with eighteen of his supporter MLAs, who checked into a resort in Manesar, situated in BJP-ruled Haryana. These developments sent shockwaves through the Congress, which had seen former union minister Jyotiraditya Scindia leave the party and join the BJP just four months ago. With him, his loyalist MLAs had also left to join the saffron party, which had led to the Congress losing its government in Madhya Pradesh.

As senior party leaders rushed to Rajasthan for damage control, a triumphant Gehlot stepped up onto the footrest of his car and launched into a long diatribe against Pilot before the media. The speech, quoted at the beginning of this section, has become famous due to the CM's unusual choice of adjectives. He also claimed that Pilot had been using disrespectful language for the last seven years, making remarks like 'I am not here to sell brinjals or vegetables, I have come here to be the CM', and accused Pilot of conspiring to topple the government for the last six months.[15]

One of the first fallouts of the political crisis was the removal of Pilot from his offices of deputy chief minister and state Congress president by the party high command. The new PCC chief was Education Minister Govind Singh Dotasra, a Jat leader and Gehlot supporter. Following his unceremonial removal, Pilot posted on X on 14 July 2020 in Hindi, '*Satya ko pareshan kiya ja sakta hai, parajit nahi* (The truth can be troubled, but not defeated).'[16] The party also dissolved all district and block Congress committees to purge them of Pilot's supporters. The heads of the Congress's student wing NSUI, Youth Congress and Congress Seva Dal were also replaced with leaders close to Gehlot.

What followed was a month-long period of great political uncertainty with both sides trying to outplay each other. The more than 100 MLAs who were supporting Gehlot were first shifted to the Hotel Fairmont in Jaipur, and later to the Suryagarh luxury resort in Jaisalmer, where they spent days chatting or indulging in activities such as cooking or yoga. This was done to ensure that no further Congress legislators defected to Pilot's camp. The number of MLAs supporting Pilot would have been much more if not for a major blow to Pilot at the very last minute, delivered by another group of MLAs.

Initially, it had been claimed that nearly forty MLAs were supported Pilot, which would have meant that the Gehlot government was in the minority. But by the end, only eighteen MLAs were found standing by Pilot. A group of legislators that did initially go to camp with the rest of the Pilot loyalist MLAs was placated and convinced to return to the party's fold by their family members; most of them were second-or third-generation politicians whose families had been associated with the Congress for many decades. Without their families' intervention, it would have been difficult to bring leaders such as Danish Abrar and Rohit Bohra to abandon their rebellion, according to a senior Congress minister in the state government between 2018 and 2023. Two years later, in September 2022, Gehlot himself acknowledged the role played by Sawai Madhopur MLA Danish Abrar in saving his government. He credited Abrar not only for extending his unyielding support to the leader, but for passing on 'timely information' that enabled Gehlot to save the party and ensure he remained CM, with Ahmed Patel, Sonia Gandhi's political secretary at the time, closely monitoring the situation. What Gehlot meant was that Abrar had tipped him off about Pilot's rebellion, which helped him spring into damage control in a timely manner and ensure that no more legislators joined the younger leader. Incidentally, thirty-nine-year-old Danish Abrar was among those considered to have been close to Pilot before the rebellion.

Congress insiders say that what led to MLAs such as Abrar, Bohra and Chetan Dudi returning from Delhi was their fear that Pilot would 'pull off a Scindia' and join the BJP. A minister from the Gehlot camp explained that Abrar's father was an MP, and Bohra's father, Pradhyuman Singh, was among the seniormost living Congress leaders. Singh and Abrar's mothers sat their children down and explained to them that would be no future for them in the BJP.[17]

The role of the BJP during the 2020 political crisis has remained a provocative subject for both the Gehlot and Pilot camps. While Gehlot publicly accused Pilot of conspiring with the BJP to topple his government, the latter has always vehemently denied the accusations. Interestingly, the BJP – usually vocal about its opinions on every issue as the opposition party – has maintained a silence on the subject of helping Pilot's camp during the crisis. The facts of the situation are as follows: it is known that when a team of officials from the Rajasthan Police went to Manesar to meet with the rebel MLAs, the BJP government obstructed their interaction. The party even remained overtly sympathetic towards Pilot throughout the duration of the political crisis in the state, springing to his defence in the face of Gehlot's accusations that the younger leader had never had to experience *ragdai* (toil) and was used to getting things easily. Senior BJP leader Rajendra Rathore, who at the time was the deputy leader of opposition, pointed out in the assembly how Gehlot had himself become an MP in 1980, when he was merely twenty-nine years old, a central minister four years later and the CM at forty-seven. He ended his retort with 'Now who should have toiled and how?'[18]

The then leader of the opposition in Rajasthan, Gulab Chand Kataria, had showered praise upon Pilot for the work done by his Panchayati Raj and Rural Development Departments in ensuring that a large section of the population benefitted from the MGNREGS after the COVID-19 pandemic. Baijayant 'Jay' Panda, then the BJP national vice president, chose to make more cryptic remarks. 'In aviation, every flight plan includes an alternate airport or airstrip to divert to in the event of technical problems or severe bad weather. Every experienced pilot knows this,' he had posted on X during the month-long standoff.[19]

Phone Tapping, Viral Audios and Court Battles

On 16 July 2020, two days after Sachin Pilot was removed from his twin posts of deputy CM and state Congress president, the Gehlot camp dropped an audio bombshell. The chief minister's officer on special duty (OSD) Lokesh Sharma sent three audio clips to media persons. The Congress claimed that one audio clip featured BJP MP from Jodhpur and union minister Gajendra Singh Shekhawat talking to Bhanwar Lal Sharma, Congress MLA from Sardarshahar in Churu, through one Sanjay Jain, who they claimed was a member of the BJP. Sharma was one of the eighteen rebel MLAs who had sided with Pilot.

In another audio clip, a voice that was alleged to be of Vishvendra Singh, an MLA from Deeg-Kumher in Bharatpur, who had earlier been removed from office by the Congress when he had been tourism minister, can purportedly be heard telling an unknown person that those in Delhi 'have taken the money'. Singh, who at the time was camping with Pilot, denied the allegations. These allegations by the Gehlot camp were meant to portray Pilot and his associates as colluding with the BJP – something that the younger leader and his loyalist MLAs have always denied.[20]

With the Gehlot camp going for the BJP's jugular, the saffron party was cornered into hitting back. While Shekhawat denied outright that it was his voice in the audio clip, his party accused Congress of illegally tapping the phones of public representatives. Two FIRs were lodged by the police, even though Shekhawat was not named by the cops as an accused; instead, the FIR mentioned one Gajendra Singh. The identity of this person was unclear, as at the time, apart from union minister Shekhawat, one of the eighteen loyalist MLAs siding with Pilot was Gajendra Singh Shaktawat, who later passed away in 2021. It was also not revealed how OSD Lokesh Sharma came into possession of the audio clips. While he maintained that he got them from 'social media', the opposition was insistent that the government was illegally tapping phones.

Months later, Shekhawat registered an FIR with the Delhi Police against OSD Sharma, accusing him of criminal conspiracy. It was at this time that a new phrase entered the glossary of Rajasthan's political and journalistic circles, 'WhatsApp calling'. Everyone from sitting cabinet ministers to government officials would agree to talk only via WhatsApp, afraid of having their phones tapped or calls recorded. Later, as the Congress was voted out of power, OSD Sharma would turn state's witness in the phone tapping case lodged by Shekhawat, claiming he received the audio files from Gehlot, even releasing an audio recording of a purported conversation between himself and the former CM discussing how the electronic devices used to share the recording of phone tapping had been destroyed.[21]

Parallelly, there was drama unfolding at the Rajasthan High Court as well, which had become a second battlefront for the two groups. Right after Pilot and his followers defied the party whip and skipped the CLP meeting called in Jaipur, assembly speaker C. P. Joshi was prompt to issue notices to them demanding explanations. The notice meant that Joshi had started the process of disqualifying all eighteen MLAs and Pilot from the assembly on account of not following the party whip. Both sides were now fighting it out in a court battle and the lawyers defending the Pilot camp justifiably invited a few raised eyebrows – advocates Harish Salve, a former Solicitor General of India who regularly represented the BJP government in the centre in legal matters and Mukul Rohatgi was the Attorney General of India during the first term of the Narendra Modi government.

Within days, a second front was opened by the BSP, which approached the court to object against the merger of six BSP MLAs into the Congress, giving Gehlot a crucial edge in the numbers game. Now there were four sides in the battle – the Gehlot camp, the Pilot camp, the former BSP MLAs and the BSP itself. What became apparent during that period of political turmoil was that despite Gehlot having the upper hand, there were more than a few MLAs willing to combine forces with Pilot to challenge the chief minister's authority. This was a first-time phenomenon in Gehlot's twenty-two-year-long rule in the Rajasthan Congress: such open defiance of his authority.

Pilot loyalist MLA Mukesh Bhakar was removed from his post as state president of the Youth Congress. Disgruntled, he said, 'I became state president of the Youth Congress after winning elections. Who is Ashok Gehlot to remove me? Gehlot and his ministers are busy trying to defeat a son of a farmer–soldier.'[22] Young leaders such as Bhakar and Ramniwas Gawriya – the fiercest supporters of Pilot during the political crisis – were products of the Pilot era. They had made their way through university politics and were some of the student leaders fielded by Pilot to contest – and win – the assembly elections.

After a month-long impasse, the Gehlot–Pilot political crisis ended just before 15 August, when Pilot and his MLAs returned to Rajasthan after a temporary truce had been brokered between the two leaders by Priyanka Vadra and Ahmed Patel. The police cases against the Pilot camp MLAs were put on the backburner and a committee was formed to address their grievances. Subsequently, the two sides met during a motion of confidence in the Rajasthan assembly, where Pilot emphatically declared that he will always be a 'soldier' of the party.

Despite the truce, the ripples of this episode could be felt throughout 2020. It was reported in October 2020 – two months after an understanding was reached by the warring factions – that the Rajasthan police had registered an FIR against Pilot's media manager and a senior journalist for running a story about his camp's allegations of phone tapping, which involved a few state police officers.[23] A few months later, in December 2020, the police closed the case and filed a final report saying that no evidence had been found.[24]

So why had Pilot's rebellion not succeeded? The fact is that the Pilot camp was lacking in numbers. Some MLAs who had initially gone to Delhi with Pilot later jumped ship, and served to deal a fatal blow to the young leader's chances of arm-twisting the Congress high command into a regime change. The main difference between the circumstances of Scindia's exit and Pilot's rebellion was that unlike Scindia – who later became a union minister under BJP – Pilot did not have any intentions of stepping away from Rajasthan's politics. His prospects in the BJP were not promising, considering how the party already had a well-established state leadership in place, along with its own share of power tussles among ambitious leaders. Unwilling to settle for anything less than the chief minister's chair, Pilot understood that even a short break from the state's political scene could jeopardize his prospects. His rebellion may have failed, but Pilot had achieved two major objectives – flexing his political muscle and sending the message to the party high command that he was not to be taken for granted.

Pilot's Second Coming Stopped

The scene near the District Congress Committee (DCC) office in Tonk – Pilot's assembly constituency – in September 2022, more than two years after the political crisis, serves as a perfect example of the impact that the Gehlot–Pilot feud had had on the Congress party's organization in Rajasthan. Situated in a busy market area adjacent to the Jama Masjid, the DCC office remained locked in September 2022 in the absence of a serving president. A government dispensary operated out of its ground floor. Even with the December 2023 assembly elections just a year away, the Congress in Tonk, like in most other districts of Rajasthan, remained without a district president and office bearers, its offices mostly closed. Large hoardings of Pilot, erected over busy roadside *dhabas* and shops selling lac bangles, carried the names of all the Congress leaders who had installed those signages, their designations prefixed with 'former'.

Lakshman Choudhary Gata had been the last district president of Tonk before all block and district Congress committees were dissolved by the party in the wake of Pilot's rebellion. Two years later, Gata was still loyal to the MLA: 'The Congress party was decimated to twenty-one seats [in the 2013 polls]. It was Pilot sahab who worked hard and brought the Congress to power,' he said in 2022.[25] This was an oft-repeated statement by both Pilot and his supporters, aimed at bolstering their argument for a leadership change in Rajasthan. The excitement of the Tonk public in anticipation of seeing their MLA occupy the chief ministerial chair fizzled out after the repeated outmanoeuvring by CM Ashok Gehlot. The town was hopeful for a second coming of Pilot in September 2022, when Gehlot was set to file his nomination for the Congress's national president elections. A close aide of Pilot's, Tonk Municipal Council chairman Ali Ahmed said at the time that it was now or never, having grown sceptical and wary of waiting since 2018. His apprehensions were proved right just a few days later.

An independent MLA in the state government received a call from Pilot requesting his support and knew the leader would be reaching out to other MLAs as well. But having worked with Gehlot for many years, he was sure the veteran leader had a card up his sleeve to snag the CM chair from Pilot's grasp once again. A senior Congress leader with connections within the party high command had revealed that the leadership had been set on making Pilot the CM and if Gehlot somehow managed to change their minds, he deserved to be saluted. After the events of 25 September 2022, the independent merely called the senior leader and asked him to go salute Gehlot.

The day will go down in the state Congress's history as a watershed moment when a fifty-year-old tradition was broken by Gehlot. Starting from the early 1970s, the Congress high command had changed sitting chief ministers of Rajasthan on a whim, never facing any resistance from the outgoing leaders. During the prime ministership of Indira Gandhi and her son Rajiv, the Congress changed five chief ministers in just one decade during the 1980s. The reasons for this ranged from criticism for the government after police encounters, to a chief minister telling a poet that he did not understand her poems. But something changed on 25 September 2022, when the Congress high command, substantially weakened after the defeat during the Narendra Modi-led BJP era, had to swallow its pride and face the ultimate humiliation – one of its own leaders openly defying its orders.

The day had started on a note of sombre acceptance. The party had announced that a meeting of party MLAs was set to be held at Gehlot's residence. Senior leader Mallikarjun Kharge, who would later become the Congress national president, had accompanied the party general secretary in-charge Ajay Maken to Jaipur for the meeting. Many felt that it was the end of the road for Gehlot, who would finally have to relinquish the chief minister's post to Pilot before filing his nomination for the party's presidential elections. Even until later in the day, Gehlot seemed to have accepted his fate. 'It is on my mind that the new generation should get a chance. Since the party has trusted me, it is my duty that whatever they tell me, I will accept it. I will brief the person who becomes the next chief minister to focus on the youth and students in the Budget,' Gehlot was seen saying in Jaisalmer, as if graciously clearing the path for Pilot.[26]

The Congress high command sensed an opportunity that could help them get two birds with one stone – silencing the opposition on its accusations of dynasty politics by elevating a non-Gandhi to the post of Congress president and bringing down the curtains on the long-standing tussle between Gehlot and Pilot. A year before the 2023 assembly elections, they were in the process of moving the veteran politician out of Rajasthan and onto the national stage, while installing Pilot as the chief minister. But the day had more drama in store. By the evening, over eighty MLAs loyal to Gehlot had assembled at the residence of Parliamentary Affairs minister Shanti Dhariwal, instead of attending the official party meeting. Dhariwal demanded to know of the high command what had offended them so about Gehlot that the leader was being asked to resign. He said the 'conspiracy' had already cost them Punjab, and they were now being set up to lose Rajasthan as well. If they were not alert, the desert state was surely going to slip from their grasp.

What followed was a repeat of the 2020 political crisis. The only difference was that it was now Gehlot camp's turn to defy the high command. These eighty MLAs of the ruling Congress walked into the premises of Bungalow number 49, Civil Lines – the residence of assembly speaker C. P. Joshi – to tender their resignations. The legislators had been brought on specially arranged buses parked outside the gates, while police personnel were busy cordoning off the area from the public. TV channel crews were reporting minute-by-minute developments, their faces illuminated by the floodlights that had been brought in on the outside broadcast vans stationed outside the speaker's house.

Some of the policemen drove away a group chanting slogans in support of former deputy chief minister Sachin Pilot, whose crowning as CM had once again been stalled by these legislators who were submitting their resignations. Just a few hundred metres away, Pilot himself was sitting and waiting for a CLP meeting to commence at 13, Civil Lines, Ashok Gehlot's official residence. Veteran Congress leaders Kharge and Maken were waiting with Pilot, watching as the state legislators openly defied the party leadership by skipping the meeting.

Minister Pratap Singh Khachariyawas, the former Pilot aide who had turned into a staunch Gehlot supporter asserted that democracy was built on the principle of numerical majority – the ten to fifteen MLAs siding with Pilot stood no chance of bending the will of 100 MLAs supporting Gehlot.[27] The latter camp of MLAs said they would attend the CLP meeting only on one condition: nobody among Pilot or his supporters would be made the chief minister. Independent MLA Sanyam Lodha said the next CM should be a party loyalist, like the 102 who were at Fairmont Hotel, Jaipur, and Suryagarh Resort, Jaisalmer, during the 2020 political crisis. He said it was their unanimous decision that none among those who conspired with the BJP to commit *gaddari* (treason) and topple the government could be allowed to be CM. The Congress high command was left red-faced and by nightfall, it was clear to the two leaders who were representing then Congress president Sonia Gandhi that the legislators were not going to turn up for the CLP meeting which was meant to pave the way for a change of guard in the state. In just two years, a second political crisis had gripped India's largest state.

With less than a year to the 2023 assembly elections, Pilot started a new chapter in his life. After serving as party president, deputy chief minister, rebel and MLA, he was now once again preparing for the assembly elections. It had merely been two months since he had been called a traitor by Gehlot, who didn't hold back while emphatically stating in an interview that come what may, Pilot can't be made the chief minister.[28]

The former deputy chief minister himself had refrained from attacking Gehlot. Instead, he had curtly denied the allegations and on some other occasions, merely made indirect jibes at his political rival. Taking the moral high ground, Pilot said at a college gathering in Jaipur in January 2023 that he did not use language for a rival he wouldn't use for himself, and that while it was easy to level personal allegations and use abusive language, there was much more to be gained from simply holding one's tongue. He was cognizant of the fact that once something was said, it could not be taken back. Flanked by his trusted group of Congress leaders and MLAs, he moved from district to district over the span of a week to address *kisan sammelans* (farmers' conference), seizing the opportunity to both mobilize his supporters before the elections later in the year, and show his strength to let the Gehlot camp know that he was still very much in the fray for the top post.

At one of his rallies, Pilot said that before the 2018 assembly elections, he had gone to Delhi to pay a visit to the Gandhis and emphasized the importance of Congress empowering the youth. For five years, there were 163 MLAs in Vasundhara Raje's government, while Congress had only twenty-one legislators. During the five years he was party president, he made the effort to reach out to every worker, which served as a reminder to Rahul Gandhi and Sonia Gandhi about his role in rallying the Congress together and bringing it to power in the state.

In another instance, he paid Gehlot back in kind, aiming an indirect jibe at the CM who is often called a 'jaadugar' – both due to his undeniable shrewdness as a politician and for belonging to a family of magicians – over questions about why examination question papers were being leaked in the state. He wondered aloud how a question paper secured inside a locker could get leaked, remarking, '*Ye toh jaadugari ho gayi bhai, aise kaise ho sakta hai*? (It must be the work of a magician, how else is it even possible?)'. It was evident that their rivalry was far from over.

Such verbal volleys have often marked the feud between the two leaders battling out for bagging the top post in the desert state.

The Congress's defeat in the 2023 assembly elections once again relegated the party to the opposition and put an interlude in the power tussle between Gehlot and Pilot. After the electoral loss, Pilot, who by now had become a member of the CWC, was put in charge of the party unit in Chhattisgarh in December 2023. Gehlot was not given any organizational duties, but he continued to act as an agent of scrutiny and criticism of the ruling BJP government led by Bhajan Lal Sharma and participated in Congress party events.

On 11 June 2025, Gehlot and many of his loyalist MLAs turned up at Pilot's father Rajesh Pilot's memorial in Dausa to pay their respects on his death anniversary. Senior *Indian Express* journalist Hamza Khan remarked at how the relations between Pilot and Gehlot seemingly came full circle at the event as it was on this exact day five years ago that Pilot had been planning to lead a rebellion ahead of the Rajya Sabha elections in the state, according to Gehlot, prompting him to sequester the MLAs in resorts a day in advance.[29] Five years later, Gehlot was heard saying that he and Sachin Pilot 'were never far apart' and that 'the love has always been there', even as Pilot himself stuck to more formal statements.

According to Khan, the June 2025 meeting showed a 'thawing' or 'resetting' of the relations between the two leaders – a marked departure from Gehlot's infamous 'nakaara' and 'nikamma' barbs levelled at Pilot.[30] However, in the authors' view, it is at best a truce aided by the fact that the party is not in power. It is undoubtedly helpful for the Congress to maintain a united front while they are not actively involved in an electoral tussle, but as Khan says, 'The Gehlot versus Pilot story is far from over.' In all likelihood, the next chapter of the feud is expected to be written as we approach the 2028 assembly elections. Regardless of who emerges as the final winner in this tug of war, this is one of the most remarkable rivalries in Rajasthan's political history.

11

A NEW DAWN

2023 Assembly Polls and After

ONE DAY, IN MARCH 2023, JOURNALISTS IN JAIPUR RECEIVED PHONE calls inviting them to dinner at 8, Civil Lines, the official residence of CM Ashok Gehlot. This was par for the course, except that the voice extending the invite did not belong to the CM's OSD Lokesh Sharma, who was usually the one communicating with the media. 'We are from DesignBoxed,'* the unfamiliar voice at the other end clarified.

For the next ten months in the run up to the assembly elections, young professionals and consultants working with this political campaigning agency based in Chandigarh could be spotted across the state in all assembly constituencies, conducting surveys and devising marketing strategies – ranging from cash prize rewards for creating videos showing the success of government schemes to enhancing Gehlot's image as a good administrator. They had a singular objective: to help the CM break from the twenty-five-year-old trend of incumbent governments being voted out every

* For more on the DesignBoxed campaign for Gehlot, see Hamza Khan, 'Rajasthan polls behind him, strategist for Cong, Gehlot lays out his role: 'Not about telling anyone how to contest', *The Indian Express*, 27 November 2023. Available at: https://indianexpress.com/article/political-pulse/rajasthan-polls-strategist-congress-gehlot-role-9042935/.

five years. The hiring of the agency was not entirely unexpected as there was certainly a need for a fresh approach – as Gehlot himself had admitted to journalists attending the aforementioned dinner at his residence in April 2023. He said that in his experience, it had been difficult to convince the public to vote for the incumbent government, although he seemed optimistic now that he had the support of his political consultants and marketing managers. 'We are getting very good response to our schemes,' Gehlot had said, armed with the insights from the extensive surveys and analyses conducted by his PR team.

In a state such as Rajasthan, where the electoral contest is primarily between the Congress and BJP with very little scope for any third player, even a slight difference in voting percentage could translate to the gain or loss of several seats.* Gehlot understood this well and was determined to use every opportunity to tilt the public favour towards the Congress. Given the historical trend, there was a dire need for the Congress to find a new narrative that had mass appeal and could convince the public to stick to the incumbent regime this time around. As per the surveys, the Gehlot government's welfare schemes were their best bet, alongside reiterating the CM's penchant for good governance. However, the feud between Gehlot and Sachin Pilot was ongoing in the background, putting the rifts within the party on full display.

In April 2023, Pilot staged a day-long fast and dharna against his own party's government for not taking action in the alleged corruption cases against the previous Vasundhara Raje government. He also organized a Jan Sangharsh Yatra to protest against corruption in the Rajasthan Public Service Commission (RPSC).[1]

---

* Back in 2018, the Congress's vote share was 39.8 per cent while that of the BJP was 39.3 per cent. However, the paper-thin margin of 0.5 per cent votes had meant that the Congress had won twenty-seven more seats than the BJP's seventy-three. Source: '2018 Vidhan Sabha/assembly election results Rajasthan', India Votes. Available at: https://www.indiavotes.com/vidhan-sabha/2018/rajasthan/268/14.

On the other hand, Gehlot claimed at an event in Dholpur that Raje had helped him during the 2020 political crisis.[2] The claim invited a strong denial from Raje,[3] but Pilot took the opportunity to allege that Gehlot's 'real leader' was not his party president, Sonia Gandhi, but Raje.[4] Verbal volleys between the two continued even as the district Congress prepared to go into election mode in the absence of any office bearers for nearly three years. In May 2023, the Congress high command finally put a stop to the Gehlot–Pilot tussle. Congress President Mallikarjun Kharge, along with Rahul Gandhi, conducted talks with the two leaders, after which they jointly declared that they would be contesting the state elections together. This was the last round of talks directed at resolving the Gehlot–Pilot conflict as the state was now gearing up to go to polls.

The professionally crafted electoral campaign of the Congress projected Gehlot as the face of good governance and highlighted his government's welfare schemes in new and innovative ways. Over the next few months, large hoardings in pink with Gehlot's smiling face were put up in every corner of the state with the details of welfare schemes listed alongside an appeal for the public to once again vote him into the CM office. As part of this latter effort, the party announced a daily prize of ₹2.75 lakh to the winner of the Jan Samman Video Contest, wherein social media influencers were asked to make videos on various flagship schemes of the Rajasthan government.[5] The Gehlot administration also started 'Mehangai Rahat Camps', or inflation relief camps, to streamline the process of registration for these government schemes. However, despite the elaborate marketing campaign designed by professional poll strategists, the public remained unconvinced. Govind Sahay, a resident of Jaipur who irons clothes for a living, was among those who attended an inflation relief camp in Jaipur and when asked about whether the effort was likely to improve the Congress's chances, responded, '*Kuch nahin hoga* (Nothing will work)'.[6]

BJP's Novel Campaign

The fact that the BJP did not want to further any existing regional monopolies was well-known, but in a completely unprecedented move, the party centred its entire 2023 electoral campaign around PM Narendra Modi, rather than a representative from the state or CM forerunner. The PM himself made an appearance at a public meeting in Bharatpur and declared, '*Jaadugar ji, koni mile vote ji* (Mr Magician, you're not getting any votes)', urging the public to vote for the BJP.[7] His prediction did come true, as was discovered on the morning of 3 December 2023, when the counting of votes for the Rajasthan assembly elections took place.

Despite CM Gehlot's painstaking efforts to bag a fourth tenure, history repeated itself and the incumbent government was once again unseated by a comfortable lead. While the Congress performed better than it had in the last two elections in 2003 and 2013, the results were nowhere close to what Gehlot had hoped for. The Congress won a mere sixty-nine seats compared to the BJP's whopping 115 with PM Narendra Modi as the only face of its campaign. It was the start of a new era, wherein for the first time, the winning party had not needed a state leader to support its electoral bid.

Vasundhara Raje, who had been projected as the official chief ministerial candidate of the saffron party previously in 2003 and 2013 and led the Parivartan Yatra and Suraj Sankalp Yatra into the state's various constituencies on behalf of the party, was now relegated to organizing yatras on her own initiative. She had made it a point to undertake Dev Darshan Yatras, or temple visits, where she would meet and mobilize her supporters, but had been relatively sidelined in the two official yatras the BJP organized against the Gehlot government – the Jan Aakrosh Yatra and the Parivartan Sankalp Yatra. Instead, these were helmed by PM Modi, Home Minister Amit Shah and the national party president

J. P. Nadda, who occupied centre-stage, addressing multiple rallies and urging the public to vote for a 'double engine' government with the centre and state governments working in tandem.

The fact that the central leadership had decided to take over the reins of the Rajasthan state unit became evident in early 2023, when it appointed Chittorgarh MP C. P. Joshi, a Brahmin leader, as the party's state president in Rajasthan. A former student leader from the Congress-affiliated NSUI, who later switched to the BJP,* Joshi was an unlikely choice for the post of the state BJP president, which was held at the time by Satish Poonia, a veteran Jat leader. In fact, Poonia had been instrumental in sidelining Raje by bringing several of her detractors back into the party fold with the blessings of the BJP central leadership. It was expected that even at the end of his three-year tenure, Poonia would be permitted to continue in his role till the December 2023 assembly elections. With Joshi's elevation, the high command surprised its own leaders and reaffirmed its authority over state-level forces. Joshi kept to the course mandated for him by the party's central leadership and would remind the public and party leaders at every turn that the elections were being contested under the banner of the PM.

The BJP's campaign was focused on attacking the Congress over issues such as deteriorating law and order, corruption and question paper leaks. The most potent weapon in its arsenal was Hindutva, with party leaders right up to Nadda and PM Modi accusing the Congress of practising 'appeasement politics' at the cost of Hindu citizens. It became routine at almost all BJP rallies to hear the party leaders bring up the murder of Kanhaiya Lal, a tailor in Udaipur, by two Muslim men alongside accusations of

---

* A detailed timeline of Joshi's career can be found here: 'Political career of CP Joshi: जोशी की NSUI से हुई शुरुआत, छात्रसंघ अध्यक्ष बनने के बाद शेखावत ने दिलाई थी भाजपा की सदस्यता', ETV Bharat, 23 March 2023. Available at: https://www.etvbharat.com/hindi/rajasthan/state/chittaurgarh/know-political-career-of-cp-joshi-from-nsui-to-joining-bjp-by-bhairon-singh-shekhawat/rj20230323193839753753350.

the Congress paying less compensation to Kanhaiya Lal's family than to the family of Iqbal, a Muslim man who was killed in a later incident by a mob in Jaipur over a dispute involving a road accident. On each of these occasions, the Congress issued counter statements and provided evidence of the compensation paid to Kanhaiyalal's family, disproving all such claims.[8]

Yet, the consistent reiteration of these allegations by the BJP appears to have succeeded in turning public perception against the Congress, going by the election results, when the several Hindu priests fielded by the BJP, including Balak Nath and Balmukund Acharya, managed to win on the basis of their highly polarized campaigns. An important factor that harmed the Congress's prospects in the 2023 polls was their inability to replace anti-incumbency-ridden MLAs with new faces. As a result, a majority of the council of ministers under Gehlot were beaten by BJP candidates. Thus, a combination of Hindutva propaganda, a campaign built on Modi's widespread popularity and the natural anti-incumbency sentiment towards the Congress worked to bring the BJP to power despite the Congress's professionally managed publicity efforts.

However, with Raje effectively distanced from the limelight and no other state leader being declared as BJP's official candidate in her place, the air was thick with suspense: who was going to be the next CM?

End of an Era

The crowd of hundreds of BJP workers buzzed with excitement as they gathered along both sides of Jaipur's Sardar Patel Marg, where the state BJP headquarters is located. They waved party flags and waited for the moment when they could finally light their firecrackers. The mood was set for the celebrations to begin, but there was a longer wait in store. The media, too, was huddled outside the BJP office, speculating as they had been doing for the last five years in preparation for this moment.

Nearly a fortnight had passed since the BJP had wrested Rajasthan from the Congress, but neither the party's supporters nor the media had any inkling about who was going to succeed Ashok Gehlot. When the party finally called a meeting of all its MLAs on the evening of 12 December 2023, all eyes were on Vasundhara Raje.

Ever since the election results had been declared on the third, journalists had been waiting near 13, Civil Lines, Raje's official residence. The newly elected MLAs – many of whom were Raje's supporters and whose campaigns were supported by the former CM in more than forty-five constituencies – arrived at her bungalow in SUVs, quietly met their leader and left, remaining tight-lipped in the face of the flurry of questions lobbed at them by the media. While some of the stauncher supporters did speak publicly in Raje's support, most remained silent. As for Raje, she confined herself to her residence throughout this period except on one occasion, when she went to Delhi to meet J. P. Nadda.

Until nine months ago, she had been far from reticent. She had put her charisma and crowd-pulling capabilities on full display on her birthday celebrations in March that year, where thousands of her supporters were seen chanting 'Rajasthan *mein* Vasundhara'. After staying in the shadows for five years and being sidelined by the state party unit under Satish Poonia, Raje's grand birthday celebrations were her way of communicating her stature and importance to her party – she could very much run for the chief minister's chair a third time.

For nearly twelve hours, the massive crowds continued to swell as various lavish cars drove in and out of the temple town of Salasar in Churu district, much to the surprise of locals. While the Salasar Balaji temple is known to be one of the holiest pilgrimages in the state, the thousands of BJP workers – including present and former Sarpanch,

MLAs, MPs and other office bearers – had not been flocking to it for that reason. They had been gathering to join in Raje's seventieth birthday celebrations. This served to enhance her image as the natural choice for the CM's post – a perception held by the majority of BJP workers, despite scepticism regarding the party's central leadership's stance on giving her another opportunity.[9] There was no doubt about her popularity far surpassing that of the other chief minister aspirants in the party. She still was the most recognizable face of the BJP in Rajasthan.

However, the party had not needed her at the helm to secure its comfortable majority of 115 seats in the 2023 polls.

12 December 2023, the day of Vasundhara Raje's reckoning, finally arrived. By now, the BJP had replaced Shivraj Singh Chouhan in Madhya Pradesh, who had ruled the state for sixteen years and had been a major reason the party could secure a brute majority in the 2023 assembly elections as well. In his place, the very junior and unlikely CM candidate Mohan Yadav had been appointed CM. This filled the Raje camp with a sense of foreboding as they realized that their leader's chances at the top post were rather bleak.[10]

The show of strength by Raje had been effective as it compelled the BJP leadership, albeit grudgingly, to acknowledge the fact that they had to take her into confidence before the name of the new CM was revealed to the other MLAs. For this, the party high command chose union minister Rajnath Singh, one of the few remaining BJP leaders from the Vajpayee era and a contemporary of Raje's. The two had a one-on-one meeting at Singh's hotel after Raje received him at the airport before the MLAs' meeting. At the MLAs' meeting, as the cameras remained squarely focused on Raje, Singh asked her to open the chit of paper bearing the name of the new CM and she could do little to conceal her surprise. Most of the other BJP leaders present in the room mirrored her initial reaction once she announced the name of Bhajan Lal Sharma.[11]

Outside the party headquarters, the supporters who had been waiting for several hours, finally found a name to chant. As the sound of firecrackers filled the air, their slogan reverberated, 'Bhajan Lal Sharma zindabad! (Long live Bhajan Lal Sharma)'.

The Surprise CM

The evening of 12 December placed an unforeseen challenge before the Rajasthan BJP media cell. As the phones in their office rang endlessly with multiple news outlets calling to ask for a short bio for the newly crowned chief minister to carry in the news, they dilly-dallied for some time before they were compelled to divulge the truth.

'We are finding details about him and putting up a bio that we will share with the media in some time,' said a party leader. He was bombarded with further questions, including if it was true that Bhajan Lal Sharma had gone to Ayodhya and been arrested for *kar seva* during the Babri agitation. The leader wryly responded, 'Even I went to Ayodhya during the Ram Janmabhoomi movement,' implying that the new CM was but one of many and the event had played no role in his appointment to the top post.[12] This conversation revealed the bafflement within the BJP after its central leadership declared its choice of CM for India's geographically largest state.

Earlier in the day, when the newly elected MLAs had presented themselves at the BJP headquarters, they had been asked to gather for a group photograph. Sharma, a first-time MLA from Sanganer – one of BJP's safest seats in Jaipur – could be seen standing in the last row, while senior leaders such as Raje were seated in the front. A few hours later, Sharma became the first person after Gehlot and Raje to occupy the CM's chair in the state since 1998.

Another telling visual from the day came in the moments before the MLAs entered the meeting room for the new CM announcement. As the newly elected legislators followed each other in, RSS's Chandrashekhar – the low-profile organizational general secretary of Rajasthan – was seen egging Bhajan Lal Sharma on with a hand on his back, leaving little doubt as to whether his appointment had the approval of the Sangh.

Sharma's appointment was so unexpected that the media cell took an unusual amount of time tracking down the details of his nondescript political journey. As the state BJP's general secretary and in-charge of the party's headquarters, Sharma had worked with all major leaders of the Rajasthan BJP, including those of considerable stature with their eyes set on the top post. Unlike the other names in the running, Sharma was neither a multiple-time legislator nor parliamentarian and had no significant political clout.

Born in Bharatpur district's Atari village in 1966, Sharma has a postgraduate degree in political science and worked his way through the ranks of the ABVP and the BJYM before being inducted into the BJP. Prior to his victory from the Sanganer assembly seat in 2023, the only experience that Sharma had in politics was as a village Sarpanch and later as a Panchayat Samiti member in Bharatpur.[13] In fact, back in 2003, he had contested the assembly elections from Nadbai, under the banner of the Rajasthan Samajik Nyay Manch (RSNM) – a breakaway outfit floated by BJP leaders, including former minister Devi Singh Bhati – against both the BJP and Congress. Sharma had finished fifth in the contest, getting just over 5,900 votes.[14] Multiple BJP leaders in Rajasthan have confirmed that as the general secretary in-charge of the party's state headquarters in Jaipur, Sharma's duties also included ensuring that all arrangements were in order during dignitary visits by senior party leaders from Delhi.

For the BJP central leadership, Sharma's appointment was one among many unconventional chief ministerial appointments, such as in Madhya Pradesh, Gujarat and Haryana, wherein low-profile – and at times first-time legislators – had been selected for the post. After the BJP emerged victorious around the same time in the Chhattisgarh, Madhya Pradesh and Rajasthan assembly elections, it chose a tribal leader – Vishnu Deo Sai – and an OBC leader – Mohan Yadav – as heads of the other two states and Sharma, a Brahmin, in Rajasthan in order to cater to the respective demographics. The upper castes in the desert state constitute the core voter base for the saffron party.

A Caste-Diverse Council of Ministers

If Sharma's choice as the CM served the dual purposes of appointing a lesser-known face to ensure loyalty to Delhi – unlike previous leaders with years of political clout – and a tip of the hat towards the upper castes of the state, the choice of the two deputy chief ministers was aimed at the other half of the caste equation. Union minister Rajnath Singh announced shortly after the news of Sharma's appointment that the two deputy chief ministers were going to be Diya Kumari and Prem Chand Bairwa.

Kumari, a Rajput, is a former legislator, two-term MP and a member of the erstwhile royal family of Jaipur and Bairwa is a two-time MLA and belongs to a Dalit community. The BJP hoped to present a diverse front and strike an equilibrium in the caste-driven political milieu of the state with these appointments. Kumari was even bestowed with a number of other powerful portfolios, including finance – which meant that she would be the one to present the state budget – reinforcing to the Rajput community that its continued participation in matters of governance was important to the democratically elected government as well. She was also made in-charge of the Public Works Department (PWD) and held the highest number of portfolios, second only to CM Sharma.

On the other hand, Bairwa's appointment as the other deputy CM was aimed at improving the party's support base among Dalits, who are traditionally Congress voters. He too was entrusted with important departments such as the Higher and Technical Education Department and Transport and Road Safety.

Once the names of other ministers holding cabinet portfolios and those of MoS were announced, it became clear that the BJP was focused on garnering the loyalty of smaller OBC groups. This is part of its ongoing experiment of grooming non-dominant backward classes across the country to shape them into its loyal vote bank. For the first time in the history of Rajasthan, so many MLAs from smaller OBC groups, such as Kumawat, Mali, Rawat and Patel were inducted as ministers. These castes have traditionally voted for the BJP. Six months after the assembly election win, the BJP appointed Madan Rathore – also from a smaller OBC group – as its party president in Rajasthan. However, larger, dominant OBC groups – such as the Jats – also found representation in Bhajan Lal Sharma's council of ministers and did not go unnoticed.[15]

The saffron party's caste arithmetic is based on the assumption that wherever there is a dominant OBC caste group, chances are that other smaller OBC groups would defy the voting trend it follows, wary of giving too much power to a specific caste. For example, in Uttar Pradesh, where the Yadav community is the largest OBC group and traditionally supports the Samajwadi Party, the BJP has strengthened its influence by relying on smaller non-Yadav OBC groups, and has, at times, also allied with regional parties formed by these sections to counter the Yadav community's voting pattern.[16] The mainstay of this strategy is that even if one large chunk of a state's OBCs votes against the BJP owing to their caste allegiances, the collective votes of the remaining communities in favour of the BJP would outweigh the impact.

The same formula has now been applied to Rajasthan in the

hope that the outcome seen in Uttar Pradesh repeats itself, wherein the party has been elected into power for two successive terms.

'Double Engine' or 'Parchi Sarkar'?

In February 2025, a white luxury car rolled out of the gates of the historic City Palace of Jaipur. The car belonged to Diya Kumari, the new deputy chief minister of the BJP government. She was heading to the Rajasthan assembly, where she was to present the state budget in her capacity as the state finance minister. It was her second year presenting the budget.

For the last twenty years, the previous governments had preferred to keep the portfolio of the finance minister with the CM. Both Vasundhara Raje and Ashok Gehlot – barring his first tenure – presented the budget themselves. Since the party's central leadership had thus far had little to do with how the ministerial portfolios were distributed within a state, the all-important finance portfolio was generally used to concentrate power in the hands of the CM and thus bolster regional monopolies. Presenting the state budget in the assembly as CM also served to inextricably link their face to all welfare policies introduced therein.

The BJP high command handpicking CM Sharma and then giving away the finance portfolio to one of two deputy CMs marked a conscious departure from this tradition and served to reaffirm that it was the centre that was driving the state in Rajasthan. This was reiterated by the fact that as part of the state budget, several welfare schemes were announced which were extensions of central schemes launched earlier by the Narendra Modi-led BJP government. In the first budget presented by the Sharma government, Kumari laid down the foundations for Viksit Rajasthan @2047, along the same lines as the centre's Viksit Bharat @2047 vision. Similarly, other initiatives of the union government too have featured in the state budgets, including plans under the Jal Jeevan

Mission (JJM) and the AMRUT 2.0 scheme. The previous Congress government's Mukhyamantri Chiranjeevi Swasthya Beema Yojana was now replaced with the Mukhyamantri Ayushman Aarogya Yojana (MAA).[17]

One of the main election pitches of the BJP in 2023 was a 'double engine' sarkar – wherein the state and centre are both governed by the party, presumably ensuring smoother functioning. This was aimed at accelerating development initiatives in the state while ensuring better coordination with the centre to ensure service delivery and better implementation of welfare schemes.

During the initial months of CM Sharma's reign, while the centre had a freer hand when it came to deciding the course of the Rajasthan government, it also landed its state counterpart in tricky situations at times. Even six months into the new government taking charge, the general public perception remained that the machinery was being run by bureaucrats taking orders from the centre. One of the major reasons for this was a natural lack of trust in the new government since all the ministers were fresh faces, with only a handful having served in ministerial capacities before. In addition to this, some of the departments continued to be run by bureaucrats who had been posted there during the previous Congress regime, which was unusual and raised further questions about the real authority vested in the new administration. An example of this was the Finance Department under Diya Kumari, which continued to be headed by the same bureaucrats who had prepared the previous Congress government's budget for two subsequent budgets.

Although the state government did not show any obvious signs of internal friction, every once in a while, the cracks became visible. Kirodi Lal Meena, the stalwart tribal leader, was one of the few leaders who was part of the council of ministers and had a large devoted following of his own. Meena had been entrusted with the Rural Development Department, but was not given the Panchayati

Raj portfolio, which had traditionally been the practice of all previous BJP and Congress regimes. After the poor performance of the BJP in the 2024 Lok Sabha elections, he tendered his resignation, only to later resume charge of his ministerial duties.[18]

Around this time, the Congress in opposition coined a new term to define BJP's unconventional style of governance: 'parchi sarkar', which was a reference to the slip handed over to Raje during the BJP MLA meeting for announcing the party's decision to appoint Sharma as the new CM. This meant 'to allege that all vital decisions are being taken by the BJP top brass in Delhi, who send instructions on chits or parchis',[19] which the state government would then have to follow. CM Sharma's frequent visits to Delhi to meet central leaders only served to underscore this. CM Sharma would also occasionally pay 'courtesy visits' to former CM Raje, who still held considerable clout in the state's politics and often toured the state to meet her supporters.

Even though Sharma and his council of ministers would routinely strike back at the Congress over corruption charges and the divided front it presented during its tenure, the 'parchi sarkar' accusations continued to haunt the new government. Owing to the comfortable majority that the BJP had in the assembly, however, there was no perceivable threat to the stability of the government and the experienced bureaucrats in office ensured that there were no hindrances to the smooth functioning of the state machinery either. But despite this, it was undeniable that the role of the new ministers remained undefined.

The Shift Towards Hardline Hindutva

In September 2025, Gopal Sharma, the BJP MLA from Civil Lines in Jaipur, made a dramatic appeal in the assembly to two Muslim legislators of the Congress party: Rafeek Khan – a legislator from Adarsh Nagar, who is also the chief whip of the party in the assembly – and Amin Kagzi, Congress's Kishanpole MLA. Expressing his support for the anti-conversion bill being introduced by his party, Sharma urged Khan and Kagzi to 'return to their original religion'.[20]

Notably, the Rajasthan Prohibition of Unlawful Conversion of Religion Bill, 2025, was passed on the same day as Sharma's appeal to the two Muslim MLAs. One of its provisions includes life imprisonment as the maximum punishment for 'illegal religious conversion', while exempting 'Ghar wapsi', a Sangh Parivar concept.*

While it is well established that the RSS and its affiliate organizations advocate for Hindutva to be the main foundation of BJP's governance, the Sangh was not able to function freely during the party's previous regimes under Shekhawat and Raje as they enjoyed strong individual influence and refused to yield to the organization. As a result, Shekhawat was able to groom young Muslim leaders, such as Yunus Khan, and later, the Raje government entrusted Khan with powerful cabinet portfolios, as detailed in Chapter 5, regardless of the Sangh's stance. However, in the new state government handpicked by the central leadership and lacking individual influence, the RSS was now able to assert itself in every sphere.

The Bhajan Lal Sharma government, with its fiery Hindutva cabinet ministers that mirrored the BJP's functioning in other states, adopted an unabashedly Hindutva stance, palpable at the ground level as well. Right after his election by a narrow margin of 974 votes, Hawa Mahal MLA Sanjay Sharma, alias Balmukund Acharya, launched a campaign against restaurants selling non-vegetarian food. In videos shared widely across social media, the MLA could

* The RSS maintains that all Indians were originally Hindus and thus converting from Christianity, Islam or any other religion to Hinduism would mean a 'return' to the 'original religion'.

be seen telling the manager of a famous Jaipur eatery that 'this is Apara Kashi, not Karachi' and claiming that women could not move around freely in the area because of the 'Sharaabi–Kebabi (those who drink and eat non-vegetarian food)' who frequent it.[21]

The saffron-clad MLA continued to be in the news thereafter for his hardline Hindutva rhetoric and actions. Within months, Balmukund Acharya had made an appearance at a government school function, where he was heard claiming that the environment was being ruined owing to the practice of wearing hijab, sparking protest from the Muslim students.[22] In April 2025, an FIR was lodged against him for sloganeering in front of the Jama Masjid in Jaipur while leading a protest against the Pahalgam terror attack despite the charged environment.[23]

Before long, the tilt towards Hindutva was not restricted to political rhetoric – it was also reflected in the overall functioning of the new government.

In August 2024, Rashid Khan, an autorickshaw driver in Udaipur, watched helplessly as the district administration demolished the house that he had purchased using his savings. While Khan was not accused of any crime, the state administration had meted out punishment to him. The immediate reason for its decision to raze Khan's house was the fact that the minor son of his Muslim tenant had fatally stabbed a fellow student – a Hindu boy – at school. While the accused had been swiftly apprehended, angry Hindu outfits had demanded bulldozer action. Following suit, the administration had immediately issued a notice in the name of the accused's father and a day later, their residence had been demolished. As a distraught Khan pointed out the absurdity of issuing a demolition notice to the tenant of a house,[24] one thing became amply clear: the Bhajan Lal Sharma government was enthusiastically following the example of Uttar Pradesh, Haryana and Madhya Pradesh when it came to bulldozer justice.

At times, the administrative orders too reflected the rhetoric of Hindutva outfits. In October 2024, for instance, MoS (Home) Jawahar Singh Bedham told reporters that he had asked the state police to come up with replacements for Urdu, Farsi, Arabic words used in police jargon since the Mughal era and to ensure that only pure Hindi was used. Soon, the state police initiated the process of identifying such words and replacing them with Hindi terms.[25] In the same vein, the passing of the anti-conversion bill in the state assembly in September 2025, as mentioned at the beginning of this section, further affirmed the fact that it was the top priority of the government to incorporate Hindutva and the Sangh Parivar's demands into its policy decisions. In fact, the anti-conversion bill is an apt example of this conscious shift towards more legislations with stringent provisions on issues close to the cause of the RSS and its allied outfits. The initial draft of the bill that was introduced in February 2025 outlined less stringent punishment and did not mention life imprisonment. The state government subsequently withdrew the bill and passed a stricter legislation including life imprisonment as the maximum punishment, greater monetary fines and granted the administration the provision to demolish premises which were being used for 'illegal conversion'.[26]

A stark difference between previous BJP state governments and the government after the 2023 polls was that while in the earlier regimes, furthering the RSS's vision was one of many important items on the administration's agenda, for the Bhajan Lal Sharma government, it is the main one. A contributing factor in this is the homogenous nature of the present government, which has no differing perspectives within its machinery. As CM, both Shekhawat and Raje had leaders from other religions or known past affiliations to different political outfits within their council of ministers, such as the Janata Dal, which did not subscribe to the Hindutva ideology. But the Sharma government, with its first-time ministers – many of whom have strong RSS backgrounds and others whose stars had ascended only in the Modi era – felt no compulsion to underplay its Hindutva inclinations. As a result, policy decisions and governance now openly espouse the Hindutva outlook, finally giving the RSS the edge it has long desired.

Changing Caste Equations and the 2024 Lok Sabha Elections

Between 1996 and 2019, Amra Ram, the face of the Communist Party of India (Marxist) (CPI (M)) in Rajasthan, unsuccessfully contested the Lok Sabha election from his home constituency of Sikar seven times. Each time, he finished after the BJP and Congress. However, Amra Ram is also a prominent leader of the AIKS – the farmer wing of the CPI (M) – and has a better track record in state elections, having been elected to the assembly multiple times from the Dhod and Danta Ramgarh constituencies, although he was unable to win the last three state elections, held in 2013, 2018 and 2023.

While Sikar has a dedicated CPI (M) cadre – mostly comprising members of the Jat community, owing to the region's history of farmers' movements – the party's support base has been no match for that of the BJP or Congress, both of which succeeded in having their candidates elected to the Lok Sabha from this constituency. Moreover, the BJP had been undefeated since 2014, the dawn of the Modi era, with the party's candidate Sumedhanand Saraswati emerging the winner in two consecutive assembly elections.

Therefore, the idea that Amra Ram would defeat the incumbent BJP MP in the 2023 assembly elections – just six months after the saffron party formed the government in the state – had seemed outlandish. Yet, in June 2024, Ram emerged the unlikely winner as the joint candidate of the Congress–CPI (M), a part of the larger INDIA alliance.

The 2024 Lok Sabha election was the first major political contest six months since the Sharma government came to power. The BJP had recorded a clean sweep in both 2014 and 2019, making it crucial for the new CM to match the record of his predecessor Raje, who had ensured that the BJP captured all twenty-five seats from the state in the 2014 parliamentary elections. In 2019, buoyed by the mass support for the saffron party in the aftermath of the Pulwama terror attack and the subsequent airstrikes in Pakistan's Balakot, the BJP had once again repeated the feat. However, 2024 was different since the Modi government was dealing with the growing anti-incumbency sentiment – an inevitable outcome of having been in power for a decade. Despite this, the BJP had maintained that it would secure a majority, campaigning under the slogan of '*Ab ki baar 400 paar* (This time, we will cross 400 seats)' in the run-up to the election.

Rajasthan is a crucial Hindi heartland state where the party had a legacy to uphold – to win every seat it contested from – its leaders would consider anything less a setback. As the Lok Sabha election results started trickling in on the morning of 4 June 2024, it was evident that in spite of the BJP's strong mandate in the assembly elections just six months ago, it had lost its footing. While it had won fourteen of the twenty-five seats, for the first time in ten years, the party and its allies had not emerged victorious in all twenty-five constituencies and ended up conceding eleven seats to the opposition parties contesting under the banner of the INDIA alliance.

The biggest blow was dealt by eastern Rajasthan and the Shekhawati region. The party lost all three seats in the Shekhawati region – Sikar, Churu and Jhunjhunu – followed by the eastern districts of Bharatpur, Karauli-Dholpur, Dausa and Tonk-Sawai Madhopur. BJP lost in areas with high Dalit and tribal populations as well, with the BAP defeating it in Banswara. A common element across all territories was the loss of the Jat community's support.

As is well known, in the shifting sands of Rajasthan's politics, the support of no single community can be taken for granted. This phenomenon was best highlighted in the voting patterns of the Jat community. In the previous two Lok Sabha elections, the Jats had voted overwhelmingly in favour of the BJP, helping the party win comfortably from both the Shekhawati region and Western Rajasthan. The fact that until a few months before the 2023 assembly elections, the BJP in Rajasthan was being headed by Satish Poonia, a Jat himself, had made many in the community hopeful that if the party won, they might finally have a Jat CM. However, as mentioned before, Poonia was replaced with C. P. Joshi just months before the polls. In March 2023, just days before this fateful transition, Poonia was at the Jat Mahakumbh – a massive community assertion event where Jat politicians across party lines gather to celebrate their heritage – and demands for a Jat CM in Rajasthan were voiced.[27]

To make matters worse, Poonia lost the elections, due to which he was denied any ministerial berth, let alone the top post. After forming the government in December 2023, when the BJP announced that it had chosen a Brahmin CM and two deputy CMs from the Rajput and Dalit communities, a sense of dissatisfaction spread through the Jat community as its hopes of a Jat CM were dashed yet again. Other factors, such as the long-standing grudge over the Agniveer army recruitment scheme, which reduced the tenure of service in the military by allowing contractual recruitment of youths, also came into play in the Shekhawati belt, from where thousands of youngsters from the Jat community join the armed forces every year.[28]

Effectively alienated by these developments, the Jats voted against the BJP in the 2024 Lok Sabha elections. Sensing the public mood, Rashtriya Loktantrik Party (RLP) chief Hanuman Beniwal joined forces with the Congress and successfully won the Nagaur assembly constituency as the INDIA alliance's candidate. Five years ago, Beniwal had allied with the BJP to win the seat, but had later left the NDA in the wake of the 2020 farmers' protests.[29]

The Road Ahead

As detailed in this chapter, the 2023 assembly elections mark a crucial moment in the politics of Rajasthan – they gave the state a new chief minister after more than two decades. The Sharma government is the first BJP state government during the Modi–Shah era wherein the council of ministers, including the chief minister and his deputies, have been handpicked by the party's central leadership and reflect its larger ambitions of establishing a centralized form of governance across the nation. State governments in the grip of regional monopolies are being dismantled as powerful leaders are being swapped out for nondescript, low-profile leaders who can further the vision of the centre on the ground.

It remains to be seen if this experimental approach holds virtue in a state where the public has primarily been personality-driven and leaders with mass appeal have enjoyed decades in office. The poll results so far have been mixed. While the BJP suffered a setback in the 2024 Lok Sabha elections, it did send a message in November 2024 by winning five of the seven seats for which assembly by-elections were held, that irrespective of the presence or absence of mass leaders, the party cadre on the ground was strong. Poor candidate selections and lack of strategy sealed the fate of the Congress in these five seats, but the results gave a boost to the Sharma government.[30]

On the other hand, in the Congress, a drastic generational shift is still overdue, despite there being no dearth of young leaders with chief ministerial ambitions and impressive track records to match. While the party is presently out of power in the state, multiple

Congress leaders are engaged in a battle of ascension. Sachin Pilot, whose feud with Gehlot grabbed headlines on the regular between 2018–23, is very much still in the fray, with Gehlot himself – now in his early 70s – giving clear signals that he is in no mood to relinquish power, least of all to Pilot, whom he once described as 'nakaara aur nikamma'.

Having overcome this obstacle for itself, the next challenge that the BJP will face in Rajasthan will arrive in 2028, when it will attempt to break the thirty-year-old trend of the state never re-electing an incumbent government for two consecutive terms. Whether it will succeed is challenging to predict at this juncture, but until then, it can be safely inferred that even as Rajasthan is caught in a tidal wave of change, its politics continue to demand an expert balancing act. Shouldering its grand legacies alongside the weight of the aspirations of its youth, every new leader will have to take caste, a feudal past and the shifting sands of allegiances and time in their stride as new surprises continue to spring and events unfolding on the national scene echo across the expanse of the desert state.

EPILOGUE

RAJASTHAN HAS LONG BEEN A LAND OF CONTRASTS, ROOTED IN tradition yet eager for change; shaped by its past, yet poised for the future. The state's vibrant political history, marked by dynasties, caste struggles and political rivalries, continues to be shaped not just by those who wield the scepter as part of party high command or as state party officials, but by the aspirations of the millions of people who live in India's largest state. While it may seem that every time a new government is elected, the people observe in silence during its five-year term, but come election time, they speak with remarkable clarity.

At the time of writing, the state is living through the aftermath of the 2024 Lok Sabha elections and the new BJP government led by CM Bhajan Lal Sharma has been in power for two years. Election results are a mere symptom of the larger forces that govern Rajasthan's society – while they certainly serve as an effective compass to determine the course of the state's politics, they are also milestones that help map its social trajectory and changing demographics. While some voter trends have remained consistent, others have evolved in response to the actions of previous governments and national events.

In recent years, one of the defining features of Rajasthan's politics has been the speedy rise of anti-incumbency sentiments against governments, including those elected with large mandates. It became evident from the last few elections that the state's voters are alert and wary of leaders preoccupied with internal rivalries and divided fronts, while neglecting their duties as political representatives to address the pressing concerns affecting the lives of citizens, including unemployment, agrarian distress and water crisis. The spectacle of recent factional battles – be it the Gehlot–Pilot tussle in the Congress, or the Raje loyalists versus new power centres in the BJP – has grabbed headlines in national news far more often than the good governance agendas declared in election manifestos.

While it is a good sign that the winds of change blow every five years across the desert sands, in the longer run, it has contributed to reducing the sense of accountability felt by elected representatives and adversely affected the execution of long-term plans by sitting governments. Two years into the new BJP government's reign, these issues persist. While the party managed to trump the Congress in the assembly elections, the latter's improved performance in the 2024 Lok Sabha elections revealed that the BJP cannot take the tilt of public favour towards itself for granted.

On the social front, Rajasthan is at a crucial crossroad. The state's women remain disadvantaged by the deeply entrenched patriarchal norms, low participation in the workforce and disparity in educational opportunities. However, while the ground reality of women wearing ghoonghats and being confined to maintaining their households persists, politics is beginning to offer an encouraging contrast for women to aspire to. The state has now seen a powerful woman chief minister for two tenures, a woman assembly speaker, two women governors, and now a deputy chief minister. In the Rajasthani hinterlands, however, such a shift remains to be witnessed. A woman sarpanch in most rural areas is but a figurehead whose decisions are made either by her husband, father or father-in-law.

An arena in which women have graduated from their status as mute spectators, however, is polling. Time and again, they have emerged as a powerful and decisive voting bloc. There has been a rise in voter turnout among women in the recent elections, suggesting that gender equality and justice is slowly gaining importance in Rajasthan's politics. In recent political discourse, few issues have impacted the perception of popular leaders as much as their approach to women's safety and empowerment. While some state governments have taken steps towards gender justice by instating security measures such as more helplines, increased recruitment of women officers in the police and promising stricter action against crimes, many challenges remain.

Media outlets frequently report the link between the alarming rise in dropout rates among secondary school girl students and growing safety concerns and a lack of women-friendly transport infrastructure. Yet, most governments announce welfare schemes for girl children or women that are tokenistic. While there is no doubt that free bicycles or scholarship schemes work to encourage girls to pursue education, there is little being done to ensure that they do not encounter logistical issues such as lack of safe transportation, infrastructure and hostels to accommodate students from remote areas, that prevent them from staying in school. Better representation of women in local bodies and focused vocational training that can translate into salaried employment is also bound to aid empowerment.

Another segment of society that continues to struggle despite the many changes in administration comprises the marginalized communities, such as Dalits and Adivasis. Despite their sizeable populations, they continue to number among the most vulnerable social groups. Atrocities, demands for job reservations and calls for social dignity continue to fuel Dalit agitations across the state and such assertions have only increased in the recent years and are expected to continue to do so. While it is true that both BJP and Congress have made overtures towards Dalit and Adivasi voters through focused welfare schemes and symbolic gestures, including appointing a leader or two from these marginalized groups to prominent posts and targeted outreach during election campaigns, discrimination has continued unabated.

Working as reporters in the field for over a decade, we have witnessed firsthand how caste violence, boycotts and exclusion have failed to inspire deeper, more lasting social transformation that translates into policy action on the political front. Ensuring that politicians from marginalized groups find fair representation, rather than being used to attract voters from a considerable fraction of the state's population that continues to feel ignored and excluded, has real potential to usher in change. Other measures include ensuring the protection of land rights for Adivasis and strengthening of the SC/ST (Prevention of Atrocities) Act to begin erasing the legacy of discrimination which haunts Rajasthan since the days of feudalism.

On the other hand, the OBC communities' fight for proportionate representation in all sectors is expected to dominate the political scene in the state for the foreseeable future, in tandem with national politics, where calls for caste census and demands for the OBC's share in power have reshaped politics in recent times.

Be it the old guard, young Turks or the voters themselves, the formidable power of social media is well recognized across Rajasthan. It has transformed the state's political landscape permanently, with WhatsApp groups, trending hashtags on X, Facebook posts and YouTube channels sometimes being treated as alternatives to traditional media.

An analysis of the elections over the last fifteen years has shown how political parties are now able to mobilize faster, spread narratives wider and bypass conventional gatekeepers and barriers to communicate with the voter directly with the help of social media. The state administration has regularly been compelled to ban internet services for short periods to prevent the rapid dissemination of harmful misinformation and worsening of caste or communal tensions.

There also exists a digital divide between the rural and urban populations in the region, with one being better acquainted with the technology than the other and thus contributing to an increased sense of distance in remote areas. Since the days of the 2020 pandemic, the authors have noted the ways in which this digital divide affects the daily lives of people and the need to remedy the issue. While improving rates of enrolment in government schools is the first step to improve opportunities for digital education, it must be followed by teacher training, greater digitization of classrooms and improvement of public school infrastructure in order to bridge the knowledge gap in this crucial aspect.

The impact of social media and the endless array of trending hashtags and reels on journalism, too, is formidable. One does not just have to be wary of fake news and misinformation and conduct more rigorous fact-checks for everything that is published, but also ensure the concerns of those lacking digital literacy and access are communicated effectively to public representatives. A major source of this information are the young and first-time voters, who use the various platforms to highlight everyday issues in their constituencies. Bringing the most important and factually accurate stories to the notice of the government has become a key aspect of reportage in the state. The fourth pillar of democracy has never before been more central to ensuring accountability of the ruling government.

For many decades, the primary image associated with the desert state has been one of long queues of women waiting to fill earthen pots or plastic containers with water from a tanker, well or tubewell in the drought-ridden districts. There is a dire need for state governments to try and change this reality by prioritizing sustainable irrigation, traditional rainwater harvesting methods and organizing awareness campaigns for judicious water use, while also accounting for climate change.

When Rajasthan next goes to polls in 2028, it is anticipated to be a close fight between the ruling BJP and the Congress. If the BJP is able to maintain focus on its key promises – employment, water and inclusive growth, while avoiding or quelling factional tensions – it has real potential to break the cycle of anti-incumbency and be re-elected in the state. The next election cycle will also offer clues into whether the unconventional approach adopted by the BJP in appointing fresh representatives and dismantling regional monopolies has found favour with the public in Rajasthan. Similarly, the Congress also has an equally strong chance to make a comeback, owing to the public's disillusionment with the incumbent government every five years. There is a dire need for the party to project a united front and resolve internal tussles in order to acquire power again.

Whichever party holds the reins in Jaipur, the next decade should be defined not by factional rivalries, but by investment in human capital – especially for girls, marginalized communities and the state's youth, who grow impatient for change. If governance remains focused on ensuring access to basic rights and amenities for the population – focusing especially on expanding secure water supply, education, healthcare and social justice – then Rajasthan can finally begin to transcend the culture of tokenism in politics and make more substantive strides in progress and development.

While dynasties and caste equations cannot be made to vanish overnight, the steady rise of assertive young leaders and aspirational, aware voters, points to a more inclusive democratic future. The people of the desert state are making their voices heard now more than ever before to demand dignity, opportunity and justice.

It is in this, perhaps, that Rajasthan's political uniqueness lies. Why, despite giving pro-Hindu politics one of its earliest, strongest footholds, it has never been a stronghold of the BJP unlike Gujarat or Madhya Pradesh. Why, despite its deeply entrenched caste divides, social justice-based parties have never been able to take root here, as they have in Uttar Pradesh or Bihar. No single community ever enjoyed absolute power in Rajasthan – much like the sand dunes that adorn its landscape, public sensibilities have shifted with the winds of time and democratic values have been upheld by politicians and voters alike.

Rajasthan's strength lies in its diversity – if it can only make a decisive shift towards greater inclusion and equitable growth across social segments and shed its traditional feudalistic hierarchies, it can emerge as a shining example of how pluralism can serve as an enduring foundation for democracy.

NOTES

1. Rajput Pride and Electoral Might

1. Rohan Valecha, '"Padmavati": Rajput Karni Sena threatens to chop off Deepika Padukone's nose', *Times of India*, 17 November 2017. Available at: http://timesofindia.indiatimes.com/articleshow/61671361.cms?utm_source=contentofinterest&utm_medium=text&utm_campaign=cppst.
2. Deep Mukherjee, 'Padmavati row: Was Padmini a fictional character or a queen who enamoured Khilji?', *Hindustan Times*, 3 February 2017. Available at: https://www.hindustantimes.com/india-news/padmavati-row-was-padmini-a-fictional-character-or-a-queen-who-enamoured-khilji/story-7wYAUtMaPEndrS2DDFlo2O.html.
3. Gyan Darpan, 'जिस Mahipal Makrana को मीडिया अनपढ़ गुंडा समझती वो राजस्थान विश्वविद्यालय का गोल्डमेडेलिस्ट है |' [video], YouTube, 2 October 2018.
4. Authors' eyewitness account, 2017.
5. 'Karni Sena members burn posters of Padmavati in Jaipur, say won't let film release unless it's pre-screened', *Hindustan Times*, 23 September 2017. Available at: https://www.hindustantimes.com/jaipur/karni-sena-members-burn-posters-of-padmavati-in-jaipur-say-won-t-let-film-release-unless-it-s-pre-screened/story-LAMLQSuLq7N99f2EdJLNNN.html.
6. Authors' eyewitness account, 2017.
7. Rajesh Asnani, 'Rajasthan: Roop Kanwar forced sati case in final stage', *The New Indian Express*, 9 September 2019. Available at: https://www.newindianexpress.com/nation/2019/Sep/09/roop-kanwar-case-in-final-stage-2031032.html.
8. Interview with Lad Kumari Jain, Jaipur, January 2023.
9. Geeta Pandey, 'Why fight for justice isn't over in India's 'horrific' widow-

burning case, 37 years on', BBC, 19 October 2024. Available at: https://www.bbc.com/news/articles/cn8ykmn2p1go.

10. Rohit Parihar, 'Sati: Roop Kanwar was cheered as she burnt on her husband's pyre, now she's a faint memory', *India Today*, 29 November 1999. Available at: https://www.indiatoday.in/magazine/states/states-uttar-pradesh/story/19991129-sati-roop-kanwar-was-cheered-as-she-burnt-on-her-husbands-pyre-now-shes-a-faint-memory-781469-1999-11-28.
11. Bombay Union of Journalists Women and Media Committee, *Trial by Fire: A Report on Roop Kanwar's Death* (Bombay: Women and Media Committee, Bombay Union of Journalists, 1987).
12. 'Padmavati row: Karni Sena slams "naachnewali" Deepika Padukone for dancing in less clothing', *India Today*, 15 November 2017. Available at: https://www.indiatoday.in/movies/bollywood/story/padmavati-protests-deepika-padukone-sanjay-leela-bhansali-1087126-2017-11-15.
13. Deep Mukherjee, 'Karni Sena founder Lokendra Singh Kalvi, who led anti-Padmaavat protests, dies', *The Indian Express*, 15 March 2023. Available at: https://indianexpress.com/article/political-pulse/karni-sena-founder-lokendra-singh-kalvi-dies-8497150/.
14. Interview with Kalyan Singh Kalvi, Jaipur, December 2021.
15. Interview with Satish Kumar, Jaipur, 2023.
16. Prakash Bhandari, 'Maharaja of Jodhpur used aircraft for LS campaigns in 1952', *Times of India*, 13 April 2014. Available at: https://timesofindia.indiatimes.com/news/maharaja-of-jodhpur-used-aircraft-for-ls-campaigns-in-1952/articleshow/33677449.cms.
17. 'India: Royalty on the Hustings', *TIME*, 14 January 1952. Available at: https://content.time.com/time/subscriber/article/0,33009,806197-1,00.html.
18. V. P. Menon, *The Story of the Integration of the Indian States* (New York: The Macmillan Company, 1956), p. 117.
19. Interview with Pratap Singh Khachariyawas, Jaipur, 2017.
20. As quoted in 'India: Royalty on the Hustings', *TIME*.
21. G. B. Pant, *Report on Rajasthan jagirdari abolition*, 1953.
22. Interview with Abhimanyu Singh Rajvi, Jaipur, 2022.
23. Official records of Rajasthan State assembly proceedings, 1956.
24. Interview with Dharmendra Kanwar, Jaipur, January 2023.

25. DHNS, 'Ex-royals hit streets as govt seals Rajmahal', *Deccan Herald*, 2 September 2016. Available at: https://www.deccanherald.com/content/568209/ex-royals-hit-streets-govt.html
26. Dev Ankur Wadhawan, 'BJP MP Diya Kumari claims her family descended from Lord Ram's son, ready to present proof in Supreme Court', *India Today*, 11 August 2019. Available at: https://www.indiatoday.in/india/story/bjp-mp-diya-kumari-claims-her-family-descended-from-lord-ram-son-ready-to-present-proof-in-supreme-court-1579830-2019-08-11.
27. Vasundhara Raje (@VasundharaBJP), 'Unveiled the statue of Maharana Pratap ji at Gogunda on the occasion of #MaharanaPratapJayanti with @BJPRajnathSingh', X, 7 June 2016. Available at: https://x.com/vasundharabjp/status/740241855808409601.
28. '"Akbar ka Quila" No Longer Akbar's, Rajasthan Minister Renames It As "Ajmer Ka Quila"', HuffPost, 5 March 2017. Available at: https://www.huffpost.com/archive/in/entry/akbar-ka-quila-no-longer-akbars-rajasthan-minister-renames-i_in_5c10bdd0e4b09dcd67fbc552. See also Tabeenah Anjum, 'The Politics Around Maharana Pratap In Rajasthan', Outlook India, 18 March 2024. Available at: https://www.outlookindia.com/national/the-politics-around-maharana-pratap-in-rajasthan-news-183169.
29. DHNS, 'Saffronisation of education in BJP-ruled Rajasthan', *Deccan Herald*, 13 June 2017. Available at: https://www.deccanherald.com/content/617205/saffronisation-education-bjp-ruled-rajasthan.html.
30. Salik Ahmad, 'Maharana Pratap turned battle to hills: How Rajasthan Class 12 textbook describes Battle of Haldighati', *Hindustan Times*, 18 August 2017. Available at: https://www.hindustantimes.com/india-news/maharana-pratap-turned-battle-to-hills-how-rajasthan-class-12-texbook-describes-battle-of-haldighati/story-LpE0FDwuB6poKOCfRnKzHP.html.
31. Tabeenah Anjum, 'Rajputs to protest against Raje's pre poll yatra', *Deccan Herald*, 29 September 2018. Available at: https://www.deccanherald.com/india/rajput-community-protest-685211.html.
32. Salik Ahmad and Deep Mukherjee, 'Who is Anandpal Singh and why Rajputs in Rajasthan erupted in anger at his killing?', *Hindustan Times*, 13 July 2017. Available at: https://www.hindustantimes.com/india-news/who-is-anandpal-singh-and-why-rajputs-in-rajasthan-erupted-in-anger-at-

his-killing/story-YPpyFhIUSPzE3XEtMBsYGJ.html.

33. Shaurya Garjana, 'अहंकार त्यागे राजपूत समाज : गजेन्द्रसिंह सांखला नेता रावणा राजपूत समाज बीकानेर' [video], YouTube, 23 August 2018. Available at: https://www.youtube.com/watch?v=cDKfJ48D9a4.

2. Tillers and Kingmakers: The Jat Vote

1. Harendra Mirdha, National Election Watch. Available at: https://myneta.info/rajasthan2018/candidate.php?candidate_id=4588.
2. Official website, Sri Baldev Ram Mirdha Govt College Nagaur (Rajasthan). Available at: https://hte.rajasthan.gov.in/college/gcnagaur.
3. Interview with Ranmal Singh, Sikar, 2023.
4. Sachin, 'महायज्ञ के नाम पर हुई किसान सभा, एक हजार किलो घी से हुआ हवन', *Patrika*, 20 January 2021. Available at: https://www.patrika.com/sikar-news/mahayagya-organised-by-farmers-in-1934-in-sikar-6640942.
5. 'व्यास ने की थी मारवाड़ हितकारिणी सभा की स्थापना', *Dainik Bhaskar*, 2020. Available at: https://www.bhaskar.com/rajasthan/jaisalmaer/news/rajasthan-news-vyas-founded-marwar-hitkarini-sabha-104616-6657317.html.
6. Rajasthan State assembly archival records.
7. Ibid.
8. Interview with Sumitra Singh, Jaipur, 2024.
9. S. B. Cr. Appeal no. 977 of 1971, Jugal Kishore vs. The State of Rajasthan, Rajasthan High Court, 19 December 1977. Available at: https://www.casemine.com/judgement/in/56e6686e607dba6b53432ae5.
10. Barmer, General Election to Parliamentary Constituencies: Trends & Results June-2024, Election Commission of India. Available at: https://results.eci.gov.in/PcResultGenJune2024/candidateswise-S2017.htm.
11. PTI, 'Bhanwari Devi murder case: Divers recover wristwatch, bone pieces', *India Today*, 7 January 2012. Available at: https://www.indiatoday.in/india/west/story/bhanwari-devi-murder-case-wristwatch-bone-pieces-recovered-88802-2012-01-06.
12. 'Bhanwari Devi murder case: Top 10 facts', NDTV, 29 February 2012. Available at: https://www.ndtv.com/india-news/bhanwari-devi-murder-case-top-10-facts-469399.
13. 'Rajasthan minister to be investigated for rape, murder', NDTV, 23

September 2011. Available at: https://www.ndtv.com/india-news/rajasthan-minister-to-be-investigated-for-rape-murder-468451.

14. TNN, 'Congress veteran Mahipal Maderna, an accused in Bhanwari murder case, dies', *Times of India*, 18 October 2021. Available at: https://timesofindia.indiatimes.com/city/jaipur/cong-veteran-an-accused-in-bhanwari-murder-case-dies/articleshow/87093939.cms.
15. Deep Mukherjee, 'Rajasthan elections: Even without any prominent face, here's why Jats can play kingmakers', *The Indian Express*, 5 November 2018. Available at: https://indianexpress.com/article/india/community-accounts-for-15-of-rajasthans-population-even-without-any-prominent-face-heres-why-jats-can-play-kingmakers-5434015/.
16. Official proceedings of the Rajasthan assembly.
17. Ibid.
18. TNN, 'Jodhpur Jats demand Gehlot's ouster', *Times of India*, 24 December 2011.
19. Deep Mukherjee, 'Gehlot, Raje have been in alliance for 22 years... Now there seems to be one between PM Modi and CM: RLP's Hanuman Beniwal', *The Indian Express*, 10 November 2022. Available at: https://indianexpress.com/article/political-pulse/rlp-hanuman-beniwal-interview-8259318/.
20. Ibid.
21. Ibid.
22. Rajasthan State assembly proceedings, September 1997.
23. Bhanu Pratap Singh, 'JC Bose gang rape case: 8 sent to jail for 10 years', *Times of India*, 27 October 2012. Available at: https://timesofindia.indiatimes.com/city/jaipur/jc-bose-gang-rape-case-8-sent-to-jail-for-10-years/articleshow/16976554.cms.
24. Deep Mukherjee, 'Gehlot, Raje have been in alliance for 22 years... Now there seems to be one between PM Modi and CM: RLP's Hanuman Beniwal', *The Indian Express*, 10 November 2022. Available at: https://indianexpress.com/article/political-pulse/rlp-hanuman-beniwal-interview-8259318/.
25. Deep Mukherjee, 'Beniwal announces split from NDA over farm laws', *The Indian Express*, 27 December 2020. Available at: https://indianexpress.com/article/india/beniwal-announces-split-from-nda-over-farm-laws/.

26. Interview with Akhil Chaudhary, Jaipur, 2024.
27. Deep Mukherjee, 'How the Congress and Allies Stopped the BJP from Getting a Hat-Trick in Rajasthan', The Wire, 5 June 2024. Available at: https://thewire.in/politics/how-the-congress-and-allies-stopped-the-bjp-from-getting-a-hat-trick-in-rajasthan.

3. A House Divided: The Congress Conundrum

1. Richard Sisson, *The Congress Party in Rajasthan: Political Integration and Institution-Building in an Indian State* (University of California Press, 1972). Available at: https://doi.org/10.2307/jj.2430587.
2. Ibid.
3. As quoted in Vijay Bhandari, *Rajasthan ki Rajneeti: Samantvad Se Jativad Ke Bhanvar Mein* (New Delhi: Vani Prakashan, 2007), p. 73. Authors' own translation.
4. Bhandari, *Rajasthan ki Rajneeti*, p. 69.
5. Interview with Bhanu Kapil, 2022.
6. Interview with Suchitra Arya, 2022.
7. K. L. Kamal, *Party Politics in an Indian State: A Study of the Main Political Parties in Rajasthan* (S. Chand & Co., 1969), p. 129.
8. Ibid.
9. Ibid, p. 185.
10. Deep Mukherjee, 'Rewind & Replay | The rise of Indira Gandhi, and the shrinking of Rajasthan CMs', *The Indian Express*, 1 October 2022. Available at: https://indianexpress.com/article/political-pulse/rise-of-indira-gandhi-and-shrinking-of-rajasthan-cms-8183379/.
11. Interview with Om Thanvi, May 2023.
12. Sunil Sethi, 'Slaying of Rajasthan MLA Raja Man Singh comes as a severe jolt to Congress(I)', *India Today*, 15 March 1985. Available at: https://www.indiatoday.in/magazine/indiascope/story/19850315-slaying-of-rajasthan-mla-raja-man-singh-comes-as-a-severe-jolt-to-congressi-769863-2013-12-01.
13. Omar Rashid, 'Rajasthan ex-royal "Raja" Man Singh murder | 11 policemen including DSP sentenced to life imprisonment', *The Hindu*, 22 July 2020. Available at: https://www.thehindu.com/news/national/other-states/rajasthan-ex-royal-raja-man-singh-murder-11-policemen-including-dsp-sentenced-to-life-imprisonment/article32161186.ece.

4. The Saffron Surge: The Roots of Anti-Congress Sentiments

1. Interview with Manak Chand, Jaipur, September 2023.
2. Ibid.
3. Gayatri Devi, *A Princess Remembers: The Memoirs of the Maharani of Jaipur* (Kolkata: Rupa, 1995), pp. 253–54.
4. Ibid.
5. Ibid. pp. 238–39.
6. Interview with Sudhir Kasliwal, Jaipur, 2023.
7. Devi, *A Princess Remembers*, pp. 329–32.
8. Interview with Sudhir Kasliwal, Jaipur, 2023.
9. Interview with Satish Poonia, Jaipur, 2024.
10. Interview with Narpat Singh Rajvi, Jaipur, 2024.
11. PTI, 'Gujarat experiment to be repeated in Delhi: Togadia', *Hindustan Times*, 16 December 2002. Available at: https://www.hindustantimes.com/india/gujarat-experiment-to-be-repeated-in-delhi-togadia/story-KKIkXFDOLZMKA3Gm1JnaWM.html.
12. Vasundhara Raje, 'Vasundhara Raje HardTalk India Interview with Karan Thapar' [video], YouTube, 3 April 2018. Available at: https://www.youtube.com/watch?v=vbZuNoFtTK8&t=381s.
13. Hamza Khan, 'Rajasthan temple row: Last time, it was Raje in the dock, as RSS flung barbs like "Aurangzeb"', *The Indian Express*, 25 April 2022. Available at: https://indianexpress.com/article/political-pulse/rajasthan-temple-row-raje-dock-rss-flung-barbs-aurangzeb-7883967/.
14. Ibid.
15. Interview with Yunus Khan, Jaipur, 2024.

5. Bovines and Bloodshed: Mob Lynchings and the Communal Cauldron

1. S. Raju, 'Mathura cult movement traces back to UP godman, battles over his legacy', *Hindustan Times*, 8 June 2016. Available at: https://www.hindustantimes.com/india-news/mathura-cult-movement-traces-back-to-up-godman-battles-over-his-legacy/story-zYjbDNqxWdqhWM8lpDVlDI.html.
2. Kaunain Sheriff M. and Ishita Mishra, 'The elusive Baba Jai Gurudev in the Mathura mix', *The Indian Express*, 12 June 2016. Available at: https://indianexpress.com/article/india/india-news-india/mathura-violence-clashes-ghurelal-maharaj-baja-jai-gurudev2847899/.

3. Interview with Gopi Chand Gurjar, Jaipur, 2021.
4. Ibid.
5. Shail Mayaram, *Resisting Regimes: Myth, Memory and the Shaping of a Muslim Identity* (New York: Oxford University Press, 1997), p. 190.
6. Rajasthan State assembly Archives.
7. Statement in the Rajasthan State assembly, ibid.
8. Hamza Khan, 'Cattle sales at Rajasthan fairs last year: 8 in Pushkar, 6 in Bharatpur', *The Indian Express*, 20 August 2018. Available at: https://indianexpress.com/article/india/cattle-sales-at-rajasthan-fairs-last-year-8-in-pushkar-6-in-bharatpur-5077020/.
9. TNN, 'Rajasthan: Ex-BJP MLA Gyan Dev Ahuja caught on tape admitting "lynching"', *Times of India*, 21 August 2022. Available at: https://timesofindia.indiatimes.com/city/jaipur/rajasthan-ex-bjp-mla-gyan-dev-ahuja-caught-on-tape-admitting-lynching/articleshow/93685957.cms.
10. Deep Mukherjee, 'Alwar lynching: Rajasthan police close probe against 6 Hindu right-wing men named by Pehlu Khan', *Hindustan Times*, 14 September 2017. Available at: https://www.hindustantimes.com/india-news/no-one-killed-pehlu-khan-probe-against-hindu-right-wing-men-named-by-dying-cattle-farmer-closed/story-SDghUwo8QQJRAArn2Gy2rK.html.
11. Deep Mukherjee, 'We won't let you pay tribute to Pehlu Khan: Hindu groups confront activists in Rajasthan', *Hindustan Times*, 15 September 2017. Available at: https://www.hindustantimes.com/india-news/we-won-t-let-you-pay-tribute-to-pehlu-khan-hindu-groups-confront-activists-in-rajasthan/story-2JoujSka5TzxB4VQOndBfN.html.
12. Interview with anonymous at Behror, Alwar, 15 September 2017.
13. Deep Mukherjee, 'Surprising that video, photos not taken on record: court on Pehlu Khan probe', *The Indian Express*, 16 August 2019. Available at: https://indianexpress.com/article/india/surprising-that-video-photos-not-taken-on-record-court-on-pehlu-khan-probe-5908723/.
14. Mohammed Iqbal, 'Pehlu Khan lynching case: Juvenile Justice Board convicts two minors', *The Hindu*, 8 March 2020. Available at: https://www.thehindu.com/news/national/other-states/pehlu-khan-lynching-case-juvenile-justice-board-convicts-two-minors/article31007297.ece.
15. 'Khan Mohammad S/O Shri Ahmad Khan vs State Of Rajasthan on

30 October, 2019', CRLMP-5935/2019, Rajasthan High Court, Jaipur. Available at: https://indiankanoon.org/doc/56103426/.

16. Deep Mukherjee, 'Doctors treated Pehlu Khan's body as dummy: JJB in verdict', *The Indian Express*, 4 March 2020. Available at: https://indianexpress.com/article/cities/pehlu-khan-body-juvenile-justice-board-6313426/.
17. Interview with Nasir Ali Naqvi, Jaipur, February 2021.
18. Deep Mukherjee, 'Rajasthan: 23 cases of cow-related violence in 2017', *The Indian Express*, 2 January 2018. Available at: https://indianexpress.com/article/india/rajasthan-23-cases-of-cow-related-violence-in-2017-5008007/.
19. Neha Mehrotra, 'After Alwar Lynching, Meo Muslims Forced to Deal With Institutions That Neglected Them', The Wire, 27 July 2018. Available at: https://thewire.in/rights/alwar-lynching-rakbar-khan-meo-muslims.
20. Deep Mukherjee, '2 found charred in their car: family alleges murder, Bajrang Dal role', *The Indian Express*, 17 February 2023. Available at: https://indianexpress.com/article/india/2-found-charred-in-their-car-family-alleges-murder-bajrang-dal-role-8450011/.
21. Ibid.
22. 'Karauli violence: 13 arrested so far, SIT formed, say police', *The Indian Express*, 3 April 2022. Available at: https://indianexpress.com/article/cities/jaipur/karauli-violence-arrested-sit-formed-say-police-7851232/.
23. BJP Rajasthan (@BJP4Rajasthan), 'बेटियों की अस्मत हो रही तार-तार गृहमंत्री गहलोत कर रहे इफ्तार...', X, 22 April 2022. Available at: https://x.com/BJP4Rajasthan/status/1517548487222902784?t=EVNiitn_sJx4lt4j6tvp-A&s=19.
24. Deep Mukherjee, '"Who did Cong project as CM face? There is no set way. BJP central leadership will pick a person as CM": Rajasthan BJP chief', *The Indian Express*, 29 April 2022. Available at: https://indianexpress.com/article/political-pulse/rajasthan-satish-poonia-bjp-congress-ashok-gehlot-vasundhara-raje-7892569/.
25. Express News Service, 'Tension in Hanumangarh after clash injures VHP man, 7 arrested for attack', *The Indian Express*, 13 May 2022. Available at: https://indianexpress.com/article/cities/jaipur/tension-in-

hanumangarh-after-clash-injures-vhp-man-7-arrested-for-attack-7914582/.

26. Deep Mukherjee, 'Rajasthan labourer hacked: Accused claimed murder in name of rescuing woman, she denies link', *The Indian Express*, 9 December 2017. Available at: https://indianexpress.com/article/india/rajasthan-hacking-accused-claimed-murder-in-name-of-rescuing-woman-she-denies-link-4974668/.
27. Deep Mukherjee, 'Udaipur protesters call Afrazul killer "symbol of Hindu anger", cite "Muslim video"', *The Indian Express*, 17 December 2017. Available at: https://indianexpress.com/article/india/udaipur-murder-afrazul-khan-killer-4986140/.
28. Ibid.
29. 'Tailor beheaded in Udaipur for social media post backing Nupur Sharma', *The Hindu*, 29 June 2022. Available at: https://www.thehindu.com/news/national/other-states/tailor-murdered-in-rajasthans-udaipur-assailants-film-crime/article65576740.ece.
30. Aishwarya Iyer, 'In Udaipur, family of murdered tailor say they don't know who wrote the post supporting Nupur Sharma', Scroll.in, 4 July 2022. Available at: https://scroll.in/article/1027508/in-udaipur-family-of-murdered-tailor-say-they-don-t-know-who-wrote-the-post-supporting-nupur-sharma.
31. Interview with anonymous, Udaipur, 29 June 2022.
32. Tabeenah Anjum, 'No Covid Vaccine Without Aadhaar For Hindu Refugees From Pakistan', Outlook, 16 January 2024. Available at: https://www.outlookindia.com/national/india-news-no-covid-vaccine-without-aadhar-for-hindu-refugees-from-pakistan-news-383691.
33. Tabeenah Anjum, 'Rajasthan HC Asks Govt To Explain Why Pakistani Refugees Are Not Eligible For Covid Vaccine', Outlook, 16 January 2024. Available at: https://www.outlookindia.com/national/india-news-rajasthan-hc-asks-govt-to-explain-why-pakistani-refugees-are-not-eligble-for-covid-vaccine-news-384290.
34. Tabeenah Anjum, 'No Work, Vaccine Or Ration: Rohingya Refugees In Jaipur Stare At A Bleak Future', Outlook, 16 January 2024. Available at: https://www.outlookindia.com/national/india-news-no-work-vaccine-or-ration-rohingya-refugees-in-jaipur-stare-at-a-bleak-future-news-384438.

6. Shackles of Caste: Exploitation and Resistance

1. Deep Mukherjee, 'A day in the life of a Manu statue in the Rajasthan High Court', *The Indian Express*, 28 October 2018. Available at: https://indianexpress.com/article/india/a-day-in-the-life-of-a-manu-statue-in-the-rajasthan-high-court-5421545/.
2. Interview with Bhanwar Meghwanshi, Jaipur, 2023.
3. Interview with Kailash Mina, Sikar, 2021.
4. Khurshed Tiwari, 'Giriraj Singh Malinga: मायावती ने मुझे नेता बनाया.., हम क्यों जाएं उदयपुर, CM के कहने पर सरेंडर करने वाले MLA मलिंगा ने कह दी खरी-खरी', *Navbharat Times*, 5 June 2022. Available at: https://navbharattimes.indiatimes.com/state/rajasthan/jaipur/girraj-malinga-said-mayawati-made-him-leader-khiladi-0lal-bairwa-express-anger-on-cm-gehlot/articleshow/92003515.cms.
5. Deep Mukherjee, 'Left hanging by Congress, Rajasthan MLA accused of assaulting Dalit engineer joins BJP', *The Indian Express*, 7 November 2023. Available at: https://indianexpress.com/article/political-pulse/rajasthan-congress-mla-accused-of-assaulting-dalit-engineer-joins-bjp-9015161/.
6. Joychen Joseph, 'BSP sells tickets to highest bidder, says party MLA in Rajasthan assembly', *Times of India*, 2 August 2019. Available at: https://timesofindia.indiatimes.com/city/jaipur/bsp-sells-tickets-to-highest-bidder-says-party-mla-in-rajasthan-assembly/articleshow/70489490.cms.
7. 'WATCH | Two BSP leaders garlanded with shoes, paraded on a donkey outside party office in Rajasthan', *The New Indian Express*, 22 October 2019. Available at: https://www.newindianexpress.com/nation/2019/Oct/22/watch--two-bsp-leaders-garlanded-with-shoes-paraded-on-a-donkey-outside-party-office-in-rajasthan-2051371.html.
8. Deep Mukherjee, 'He wanted to become a lecturer, says father of Dalit youth killed in Rajasthan', *The Indian Express*, 3 April 2018. Available at: https://indianexpress.com/article/india/he-wanted-to-become-a-lecturer-says-father-of-dalit-youth-killed-in-rajasthan-5121245/.
9. Deep Mukherjee, 'At the receiving end in one Rajasthan town, Dalits say may embrace Islam', *The Indian Express*, 5 April 2018. Available at: https://indianexpress.com/article/india/dalit-bharat-bandh-protests-rajasthan-hindaun-bjp-mla-house-fire-5123746/.
10. TNN, '"State Trying To Supress Demands"', *Times of India*, 9 May 2018.

Available at: https://timesofindia.indiatimes.com/city/jaipur/state-trying-to-supress-demands/amp_articleshow/64086097.cms.

11. Vindhya First, 'SC/ST एक्ट पर सुखदेव सहि गोगामेड़ी का वीडियो वायरल' [video], YouTube, 8 December 2023. Available at: https://www.youtube.com/watch?v=Psllo5SKXnU.
12. Interview with Anil Kumar Dhenwal, Jaipur, 2022.
13. PTI, 'Over 57,000 Cases Registered For Committing Crimes Against Scheduled Castes In 2023: Data', NDTV, 1 October 2025. Available at: https://www.ndtv.com/india-news/over-57-000-cases-registered-for-committing-crimes-against-scheduled-castes-in-2023-data-9373186.
14. Geeta Pandey, 'Bhanwari Devi: The rape that led to India's sexual harassment law', BBC, 17 March 2017. Available at: https://www.bbc.com/news/world-asia-india-39265653.
15. Interview with Lad Kumari Jain, Jaipur, 2023.
16. 'Rajasthan CM Ashok Gehlot on high rape cases: Mandatory FIRs, 56% charges false', *The Indian Express*, 3 September 2022. Available at: https://indianexpress.com/article/cities/jaipur/rajasthan-ashok-gehlot-congress-ncrb-data-rape-cases-8127398/.
17. Deep Mukherjee, 'Rajasthan CM Ashok Gehlot says death penalty for rape leading to murders, faces backlash', *The Indian Express*, 8 August 2022. Available at: https://indianexpress.com/article/political-pulse/gehlot-death-penalty-rape-leading-murders-faces-backlash-8076676/.
18. Deep Mukherjee, 'Rajasthan Police data refutes Ashok Gehlot's claim of rising rape-murder cases, shows decline in two years', *The Indian Express*, 12 August 2022. Available at: https://indianexpress.com/article/cities/jaipur/rajasthan-police-data-rape-murder-cases-ashok-gehlot-8084100/.
19. Deep Mukherjee, 'Dalit youth killed in Rajasthan after row over Ambedkar poster: Police', *The Indian Express*, 10 June 2021. Available at: https://indianexpress.com/article/india/dalit-youth-killed-in-rajasthan-after-row-over-ambedkar-poster-police-7351729/.
20. Deep Mukherjee, 'Despite Rajasthan HC protection, father kills teen who eloped with Dalit man', *The Indian Express*, 5 March 2021. Available at: https://indianexpress.com/article/cities/jaipur/days-after-rajasthan-hc-ordered-police-protection-18-yr-old-in-relationship-with-dalit-man-abducted-by-family-killed-7214041/.

21. Tabeenah Anjum, 'Killed For Sporting A Moustache: Dalits In Rajasthan's Feudal Villages Face Rising Tide Of Caste Violence', Article 14, 6 April 2022. Available at: https://article-14.com/post/killed-for-sporting-a-moustache-dalits-in-rajasthan-s-feudal-villages-face-rising-tide-of-caste-violence-624cf9afb65f5.
22. Deep Mukherjee, 'Rajasthan: "Were asked to compromise, not file case", says family of Dalit boy killed for "drinking water from pot meant for upper caste teacher"', *The Indian Express*, 14 August 2022. Available at: https://indianexpress.com/article/cities/chandigarh/haryana-ips-officer-suicide-bjp-leaders-allies-demand-action-against-dgp-former-rohtak-sp-10304378/?ref=infinite.
23. Deep Mukherjee, '"I Cannot Live": Dalit Cop in Rajasthan Kills Self Over Alleged Harassment by Superiors, Journalist', The Wire, 24 August 2024. Available at: https://thewire.in/news/i-cannot-live-dalit-cop-suicide-rajasthan-alleged-harassment.
24. Deep Mukherjee, '"He Was Our Only Support": Kin of Dalit Man Beaten to Death by Liquor Mafia Demand Justice', The Wire, 22 May 2024. Available at: https://thewire.in/caste/he-was-our-only-support-kin-of-dalit-man-beaten-to-death-by-liquor-mafia-demand-justice.
25. Deep Mukherjee, 'In Damage-Control Mode, Rajasthan BJP Suspends Leader Who Sprinkled Gangajal in Temple Visited by Dalit LoP', The Wire, 8 April 2025. Available at: https://thewire.in/caste/rajasthan-bjp-gangajal-temple-dalit-congress-leader.
26. Deep Mukherjee, 'In Rajasthan village, with some official help: "I'm first Dalit groom to ride mare"', *The Indian Express*, 25 January 2022. Available at: https://www.removepaywall.com/search?url=https://indianexpress.com/article/cities/jaipur/in-rajasthan-village-with-some-official-help-im-first-dalit-groom-to-ride-mare-7739911/.
27. Ibid.
28. Chhotubhai Vasava (@Chhotu_Vasava), 'BTP नेक है इसलिए बीजेपी कोंग्रेस एक है @ashokgehlot51 जी आपको …', X, 10 December 2020. Available at: https://x.com/Chhotu_Vasava/status/1337071260946243585.
29. Interview with Rajkumar Roat, Jaipur, 2020.
30. Fact Fold, 'Adivasi Dharm Code in Rajsthan assembly by Ganesh Ghoghra' [video], YouTube, 12 March 2021. Available at: https://www.youtube.com/watch?v=AkAzFXmmcoA.

31. PTI, 'No input about Naxal activities in Rajasthan: Top cop', *The Economic Times*, 11 January 2021. Available at: https://economictimes.indiatimes.com/news/defence/no-input-about-naxal-activities-in-rajasthan-top-cop/articleshow/80215371.cms?utm_source=contentofinterest&utm_medium=text&utm_campaign=cppst.
32. Interview with anonymous Congress leader, Jaipur, 2021.
33. Deep Mukherjee, 'Rajasthan MLA demands tribal code, Cong underplays remarks, BJP cries foul', *The Indian Express*, 12 March 2021. Available at: https://indianexpress.com/article/cities/jaipur/rajasthan-mla-demands-tribal-code-cong-underplays-remarks-bjp-cries-foul-7224861/.
34. Deep Mukherjee, 'Old player, new avatar: A new tribal party looks to upend poll math in south Rajasthan', *The Indian Express*, 21 October 2023. Available at: https://indianexpress.com/article/political-pulse/tribal-party-south-rajasthan-assembly-elections-8990501/.
35. Deep Mukherjee, 'The "parallel force" in Rajasthan BJP, Kirodi Lal Meena takes the fight to Congress', *The Indian Express*, 17 October 2023. Available at: https://indianexpress.com/article/political-pulse/rajasthan-bjp-kirodi-lal-meena-congress-8987616/.

7. A Wily Survivor: Ashok Gehlot's Political Craft

1. Deep Mukherjee, 'Ashok Gehlot revives a poll battle with rival from varsity days', *The Indian Express*, 5 December 2018. Available at: https://indianexpress.com/article/india/ashok-gehlot-revives-a-poll-battle-with-rival-from-varsity-days-5478874/.
2. Ashok Gehlot (ashokgehlot51), 'After the foundation of NSUI … became the first president of #Rajasthan NSUI …', X, 10 April 2020. Available at: https://x.com/ashokgehlot51/status/1248472313604919296.
3. Interview with Mahesh Bora, Jodhpur, August 2021.
4. Interview with Mahesh Bora, 2021.
5. News Tak, 'राजस्थान के CM अशोक गहलोत ने दो साल पहले एक वीडियो में कहा था: "मैं जादूगर हूं…', Facebook, 25 August 2022. Available at: https://www.facebook.com/newstakofficial/videos/5575178745877333/.
6. TNN, 'First-time MLA Divya Maderna reminds Gehlot camp of history', *Times of India*, 27 September 2022. Available at: https://timesofindia.indiatimes.com/city/jaipur/first-time-mla-divya-maderna-reminds-gehlot-camp-of-history/articleshow/94466808.cms.

7. Interview with Rohit Parihar, Jaipur, 2025.
8. Ibid.
9. Official records of the proceedings of Rajasthan State assembly.
10. Kamla Bora, 'Rajasthan employees give in, end 64-day strike', Rediff, 17 February 2000.Available at: https://m.rediff.com/news/2000/feb/17strike.htm.
11. Ruhi Tewari, 'Congress comes up tops in Rajasthan with 96 seats', Mint, 8 December 2008. Available at: https://www.livemint.com/Politics/iQRykeSte2yOspMhwCxtAI/Congress-comes-up-tops-in-Rajasthan-with-96-seats.html.
12. 'Gujarat Election Result: Ashok Gehlot, man who gave BJP a fight in Modi's home ground', Moneycontrol, 18 December 2017. Available at: https://www.moneycontrol.com/news/india/gujarat-election-result-ashok-gehlot-man-who-gave-bjp-a-fight-modis-home-ground-2463471.html.
13. Special release-1: Free Medicines for serious diseases proving boon for patients Rajasthan ranks first in country in Free Medicine Scheme, Health Department, Government of Rajasthan, Jaipur, 20 December 2019. Available at: https://diprfile.rajasthan.gov.in/news/182988/document/SpecialRelease1.pdf.
14. PTI, 'Rajasthan assembly passes anti lynching bill', *The Hindu*, 5 August 2019. Available at: https://www.thehindu.com/news/national/rajasthan-assembly-passes-anti-mob-lynching-bill/article28823205.ece.
15. Mohammed Iqbal, 'Anti-violence Bills still await presidential nod', *The Hindu*, 1 September 2019. Available at: https://www.thehindu.com/news/national/other-states/anti-violence-bills-still-await-presidential-nod/article29311151.ece.
16. Deep Mukherjee, 'Decode Politics: What is the Rajasthan health scheme Rahul is talking about', *The Indian Express*, 2 December 2023. Available at: https://indianexpress.com/article/political-pulse/rajasthan-health-scheme-rahul-gandhi-decoded-9051036/.
17. Sidhartha Dutta, 'Rajasthan to launch Jan Soochna Portal on Friday; first state to do so', *Times of India*, 12 September 2019. Available at: https://timesofindia.indiatimes.com/city/jaipur/rajasthan-to-launch-jan-soochna-portal-on-friday-first-state-to-do-so/articleshow/71096727.cms.

18. PTI, 'Rajasthan Increases Workdays To 125 Days In Job Guarantee Scheme', NDTV, 23 February 2023. Available at: https://www.ndtv.com/india-news/rajasthan-increases-workdays-to-125-days-in-job-guarantee-scheme-3809031.
19. Sobhana K. Nair, 'Eye on Rajasthan polls, CM Gehlot reaches out to gig workers with welfare measures', *The Hindu*, 24 April 2023. Available at: https://www.thehindu.com/news/national/eye-on-rajasthan-polls-cm-gehlot-reaches-out-to-gig-workers-with-welfare-measures/article66770109.ece.
20. PTI, 'Education, healthcare shouldn't be used for making profit: Gehlot on protest against Right to Health Bill', *The Hindu*, 4 March 2023. Available at: https://www.thehindu.com/news/national/other-states/education-healthcare-shouldnt-be-used-for-making-profit-gehlot-on-protest-against-right-to-health-bill/article66579929.ece.
21. Rohit Parihar, 'Pub culture comment lands Gehlot in controversy', *India Today*, 28 January 2009. Available at: https://www.indiatoday.in/latest-headlines/story/pub-culture-comment-lands-gehlot-in-controversy-38323-2009-01-28.
22. 'Missing nurse case: Gehlot sacks tainted minister', NDTV, 16 October 2011. Available at: https://www.ndtv.com/india-news/missing-nurse-case-gehlot-sacks-tainted-minister-565519.
23. 'Vajpayee woos Rajasthan's Jats with reservation promise', Rediff, 30 August 1999. Available at: https://m.rediff.com/election/1999/aug/30jat1.htm.
24. 'Sachin Pilot should be made Rajasthan CM: Congress MLA', *The Indian Express*, 6 June 2019. Available at: http://indianexpress.com/article/india/sachin-pilot-should-be-made-rajasthan-cm-congress-mla-5767487/.
25. Deep Mukherjee, 'Will return to power, I am here for 15-20 years, says Ashok Gehlot', *The Indian Express*, 3 October 2021. Available at: https://indianexpress.com/article/cities/jaipur/will-return-to-power-i-am-here-for-15-20-years-says-ashok-gehlot-7548619/.
26. 'Ashok Gehlot apologises to Sonia Gandhi for Rajasthan crisis, says won't contest Congress presidential poll', *The Indian Express*, 29 September 2022. Available at: https://indianexpress.com/article/india/wont-contest-congress-presidential-polls-apologised-to-sonia-gandhi-ashok-gehlot-8180393/.

27. 'Parallel meeting of Gehlot loyalist MLAs amounts to indiscipline: Maken', *Times of India*, 26 September 2022. Available at: https://timesofindia.indiatimes.com/india/parallel-meeting-of-gehlot-loyalist-mlas-amounts-to-indiscipline-maken/articleshow/94451691.cms.
28. Deep Mukherjee, 'Brand Ashok Gehlot seeks fourth term on back of welfare schemes, publicity blitz', *The Indian Express*, 10 June 2023. Available at: https://indianexpress.com/article/political-pulse/ashok-gehlot-welfare-schemes-rajasthan-8655785/.
29. Deep Mukherjee, 'Two rivals, one stone: Ashok Gehlot tries to corner Sachin Pilot, Vasundhara Raje at one go', *The Indian Express*, 9 May 2023. Available at: https://indianexpress.com/article/political-pulse/two-rivals-one-stone-ashok-gehlot-tries-to-corner-sachin-pilot-vasundhara-raje-at-one-go-8599360/.
30. '"Same car for 15 years? Buy a black Defender": Jaipur tea seller urges former CM Ashok Gehlot to upgrade wheels; video goes viral', *Times of India*, 29 July 2025. Available at: https://timesofindia.indiatimes.com/city/jaipur/same-car-for-15-years-buy-a-black-defender-jaipur-tea-seller-urges-former-cm-ashok-gehlot-to-upgrade-wheels-video-goes-viral/articleshow/122966645.cms.

8. The Game Changer: Vasundhara Raje's Raj

1. Tabeenah Anjum, 'Aggressive Raje targets 180 of 200 Rajasthan seats', *Deccan Herald*, 7 August 2018. Available at: https://www.deccanherald.com/archives/aggressive-raje-targets-180.html.
2. Vasundhara Raje, 'Vasundhara Raje HardTalk India Interview with Karan Thapar' [video], Youtube, 3 April 2018. Available at: https://www.youtube.com/watch?v=vbZuNoFtTK8.
3. Rohit Parihar and Priya Sahgal, 'Rajasthan: Vasundhara Raje, BJP turn the tables on Congress by focusing on local issues', *India Today*, 15 December 2003. Available at: https://www.indiatoday.in/magazine/cover-story/story/20031215-rajasthan-vasundhara-raje-bjp-turn-the-tables-on-congress-by-focusing-on-local-issues-791311-1999-11-29.
4. Interview with Suman Sharma, Jaipur, January 2023.
5. T. K. Rajalakshmi, 'Stopping Togadia', *Frontline*, 9 May 2003. Available at: https://frontline.thehindu.com/other/article30216876.ece.

6. Rohit Parihar, 'Rajasthan CM Ashok Gehlot orders Pravin Togadia arrest for displaying tridents', *India Today*, 28 April 2003. Available at: https://www.indiatoday.in/magazine/indiascope/story/20030428-rajasthan-cm-ashok-gehlot-orders-pravin-togadia-arrest-for-displaying-tridents-792858-2003-04-27.
7. The Rajasthan Sports (Registration, Recognition and Regulation of Associations) Act, 2005, India Code. Available at: https://www.indiacode.nic.in/bitstream/123456789/21618/1/sports%2Bact%2B2005.pdf.
8. Interview with Suman Sharma.
9. PTI, 'Five killed in Gurjar-Meena clash in Rajasthan', *Times of India*, 1 June 2007. Available at: https://timesofindia.indiatimes.com/india/five-killed-in-gujjar-meena-clash-in-rajasthan/articleshow/2091973.cms.
10. Siddharth S. Bose, 'Full-blown caste war rages on in R'sthan, 8 killed', *Hindustan Times*, 2 June 2007. Available at: https://www.hindustantimes.com/india/full-blown-caste-war-rages-on-in-r-sthan-8-killed/story-YP3gLQTIDl0RYUIlXRPptK.html.
11. TNN, 'SC quizzes Raje government over dip in ads to newspaper', *Times of India*, 6 September 2016. Available at: https://timesofindia.indiatimes.com/india/sc-quizzes-raje-government-over-dip-in-ads-to-newspaper/articleshow/54026489.cms.
12. Based on the authors' own experience.
13. Sharat Kumar, 'Rajasthan rewrites history: Maharana Pratap, not Akbar, won Battle of Haldighati', *India Today*, 25 July 2017. Available at: https://www.indiatoday.in/india/story/maharana-pratap-not-akbar-won-battle-of-haldighati-rajasthan-history-book-1026240-2017-07-25.
14. Mahim Pratap Singh, 'Jawaharlal Nehru erased from Rajasthan school textbook, Congress angry', *The Indian Express*, 26 May 2016. Available at: https://indianexpress.com/article/india/india-news-india/jawaharlal-nehru-erased-from-rajasthan-school-textbook-2789754/.
15. Interview with Manvendra Singh, Jaipur, 2023.
16. Deep Mukherjee, 'Sachin Pilot interview: "No clearer camps today than in BJP — of Vasundhara Raje and central leadership"', *The Indian Express*, 12 November 2018. Available at: https://indianexpress.com/article/india/sachin-pilot-interview-no-clearer-camps-today-than-in-bjp-of-vasundhara-raje-and-central-leadership-5441648/.

17. Interview with Suman Sharma.
18. Harsha Kumari Singh, 'Rajasthan Recommends CBI Probe Into Gangster Anand Pal Singh's Encounter', NDTV, 18 July 2017. Available at: https://www.ndtv.com/india-news/rajasthan-gangster-anand-pal-singhs-encounter-to-be-investigated-by-cbi-1726290.
19. Deep Mukherjee, 'Vasundhara Raje interview: "I have worked very hard, will not use Congress as benchmark"', *The Indian Express*, 7 August 2018. Available at: https://indianexpress.com/article/india/rajasthan-elections-vasundhara-raje-rajasthan-gaurav-yatra-bjp-congress-5294893/.
20. 'Against Horse-trading Going on to Topple Elected Govt in Rajasthan, Says BJP MLA Kailash Meghwal', News18, 18 July 2020. Available at: https://www.news18.com/news/politics/against-horse-trading-going-on-to-topple-elected-govt-in-rajasthan-says-senior-bjp-mla-kailash-meghwal-2722569.html.
21. PTI, 'BJP leaders Raje, Kailash Meghwal refused to support conspiracy to topple my govt in 2020: Gehlot', ThePrint, 8 May 2023. Available at: https://theprint.in/india/bjp-leaders-raje-kailash-meghwal-refused-to-support-conspiracy-to-topple-my-govt-in-2020-gehlot/1561401/.
22. 'Rajasthan political crisis | Union Minister Gajendra Singh Shekhawat hints at Sachin Pilot's entry into BJP', *The Hindu*, 14 July 2020. Available at: https://www.thehindu.com/news/national/rajasthan-political-crisis-union-minister-gajendra-singh-shekhawat-hints-at-sachin-pilots-entry-into-bjp/article32081793.ece.
23. Joychen Joseph, 'BJP ally Beniwal accuses former CM Raje of helping Gehlot', *Times of India*, 17 July 2020. Available at: https://timesofindia.indiatimes.com/city/jaipur/bjp-ally-beniwal-accuses-former-cm-raje-of-helping-gehlot/articleshow/77008886.cms.
24. Interview with Kali Charan Saraf, Jaipur, 2021.
25. Interview with Bhawani Singh Rajawat, 2021.
26. '"Undeclared emergency more dangerous": Ghanshyam Tiwari quits BJP', *The Indian Express*, 26 June 2018. Available at: https://indianexpress.com/article/cities/jaipur/undeclared-emergency-more-dangerous-ghanshyam-tiwari-quits-bjp-5233186-5233186/.
27. Deep Mukherjee, 'Vasundhara Raje detractor Ghanshyam Tiwari returns to BJP', *The Indian Express*, 13 December 2020. Available at: https://

indianexpress.com/article/india/vasundhara-raje-detractor-ghanshyam-tiwari-returns-to-bjp-7102238/.

28. Vasundhara Raje, 'भाजपा राजस्थान से राज्य सभा प्रत्याशी श्री घनश्याम तिवाड़ी जी ने मेरे जयपुर आवास पहुँच मुलाक़ात की। …', Facebook, 30 May 2022. Available at: https://www.facebook.com/photo.php?fbid=596486288504334&id=100044289046557&set=a.570758184410478.
29. Interview with anonymous senior BJP leader, 2021.
30. Deep Mukherjee, 'Vasundhara Raje on next CM face of Rajasthan: "Person loved by all communities gets to rule"', *The Indian Express*, 23 October 2021. Available at: https://indianexpress.com/article/cities/jaipur/next-cm-rajasthan-preferred-people-vasundhara-raje-7584950/.
31. Shahnawaz Akhtar, 'Fighting female foeticide in India', Al Jazeera, 2 December 2013. Available at: https://www.aljazeera.com/news/2013/12/2/fighting-female-foeticide-in-india.
32. Interview with Harsha Kumari Singh, Jaipur, July 2025.

9. The Ascent of the Challenger: Sachin Pilot's Rise

1. Interview with Sachin Pilot, Jaipur, 2022.
2. PTI, 'Rajasthan PCC chief Chandrabhan resigns', *The Economic Times*, 8 December 2013. Available at: https://economictimes.indiatimes.com/news/politics-and-nation/rajasthan-pcc-chief-chandrabhan-resigns/articleshow/27085369.cms?from=mdr.
3. PTI, 'Companies Bill passed, government calls it "historic feat"', *Times of India*, 8 August 2013. Available at: https://timesofindia.indiatimes.com/business/india-business/companies-bill-passed-govt-calls-it-historic-feat/articleshow/21708613.cms.
4. 'Rama Pilot wins Dausa LS seat', Zee News, 3 October 2000. Available at: https://zeenews.india.com/exclusive/what-global-warming-has-done_2472.html/amp.
5. Deep Mukherjee, 'Rewind & Replay | The rise of Indira Gandhi, and the shrinking of Rajasthan CMs', *The Indian Express*, 1 October 2022. Available at: https://indianexpress.com/article/political-pulse/rise-of-indira-gandhi-and-shrinking-of-rajasthan-cms-8183379/.
6. Lipi, 'सचिन पायलट के लिए खून का एक एक कतरा बहाने को तैयार... जानिए कौन हैं राकेश पारीक', *Navbharat Times*, 12 September 2022. Available at: https://navbharattimes.

indiatimes.com/state/rajasthan/jaipur/rajasthan-politics-congress-mla-rakesh-pareek-on-sachin-pilot/articleshow/94160544.cms.

7. Interview with Vibha Mathur, January 2023.
8. RUBARU, 'Rubaru: old interview Rajesh Pilot with Rajeev Shukla (part 1)' [video], YouTube, 8 June 2017. Available at: https://www.youtube.com/watch?v=5msA3V3PzyM&t=133s.
9. Deep Mukherjee, 'Rajasthan elections: Up against BJP's only Muslim candidate, Sachin Pilot dares Yogi Adityanath to come and seek votes', *The Indian Express,* 2 December 2018. Available at: https://indianexpress.com/elections/rajasthan-assembly-elections-up-against-bjps-only-muslim-candidate-sachin-pilot-dares-yogi-adityanath-to-come-and-seek-votes-5474607/. See also 'Tonk (Rajasthan) assembly Constituency Elections', Elections.in. Available at: https://www.elections.in/rajasthan/assemblyconstituencies/tonk.html.
10. Aabshar H. Quazi, 'Garlic glut, price crash leave Rajasthan farmers in distress', *Hindustan Times*, 1 June 2018. Available at: https://www.hindustantimes.com/jaipur/garlic-glut-price-crash-leave-rajasthan-farmers-in-distress/story-suy3A2fCnLn85CYV6uiQzJ.html.
11. DHNS, 'Congress to take out 100km Kisan Nyay Yatra in CM Raje's home district', *Deccan Herald*, 27 September 2017. Available at: https://www.deccanherald.com/content/635241/congress-take-100km-kisan-nyay.html.
12. D. K. Singh, 'Rama Pilot to contest against Vasundhara Raje', *Hindustan Times,* 15 November 2003. Available at: https://www.hindustantimes.com/india/rama-pilot-to-contest-against-vasundhara-raje/story-sJ72TsdHN655zwslnsgFmN.html.
13. N. K. Singh, 'Sitaram Kesri wins Congress presidential polls, now must put party on the road to recovery', *India Today*, 23 June 1997. Available at: https://www.indiatoday.in/magazine/nation/story/19970623-sitaram-kesri-wins-congress-presidential-polls-now-must-put-party-on-the-road-to-recovery-831659-1997-06-22.
14. Interview with Sachin Pilot, Jaipur, 2023.
15. Aabshar H. Quazi, 'Will not wear Rajasthani turban until Congress comes to power: Sachin Pilot', *Hindustan Times*, 8 October 2017. Available at: https://www.hindustantimes.com/jaipur/will-not-wear-

rajasthani-turban-until-congress-comes-to-power-sachin-pilot/story-1ZhdKeLac8j2FZxY8FCW0I.html.

16. Deep Mukherjee, 'Sachin Pilot interview: "No clearer camps today than in BJP — of Vasundhara Raje and central leadership"', *The Indian Express*, 12 November 2018. Available at: https://indianexpress.com/article/india/sachin-pilot-interview-no-clearer-camps-today-than-in-bjp-of-vasundhara-raje-and-central-leadership-5441648/.
17. Tabeenah Anjum, 'In this border Dalit village, no girl attends school', *Deccan Herald,* 19 April 2019. Available at: https://www.deccanherald.com/india/in-this-border-dalit-village-no-girl-attends-school-729621.html; Anjum, 'Delta Meghwal Case: Rajasthan Court Convicts All Accused; Victim's Father Says "Justice Delivered"', Outlook India, 16 January 2024. Available at: https://www.outlookindia.com/national/india-news-delta-meghwal-case-rajasthan-court-convicts-all-accused-victims-father-says-justice-delivered-news-397094.
18. Interview with Sachin Pilot, Jaipur, 2023.
19. ANI, 'Lalit Modi row: Congress to protest against Vasundhara Raje in Jaipur today', *Financial Express,* 24 June 2015. Available at: https://www.financialexpress.com/india-news/lalit-modi-row-congress-to-protest-against-vasundhara-raje-in-jaipur-today/89296/.
20. Amit Agnihotri, 'Sachin Pilot wants Vasundhara Raje removed for helping Lalit Modi', *India Today*, 18 June 2015. Available at: https://www.indiatoday.in/mail-today/story/lalit-modi-interview-sachin-pilot-vasundhara-raje-258149-2015-06-17.
21. Sweta Dutta, 'Raje-Modi controversy: Congress gets a shot in the arm in Rajasthan but stands divided', *The Indian Express,* 22 June 2015. Available at: https://indianexpress.com/article/india/india-others/raje-modi-controversy-congress-gets-a-shot-in-the-arm-in-rajasthan-but-stands-divided/.
22. Bhanu Pratap Singh, 'Rajasthan Congress takes out rally on animal-carts to protest against hiked fuel prices', *Times of India*, 26 September 2017. Available at: https://timesofindia.indiatimes.com/city/jaipur/rajasthan-congress-takes-out-rally-on-animal-carts-to-protest-against-hiked-fuel-prices/articleshow/60843747.cms.
23. TNN, 'Congress alleges Rs 45,000 crore mines scam in Rajasthan', *Times of India*, 26 September 2015. Available at: https://timesofindia.indiatimes.

com/india/congress-alleges-rs-45000-crore-mines-scam-in-rajasthan/articleshow/49105084.cms.

24. 'Rajasthan Patrika won't write about government till ordinance shielding public servants is repealed', Scroll.in, 1 November 2017. Available at: https://scroll.in/latest/856303/rajasthan-patrika-wont-write-about-government-till-ordinance-shielding-public-servants-is-repealed.
25. 'Rajasthan elections: Row over who is "outsider", Sachin Pilot or Vasundhara Raje', *The New Indian Express*, 6 November 2018. Available at: https://www.newindianexpress.com/elections/rajasthan-elections/2018/Nov/05/rajasthan-elections-row-over-who-is-outsider-sachin-pilot-or-vasundhara-raje-1894673.html.
26. Rahul Pandita, 'Uneasy in a Turban', Open, 23 June 2009. Available at: https://openthemagazine.com/features/india/uneasy-in-a-turban/.
27. Interview with Umashankar Meena, Dausa, 2020.
28. Interview with anonymous.
29. Interview with Indraj Gurjar, Jaipur, 2022.
30. Interview with Himmat Singh Gurjar, Jaipur, 2021.
31. TNN, 'Shoes for minister Ashok Chandna as protesters hail Sachin Pilot at Gujjar event in Rajasthan's Pushkar', *Times of India*, 13 September 2022. Available at: https://timesofindia.indiatimes.com/city/ajmer/shoes-for-minister-ashok-chandna-as-protesters-hail-sachin-pilot-at-gujjar-event-in-rajasthans-pushkar/articleshow/94163770.cms.
32. 'समाज का आशीर्वाद रहा तो अकेले ही कबड्डी खेल जाऊंगा : सचिन पायलट', *Dainik Bhaskar*. Available at: https://www.bhaskar.com/rajasthan/niwai/if-you-have-been-blessed-with-society-i-will-play-kabaddi-alone-sachin-pilot-060548-2741424.html.
33. TNN, 'Four days after Dalit boy beaten to death, friend burnt alive', *Times of India*, 6 March 2018. Available at: https://timesofindia.indiatimes.com/city/jaipur/4-days-after-dalit-boy-beaten-to-death-18-yr-old-found-burnt/articleshow/63177809.cms.
34. Deep Mukherjee, 'Alwar killing: Mahapanchayat warns upper castes over Dalit's death', *The Indian Express*, 5 March 2018. Available at: https://indianexpress.com/article/india/alwar-killing-mahapanchayat-warns-upper-castes-over-dalits-death-5086047/.
35. Deep Mukherjee, 'Two teens dead within days of each other, one community lives "in fear" of another in Rajasthan's Bhiwadi', *The Indian*

Express, 8 March 2018. Available at: https://indianexpress.com/article/india/two-teens-dead-within-days-of-each-other-one-community-lives-in-fear-of-another-in-rajasthans-bhiwadi-5090096/.

36. TNN, 'Rs 25 lakh compensation sought for kin of murdered Alwar boys', *Times of India*, 8 March 2018. Available at: https://timesofindia.indiatimes.com/city/jaipur/rs-25l-compensation-sought-for-kin-of-murdered-alwar-boys/articleshow/63209213.cms.
37. Mukherjee, 'Two teens dead within days of each other'.
38. Interview with Sachin Pilot, Jaipur, 2018.
39. Deep Mukherjee, Hamza Khan and Apurva, 'Campaign winds up in Rajasthan, rebels give both sides the jitters', *The Indian Express*, 6 December 2018. Available at: https://indianexpress.com/elections/campaign-winds-up-rajasthan-rebels-bjp-congress-jitters-5480581/.
40. Mohammed Iqbal, 'Congress wins 12 seats in panchayat by-polls in Rajasthan', *The Hindu*, 26 September 2017. Available at: https://www.thehindu.com/news/national/other-states/congress-wins-12-seats-in-panchayat-by-polls-in-rajasthan/article19756047.ece. See also PTI, 'Congress wins 19 out of 37 seats in local bodies by-polls in Rajasthan', *The New Indian Express*, 8 August 2016. Available at: https://www.newindianexpress.com/nation/2016/Aug/08/congress-wins-19-out-of-37-seats-in-local-bodies-by-polls-in-rajasthan-1506721.html.
41. Interview with Sachin Pilot, Jaipur, 2022.
42. 'Rajasthan by-polls: Congress wrests three assembly seats from BJP', *The Hindu*, 16 September 2014. Available at: https://www.thehindu.com/news/national/rajasthan-bypoll-results/article6414998.ece.
43. Deep Mukherjee, 'Rajasthan: Ex-Congress, 10 of 13 "kingmaker" Independents likely to back CM Gehlot', *The Indian Express*, 16 July 2020. Available at: https://indianexpress.com/article/india/rajasthan-ex-congress-10-of-13-kingmaker-independents-likely-to-back-cm-ashok-gehlot-6507790/.

10. Old Guard Vs Young Turk: Games for the Gaddi

1. Rahul Gandhi (@RahulGandhi), 'The united colours of Rajasthan!', X, 14 December 2018. Available at: https://x.com/RahulGandhi/status/1073504931041173504?ref_src=url.cms.

2. 'Parleys begin for cabinet formation', *Times of India*, 22 December 2018. Available at: https://timesofindia.indiatimes.com/city/jaipur/parleys-begin-for-cabinet-formation/articleshow/67200516.cms.
3. Interview with Ramkesh Meena, Jaipur, 12 December 2018.
4. Interview with senior incumbent MLA, Jaipur, October 2022.
5. Deep Mukherjee, 'Portraits of neglect: 10 deaths in 48 hrs, parents can't afford pvt hospital', *The Indian Express*, 4 January 2020. Available at: https://indianexpress.com/article/india/pm-urges-people-to-have-darshan-of-jore-sahib-during-guru-charan-yatra-10321219/?ref=infinite.
6. Deep Mukherjee, 'Sachin raps his govt on Kota deaths: "We could have been more sensitive"', *The Indian Express*, 5 January 2020. Available at: https://indianexpress.com/article/india/sachin-pilot-rajasthan-kota-children-deaths-6200109/.
7. Interview with Sachin Pilot's close aide, Jaipur, January 2020.
8. Deep Mukherjee, 'Ashok Gehlot govt flip-flop on civic elections, faultlines lie within', *The Indian Express*, 24 October 2019. Available at: https://indianexpress.com/article/india/ashok-gehlot-govt-flip-flop-on-civic-elections-faultlines-lie-within-6084814/.
9. Manoj C G, 'Scindia shadow: Rs 25 crore-worth advertisements for CM Ashok Gehlot, 0 for Deputy Sachin Pilot', *The Indian Express*, 13 March 2020. Available at: https://indianexpress.com/article/india/rajasthan-jyotiraditya-scindia-ashok-gehlot-ads-sachin-pilot-6311648/.
10. PTI, 'People who struggled for ensuring poll victory must be recognised, rewarded by Raj govt: Pilot', *The Indian Express*, 26 January 2020. Available at: https://indianexpress.com/article/india/people-who-struggled-for-ensuring-poll-victory-must-be-recognised-rewarded-by-raj-govt-pilot-6236264/.
11. Hamza Khan, 'Rajasthan SOG drops sedition charge, transfers cases to ACB', *The Indian Express*, 5 August 2020. Available at: https://indianexpress.com/article/india/rajasthan-sog-drops-sedition-charge-transfers-cases-to-acb-6539653/.
12. TNN, 'Rajasthan assembly elections 2018: Gehlot can't decide who will become CM: Khachariyawas', *Times of India*, 9 December 2018. Available at: https://timesofindia.indiatimes.com/city/jaipur/gehlot-cant-decide-who-will-become-cm-khachariyawas/articleshow/67006881.cms.

13. Deep Mukherjee, 'Pilot's right-hand man to detractor, the arc of a Gehlot loyalist's journey', *The Indian Express*, 30 November 2023. Available at: https://indianexpress.com/article/political-pulse/pilot-right-hand-man-detractor-gehlot-loyalist-8176543/.
14. Deep Mukherjee, 'Pilot loyalists stay firm on support: Leader's humiliation unacceptable', *The Indian Express*, 15 July 2020. Available at: https://indianexpress.com/article/india/sachin-pilot-loyalists-stay-firm-on-support-leaders-humiliation-unacceptable-6506034/.
15. Hamza Khan, 'Gehlot steps up attack on Pilot: Nikamma, stabbed party in the back', *The Indian Express*, 20 July 2020. Available at: https://indianexpress.com/article/india/gehlot-steps-up-attack-on-pilot-nikamma-stabbed-party-in-the-back-6515276/.
16. Sachin Pilot (@SachinPilot), 'सत्य को परेशान किया जा सकता है पराजित नहीं।', X, 14 July 2020. Available at: https://x.com/sachinpilot/status/1282960796037742598?mx=2.
17. Interview with anonymous, Jaipur, 2022.
18. Deep Mukherjee, 'Nikamma, ragdai, a no-words-barred Gehlot-Pilot tussle', *The Indian Express*, 28 July 2022. Available at: https://indianexpress.com/article/political-pulse/nikamma-ragdai-no-words-barred-gehlot-pilot-tussle-8025164/.
19. Baijayant Jay Panda (@PandaJay), 'In aviation, every flight plan includes an alternate airport or airstrip ...', X, 14 July 2020. Available at: https://x.com/PandaJay/status/1282966096233091073.
20. Neelam Pandey, 'Gehlot camp leaks tapes featuring Pilot camp MLAs talking about accepting money from BJP', The Print, 16 July 2020. Available at: https://theprint.in/politics/gehlot-camp-leaks-tapes-featuring-pilot-camp-mlas-talking-about-accepting-money-from-bjp/462617/.
21. TNN, 'Audio clip of talk "between former Rajasthan CM Ashok Gehlot, ex-OSD Lokesh Sharma" surfaces', *Times of India*, 14 July 2024. Available at: https://timesofindia.indiatimes.com/city/jaipur/audio-clip-of-talk-between-former-rajasthan-cm-ashok-gehlot-ex-osd-lokesh-sharma-surfaces/articleshow/111724400.cms.
22. Authors' own translation. Mukesh Bhakar (@MukeshBhakar_), 'मैं तो चुनाव जीतकर यूथ कांग्रेस का प्रदेश अध्यक्ष बना हूँ। अशोक गहलोत कौन ...', X, 14 July 2020. Available at: https://twitter.com/MukeshBhakar_/status/1282956309298438145.

23. Hamza Khan, 'Rajasthan phone tapping case: FIR against Sachin Pilot's media manager, journalist', *The Indian Express*, 7 October 2020. Available at: https://indianexpress.com/article/india/rajasthan-sachin-pilot-mlas-phone-tapping-fir-journalist-6706500/.
24. 'Police close case against Sachin Pilot's media manager, journalist', *The New Indian Express*, 6 December 2020. Available at: https://www.newindianexpress.com/nation/2020/Dec/06/police-close-case-against-sachin-pilots-media-manager-journalist-2232516.html.
25. Deep Mukherjee, 'Among Pilot supporters in Tonk, a glimmer of hope: "Will he get a chance to lead now?"', *The Indian Express*, 25 September 2022. Available at: https://indianexpress.com/article/political-pulse/a-letter-from-tonk-rajasthan-will-pilot-get-a-chance-to-lead-at-least-now-among-supporters-a-glimmer-of-hope-8170845/.
26. Deep Mukherjee, 'Gehlot hints at stepping down as Rajasthan CM: "New generation should get a chance"', *The Indian Express*, 25 September 2022. Available at: https://indianexpress.com/article/political-pulse/gehlot-hints-at-stepping-down-as-rajasthan-cm-new-generation-should-get-a-chance-8172085/.
27. Deep Mukherjee, 'Pilot's right-hand man to detractor, the arc of a Gehlot loyalist's journey', *The Indian Express*, 30 November 2023. Available at: https://indianexpress.com/article/political-pulse/pilot-right-hand-man-detractor-gehlot-loyalist-8176543/.
28. Sreenivasan Jain, 'Exclusive: Ashok Gehlot's Total Takedown Of Sachin Pilot', NDTV, 24 November 2022. Available at: https://www.ndtv.com/india-news/ashok-gehlot-to-ndtv-sachin-pilot-is-gaddar-3549213.
29. Rohit Parihar, 'Pilot had been planning this coup for six months: Ashok Gehlot', *India Today*, 25 July 2020. Available at: https://www.indiatoday.in/india-today-insight/story/pilot-had-been-planning-this-coup-for-six-months-ashok-gehlot-1703769-2020-07-23.
30. Interview with Hamza Khan, Jaipur, August 2025.

11. A New Dawn: 2023 Assembly Polls and After

1. 'Sachin Pilot concludes Jan Sangharsh Yatra in Rajasthan, threatens agitation against corruption', CNBC TV18, 15 May 2023. Available at: https://www.cnbctv18.com/politics/sachin-pilot-concludes-jan-sangharsh-yatra-in-rajasthan-threatens-agitation-against-corruption-16669391.htm.

2. Jaykishan Sharma, 'Ashok Gehlot's big claim: "Vasundhara Raje, 2 BJP leaders helped save my govt in 2020"', *India Today*, 7 May 2023. Available at: https://www.indiatoday.in/india/story/ashok-gehlot-vasundhara-raje-bjp-leaders-helped-save-govt-during-2020-rebellion-by-congress-mlas-2376115-2023-05-07.
3. 'Outrageous and untrue: Vasundhara Raje on Ashok Gehlot's claim that she saved his govt. in 2020', *The Hindu*, 8 May 2023. Available at: https://www.thehindu.com/news/national/other-states/outrageous-and-untrue-vasundhara-raje-on-ashok-gehlots-claim-that-she-saved-his-govt-in-2020/article66825769.ece.
4. 'Pilot targets Gehlot over his claim that some BJP leaders helped save the Congress government in Rajasthan during 2020 rebellion', *The Hindu*, 9 May 2023. Available at: https://www.thehindu.com/news/national/other-states/seems-gehlots-leader-is-vasundhara-raje-not-sonia-gandhi-sachin-pilot/article66829780.ece.
5. Deep Mukherjee, 'Video contest to influencers, Gehlot steps up to project welfare model to buck 25-year poll trend', *The Indian Express*, 21 July 2023. Available at: https://indianexpress.com/article/political-pulse/rajasthan-assembly-elections-ashok-gehlot-social-welfare-mode-congress-8852046/.
6. Deep Mukherjee, 'Ashok Gehlot's 'Mehangai Rahat' camps: "Good, but too late", say beneficiaries', *The Indian Express*, 28 April 2023. Available at: https://indianexpress.com/article/political-pulse/ashok-gehlots-mehangai-rahat-camps-good-but-too-late-beneficiaries-8581740/.
7. Deep Mukherjee, 'PM Modi targets Ashok Gehlot: Some call themselves jaadugar… on Dec 3, Cong chumantar', *The Indian Express*, 19 November 2023. Available at: https://indianexpress.com/article/political-pulse/pm-modi-targets-ashok-gehlot-rajasthan-polls-congress-9032514/.
8. Abhishek Anand, 'False Communal Spin Given to Compensation Offered by Rajasthan Government', The Quint, 4 October 2023. Available at: https://www.thequint.com/news/webqoof/viral-claim-comparing-kanhaiya-lal-and-iqbal-compensation-fact-check#read-more.
9. Deep Mukherjee, '"Rajasthan mein Vasundhara": Raje loyalists' message to BJP from mega birthday show as rival group holds stir', *The Indian Express*, 4 March 2023. Available at: https://indianexpress.com/article/political-pulse/rajasthan-mein-vasundhara-raje-mega-birthday-show-8479529/.

10. Deep Mukherjee, 'MP CM picked, the wait outside and inside 13, Civil Lines, Jaipur', *The Indian Express*, 12 December 2023. Available at: https://indianexpress.com/article/political-pulse/mp-cm-picked-the-wait-outside-and-inside-13-civil-lines-jaipur-9063971/.
11. Hamza Khan, 'BJP drops another surprise: Grass-roots worker, first-time MLA is new Rajasthan CM', *The Indian Express*, 12 December 2023. Available at: https://indianexpress.com/article/political-pulse/bhajan-lal-sharma-rajastha-new-chief-minister-bjp-first-time-mla-9065536/.
12. Based on the authors' own interactions with the BJP media cell.
13. Sh. Bhajan Lal Sharma, Chief Minister profile, Chief Minister Office, Government of Rajasthan. Available at: https://cmo.rajasthan.gov.in/cm-profile.
14. 'Rajasthan Vidhan Sabha General Election – 2003', Office of the Chief Electoral Officer Rajasthan, Government of Rajasthan. Available at: https://election.rajasthan.gov.in/acanalysis/ac74.htm.
15. Deep Mukherjee, 'BJP bets on new faces in Rajasthan cabinet, focus on non-dominant OBCs', *The Indian Express*, 1 January 2024. Available at: https://indianexpress.com/article/political-pulse/bjp-new-faces-rajasthan-cabinet-focus-non-dominant-obc-9088914/.
16. Manish Chandra Pandey, 'OBC outreach marks PM Modi, Amit Shah's visits to Uttar Pradesh', *Hindustan Times*, 9 July 2023. Available at: https://www.hindustantimes.com/cities/lucknow-news/obc-outreach-marks-pm-modi-amit-shah-s-visits-to-uttar-pradesh-101688839223563.html.
17. '4 lakh jobs, Rs 27,000 crore for health and Rs 15,000 crore for tap water in Rajasthan's budget 2024-25', *The Indian Express*, 10 July 2024. Available at: https://indianexpress.com/article/cities/jaipur/rajasthan-finance-minister-diya-kumari-presents-budget-9444302/.
18. Shanker Arnimesh, 'Kirodi Lal Meena resumes duties as minister, but truce in Rajasthan BJP is fragile', The Print, 1 April 2025. Available at: https://theprint.in/politics/kirodi-lal-meena-resumes-duties-as-minister-but-truce-in-rajasthan-bjp-is-fragile/2573549/.
19. Rajesh Asnani, 'JP Nadda hails Rajasthan's double-engine government, draws flak from Opposition', *The New Indian Express*, 31 May 2025. Available at: https://www.newindianexpress.com/nation/2025/May/31/jp-nadda-hails-rajasthans-double-engine-government-draws-flak-from-opposition.

20. Deep Mukherjee, 'Rajasthan Passes Anti-Conversion Bill, BJP MLA Asks Muslim Legislators to "Return to Original Religion"', The Wire, 10 September 2025. Available at: https://thewire.in/communalism/rajasthan-passes-anti-conversion-bill-bjp-mla-asks-muslim-legislators-to-return-to-original-religion.
21. Hamza Khan, 'Balmukundacharya, Hawa Mahal BJP MLA, whose tirade against meat vendors went viral', 10 December 2023. Available at: https://indianexpress.com/article/political-pulse/balmukundacharya-hawa-mahal-bjp-mla-whose-tirade-against-meat-vendors-went-viral-9061667/.
22. PTI, 'Jaipur Muslim girl students protest against BJP MLA Balmukund Acharya for objecting to girls wearing hijab', *Times of India*, 29 January 2024. Available at: https://timesofindia.indiatimes.com/india/jaipur-muslim-girl-students-protest-against-bjp-mla-balmukund-acharya-for-objecting-to-girls-wearing-hijab/articleshow/107237945.cms.
23. Rajesh Asnani, 'BJP MLA Acharya apologises amid outrage over controversial protest at Jaipur's Jama Masjid', *The New Indian Express*, 26 April 2025. Available at: https://www.newindianexpress.com/nation/2025/Apr/26/bjp-mla-acharya-apologises-amid-outrage-over-controversial-protest-at-jaipurs-jama-masjid.
24. Deep Mukherjee, '"Is This Justice?": Muslim Auto Driver's House Bulldozed After Tenant's Minor Son Injures Classmate', The Wire, 19 August 2024. Available at: https://thewire.in/communalism/is-this-justice-muslim-auto-drivers-house-bulldozed-after-tenants-minor-son-injures-classmate.
25. Deep Mukherjee, 'Rajasthan Govt to Replace "Mughal Era" Urdu Words Used in Police Terminology with "Shudh Hindi"', The Wire, 16 December 2024. Available at: https://thewire.in/government/rajasthan-govt-to-replace-mughal-era-urdu-words-used-in-police-terminology-with-shudh-hindi.
26. Deep Mukherjee, 'New, "Stricter" Rajasthan Anti-Conversion Bill Has Provision For Life Term But "Ghar Wapsi" Exempted', The Wire, 1 September 2025. Available at: https://thewire.in/government/new-stricter-rajasthan-anti-conversion-bill-has-provision-for-life-term-but-ghar-wapsi-exempted.
27. TNN, 'Jat Mahakumbh bats for CM from community, increase in OBC quota in Rajasthan', *Times of India*, 6 March 2023. Available at:

https://timesofindia.indiatimes.com/city/jaipur/jat-mahakumbh-bats-for-cm-from-community-increase-in-obc-quota-in-rajasthan/articleshow/98438169.cms.

28. Deep Mukherjee, 'How Jats Halted the BJP's Poll Wagon in the Hindi Heartland', The Wire, 13 June 2024. Available at: https://thewire.in/politics/bjp-jats-election-uttar-pradesh-rajasthan-haryana.
29. Deep Mukherjee, 'How the Congress and Allies Stopped the BJP from Getting a Hat-Trick in Rajasthan', The Wire, 5 June 2024. Available at: https://thewire.in/politics/how-the-congress-and-allies-stopped-the-bjp-from-getting-a-hat-trick-in-rajasthan.
30. Deep Mukherjee, 'BJP's Victory in Rajasthan Bypolls: Poor Candidate Selection by Congress, Crumbling Alliances', The Wire, 24 November 2024. Available at: https://thewire.in/politics/bjps-victory-in-rajasthan-bypolls-poor-candidate-selection-by-congress-crumbling-alliances.

ACKNOWLEDGEMENTS

We want to begin by thanking the people of Rajasthan – voices both heard and unheard – who have reminded us of the importance of storytelling and truth in these times.

As we chronicled the journey of India's largest state, our forays into its small towns and villages taught us that every conversation, every silence carried a fragment of history and a story of the present that needs to be told. Be it the aspirations of children sitting inside dilapidated school buildings in remote hamlets, or the grit displayed by people from marginalized communities taking a stand against caste atrocities and oppression, our attempt has been to include them in the larger narrative through this book and acquaint the world with their lives.

We owe a special gratitude to our favourite cafés across Rajasthan for countless cups of tea and coffee, over which the idea of this book slowly took shape amidst the uncertainty of the pandemic, work tours and numerous tight deadlines. Long evenings of scribbling notes, laughter and arguments marked the beginning of this manuscript.

We were fortunate to find our perfect co-travellers in A Suitable Agency, especially Hemali Sodhi, Ranjana Sengupta and Ambar Sahil Chatterjee, who believed in this project from its earliest spark and walked beside us through every high and low, reassuring us at every step.

Our heartfelt thanks to the brilliant editorial team at Pan

Macmillan India; to Rajdeep Mukherjee and Teesta Guha Sarkar for spotting and acquiring this book. And later, Pujitha Krishnan and Udyotna Kumar, whose invaluable guidance and support greatly enriched the book. Your insight, clarity and generosity have shaped this work into what it is today. A special thanks as well to our book cover designer, Bhavana, for being open to our ideas and translating the essence of Rajasthan into an apt visual.

To our fellow journalists, trusted sources, the politicians we interviewed and the many people who gave us their time and stories – this book belongs as much to you as it does to us.

We are also grateful to the media houses where we have worked over the past decade and a half for giving us the space to witness firsthand and then tell Rajasthan's stories. To our editors – thank you for your faith and guidance through the years.

As first-time authors, this journey has been a labour of love – filled with learning, humility and moments of wonder. We owe much to our friends, family and the subject-matter experts who read early drafts, offered advice and wrote generous endorsements that encouraged us to keep going.

Finally, thank you, Rajasthan – miles away from our roots in West Bengal and Kashmir and yet so intimately intertwined with our lives – this book celebrates the resilience of your people, their warmth and endless courage.